Genesis and Jewish Thought

Genesis and Jewish Thought

By Chaim Navon

Translated by David Strauss

KTAV Publishing House, Inc.
JERSEY CITY, NEW JERSEY

in association with

Yeshivat Har Etzion
ALON SHEVUT, ISRAEL

Library of Congress Cataloging-in-Publication Data

Navon, Hayim, 1973–
[Mahshevet Yisra'el be-Sefer Bereshit. English]
Genesis and Jewish thought / by Chaim Navon ; translated by David Strauss.
p. cm.
ISBN 978-1-60280-000-7

1. Bible. O.T. Genesis – Criticism, interpretation, etc. 2. Philosophy, Jewish. 3. Judaism. I. Title.
BS1235.52.N38 2007
222'.1106--dc22

2007040223

Typesetting by Jerusalem Typesetting, www.jerusalemtype.com

Contents

This book is dedicated to the memory of our ancestors:

R. Yeshayahu David b. R. Moshe Navon, z"l

R. Moshe b. R. Menachem Mendel Navon, z"l

Tzippora b. R. Chayyim Alexander (Feldblum) Navon, z"l

R. Reuven b. R. Eliyah Kahana, z"l

Carola b. R. Shemuel (Oppenheimer) Kahana, z"l

R. Abraham Abish b. R. Moshe Menachem Firer, z"l

R. Kalman b. R. Binyamin Gordon, z"l

We thank The University of Chicago Press for permission to reprint selections from Shlomo Pines, translator, *The Guide of the Perplexed*, © 1963 by the University of Chicago.

Introduction

The book of Genesis is the most familiar book of the Torah but also the most mysterious. We have all studied it from the earliest days of childhood, yet no one pretends to understand it. The present volume is based on a course on theological issues in the book of Genesis that I taught at Yaacov Herzog Teachers' College and on Yeshivat Har Etzion's Virtual Beit Midrash (www.vbm-torah.org), headed by Rav Ezra Bick and Rav Reuven Ziegler.

My approach to the issues under discussion was shaped by several important principles.

First, ideas greatly contribute to our understanding of the Torah. As Maimonides noted many years ago, it is impossible to understand the plain sense of Scripture without a knowledge of philosophy. A certain conceptual background is necessary even to understand that the expression *charon af Hashem* refers neither to God's nose (*af*) nor to His anger (*charon*).

Second, the words of the Torah embody important and complex ideas. Scripture takes a stand on theological issues. Therefore, just as conceptual knowledge is necessary to understand better the Torah, so is Torah knowledge necessary to shape a more correct position in the conceptual realm.

Third, the world of Jewish thought is not uniform. Jewish thinkers have held diverse opinions on almost every imaginable issue. In equal measure, it is difficult to extract unequivocal positions from

Scripture. Every verse in Scripture is open to multiple interpretations and gives rise to a variety of views. Nevertheless, there are clear lines that distinguish Jewish thought from the other religions. In some cases, a clear majority of Jewish thinkers agrees to a certain position. In others, the disparate Jewish positions are all relatively similar, at least in rejecting some particular alternative. In my discussions of the theological issues arising in the book of Genesis, I have tried both to present the richness of Jewish thought and to note its uniqueness in comparison to non-Jewish approaches.

Finally, despite the uniqueness of the world of Jewish thought, Jewish thinkers have drawn – and continue to draw – many insights from the world of general philosophy. Maimonides taught us in his introduction to tractate *Ethics of the Fathers*: "Accept the truth from him who speaks it." Therefore, any serious discussion of an issue must make reference to the ideas of non-Jewish thinkers.

It is in light of these four principles that I have undertaken to discuss some important theological issues that arise in the study of Genesis. I have chosen issues that are central in the world of Jewish thought. Given the limited framework of this book, I was unable to exhaust the subjects under discussion; thousands of works have been written about some of them, and I could not offer comprehensive treatment in a few pages. Moreover, I have not compiled a detailed bibliography, and instead have focused on the most fundamental sources pertaining to the matters at hand. In general, I have tried to present the essence of each issue in several circles: the scriptural message, the words of the commentators, the positions of Jewish thinkers, and the views of the sages of the nations. Regarding each issue, however, I chose the structure that seemed most appropriate in light of the material.

It is my prayer that I have contributed to the understanding of the rich world of ideas created by Jews standing before the Creator of heaven and earth.

Chaim Navon
Modi'in 5767

God and the World

"In the Beginning..."

The biblical commentators disagree about the meaning and function of the opening verse of Scripture. Rashi understands the words *Bereishit bara Elohim* to mean "At the beginning of God's creation." These words function as a heading, setting the time framework for what follows. Ibn Ezra implies that the next verse is also a subordinate clause, serving to describe the state of the world at the beginning of time: "And the earth was without form and void." The actual description of the creation of the world begins only in the third verse: "And God said, Let there be light." Nachmanides, on the other hand, understands the first verse as standing on its own: "In the beginning, God created the heaven and the earth," that is to say, heaven and earth were created first.

In addition to the textual problem ("in the beginning" of what?), both interpretations raise serious difficulties: According to Rashi, it seems that the world already existed before the initial act of creation – "let there be light." According to Nachmanides, it appears that the heaven was created at the very beginning of creation, but a later verse states explicitly that the heaven was only created on the second day.[1]

1. Nachmanides himself argues that in the beginning God created the primeval materials that would later be used for the fashioning of the heaven and the earth.

In any event, the plain sense of the verse supports the interpretation proposed by Nachmanides that the opening verse of the Torah is a description of the primal act of creation: In the beginning, God created the heaven and the earth. It follows from this that the next verse describes the state of the world following the primal creation. We are now presented with a difficult problem: If the heaven was created first, what exactly happened on day two? This, however, is only one of the many difficulties in understanding the order of creation and the relationship between the various things that were created. For example, what does it mean that light was created on the first day when the lights of the firmament – the sun and the moon – were created on the fourth day? Moreover, what is the meaning of "and there was evening and there was morning" before there was a sun and a moon? All that we can do is accept our inability to understand the particulars of how the world was created.

God Is Not Nature

There is also a conceptual reason for preferring Nachmanides' interpretation. It would be somewhat disappointing for Scripture to begin with a verse that merely indicates the time and background of what follows. If, however, we understand the first verse as a sharp and unequivocal proclamation, it has special intensity. This is what Hermann Gunkel, one of the more prominent non-Jewish biblical scholars, had to say:

> The verse can be best taken as a main clause "in the beginning God created heaven and earth" – a powerful statement! Simply and powerfully, the author first establishes the doctrine that God created the world. No statement in the cosmogonies of other peoples approaches this first statement in the Bible. Everything that follows has the goal, then, of illustrating this clause. (Gunkel, Genesis, p. 103)

Gunkel is certainly not one of our authorities; but it is

interesting and instructive to see the impression made by this verse on a gentile who was not known for excessive love of the Jewish people. We sometimes miss the force of certain scriptural passages precisely because they are so familiar to us from our earliest childhood. In such cases, the musings of an outsider can be very illuminating.

What is so unique about the first verse in the Torah? Let us compare it to the opening lines of one of the ancient Babylonian creation myth:

> When in the height heaven was not named, and the earth beneath did not yet bear a name, and the primeval Apsu, who begat them, and chaos, Tiamut, the mother of them both – their waters were mingled together. (*Enuma Elish*)

The *Enuma Elish* opens with a description of a world consisting solely of Tiamut, the primal sea, and her mate, Apsu, the sweet waters. As their waters mingled together, they gave rise to the gods, this being the beginning of the history of the world.

What is the most striking difference between our Bible and the *Enuma Elish*, between the word of God and the vanities of man? One point stands out: the distinction and gap between God and the world. According to ancient Near Eastern myth, there is no clear demarcation between the gods and the world. The gods are part of the world. Tiamut and Apsu are the two primordial seas, and it is they who give rise to the gods, as well as to the forces of nature.

Generally speaking, the world of idolatry did not distinguish between the gods and nature. On the one hand, the forces of nature were identified with individual gods: "the god of thunder," "the god of the sea," "the god of fertility," and the like. On the other hand, the gods were occasionally depicted as subject to the forces of nature. In Greek mythology, we find gods who fight with one another, are wounded, and act treacherously, gods who belong to the natural order. They resemble living creatures, only they are more powerful.

The first verse of the Torah rejects this idolatrous outlook: God is not nature, and nature is not God. The biblical scholar Ezekiel Kaufmann notes the fundamental importance of this principle:

> The Israelite religion overcame the doctrine of the corporeality of God in a fundamental and decisive manner: it imagined God as being totally unconnected to the matter of the world.... God is "spirit and not flesh," He is not a "body." And furthermore, it imagined Him above and beyond any connection to the laws of the universe, to nature, to fate. This is the point that distinguishes it from idolatry; it is from here that it rose to its own unique sphere. Its God is super-mythological and supernatural – this is its fundamental idea. (Kaufmann, *History of the Religion of Israel,* vol. 1, p. 227)

This idea finds expression in many parts of the Torah. For example, consider this passage from the book of Deuteronomy:

> Take therefore good heed to yourselves; for you saw no manner of form on the day that the Lord spoke to you in Chorev out of the midst of the fire. Lest you become corrupt, and make a carved idol, the similitude of any figure, the likeness of male or female, the likeness of any beast that is on the earth, the likeness of any winged bird that flies in the air, the likeness of any thing that creeps on the ground, the likeness of any fish that is in the waters beneath the earth. And lest you lift up your eyes to heaven, and you see the sun, and the moon, and the stars, all the host of heaven. (Deuteronomy 4:15–19)

King Solomon's prayer offered at the dedication of the Temple is a perfect example of the repudiation of idolatry and the rejection of the identification of God with nature:

> For will God indeed dwell on the earth? Behold, the heaven and heaven of heavens cannot contain You; how much less

> this house which I have built. Have consideration therefore to the prayer of Your servant, and to his supplication, O Lord my God, to hearken to the cry and to the prayer that Your servant prays before You today; that Your eyes may be open toward this house night and day, toward the place of which You have said, My name shall be here; that You may hearken to the prayer which Your servant shall make toward this place. And hearken You to the supplication of Your servant, and of Your people Israel, when they shall pray toward this place: and hear You in heaven, Your dwelling place; and when You hear, forgive. (1 Kings 8:27–30)

Solomon asserts that God is "found" nowhere, at least in the plain sense of the term, not even in the Temple. The Temple was not built as a "house" for God; it was intended to serve as a center for the worship and prayer of the Jewish people.

We repeatedly find that the Sages reject creeds that identify God with particular forces or parts of the world:

> Rabbi Yose says: The *Shekhina* never descended to the world, and Moses and Eliyahu never ascended to heaven, as the verse states: "The heavens are the heavens of the Lord, but He has given the earth to the children of men" (Psalms 115:16). (Sukka 5a)

The Midrash certainly does not mean to describe the whereabouts of God. It is trying to teach us an important principle: there will always be a great separation between heaven and earth: "The heavens are the heavens of the Lord, but He has given the earth to the children of men." Man cannot climb up to God, and God is not found in nature. We have here a forceful rejection of idolatry's approach to God and the world.

In philosophical terms, two different religious approaches are commonly spoken of: the "immanent" approach, which perceives the presence of God as pervading the world, and the "transcendent" approach, which views God as elevated above and beyond the universe, and external to it. We are speaking here of transcendent motifs in Judaism. There were thinkers who argued that this is the primary teaching of the first verse in the Torah:

> An expression of the liberation of God from subjugation to fate, to nature, to myth and to magic, is found in the first verse of the Torah: "In the beginning God created the heaven and the earth" – God on the one side, and heaven and earth on the other."
>
> (Levinger, *Bein Shigra le-Chiddush*, p. 22)[2]

> God's relationship to the world: He is the Creator, He says and does, He stands above the world. Surely there are other religious attitudes: the god of pantheism is in the world. He is supreme unity, the powers of which fill the world.... Judaism's God of ethics has a different relationship to the world. He is perforce separate from the world, He gives direction, He provides the world with an objective, but He is not part of the world. This is the secret of the greatness of Genesis 1.
>
> (Guttmann, *Dat u-Mada*, p. 265)[3]

> It is impossible to attribute to the first verse in the Torah any meaning other than a grand proclamation regarding the state of the world before God.... We, perforce, must understand "In the beginning, God created" as a great call directed at man to recognize the insignificance of the heaven and the earth – "For fear of the Lord, and for the glory of His majesty" (Isaiah 2:10): the world ("the heaven and the earth") is not God! A great negation of the essence of idolatry, pantheism, and atheism.
>
> (Leibowitz, *Yahadut, Am Yehudi, u-Medinat Yisra'el*, p. 321)

---

2. See also ibid., p. 51.
3. See also Julius Guttmann, *Devarim al ha-Filosofiya shel ha-Dat*, pp. 38, 68; idem, *Philosophies of Judaism*, pp. 6–8.

Guttmann and Leibowitz understand that the Torah rejects not only idolatrous ancient concepts but also certain modern philosophical ideas. They are referring, first and foremost, to Spinoza. The Jewish philosopher Baruch (Benedict) Spinoza developed a philosophical system whose total focus is pantheism, that is, the identification of God with nature. Spinoza said: God is nature. According to Spinoza, God is not a distinct, independent, and autonomous Being. When Spinoza speaks of God, he means the totality of beings and forces that exist in the world, both the physical and the mental world. The entirety of being, including you, me, our thoughts, flies and stones – everything together constitutes God. Spinoza's world view has been enormously influential, both philosophically and also existentially.

One of the most important developments of physics in the twentieth century was quantum mechanics, which maintains that the laws of nature are statistical; there is a one in many billions chance that if you drop a vase it will not smash on the ground but rise in the air. Albert Einstein refused to accept the principle of chance in quantum mechanics. As he once famously commented, God does not play dice with the universe. This comment stemmed from a deep sense of the religious dimension in the laws of nature. The violation of the absoluteness of the laws of nature was an insult to Einstein's religious sensibility. Einstein was essentially a pantheist in the spirit of Spinoza. This approach gave rise to profoundly religious feeling. Thus, when a child asked him whether scientists pray, Einstein answered:

> Anyone seriously involved in scientific investigation gradually becomes convinced that the laws of nature embody a spirit – a spirit immeasurably higher than that of man.... In this way, scientific investigation leads to a unique religious feeling, altogether different from the religiosity of one who is more naive.

My revered teacher, Rabbi Aharon Lichtenstein, found another shade of ancient idolatry in the modern world. He argues that idolatrous motifs that sanctify nature may be found in some of the ecological movements prevailing in our time. He notes that the emphasis of secular ecology is aesthetic:

> It seems that it would not be wrong to suggest that what generally hovers over this movement is an idolatrous worship of the land, one of the oldest and also one of the newest forms of idolatry in the world. It is difficult not to hear echoes of the worship of the fertility gods of the ancient world. It is as if at any moment we expect to see those women who would cry over Tammuz in one season, and rejoice over his ascendancy at another time.
>
> ("Ha-Adam ve-ha-Teva," *Hagut* 4 [1980])

In contrast, Halakha recognizes an obligation to preserve the wholeness of nature, but this obligation is merely one component of the more embracing prohibition of *bal tashchit* (wanton destruction):

> The prohibition against wanton destruction does not come to bestow honor on nature in and of itself, but rather as a creation and possession of the Holy One, blessed be He.... A proof for this point: the very fact that the prohibition does not discriminate between divine and human creation, between one who tears clothing and one who seals a spring. We are not interested in preserving nature, but rather in maintaining reality.
>
> (Ibid.)

Environmentalist groups occasionally give expression not only to an honest concern about man's fate in a destroyed world, but also to a mystical-idolatrous attitude that relates to nature as an organic being, filled with vitality and holiness, which we are forbidden to violate. This is a modern version of ancient idolatry.

The Torah rejects these religious attitudes. When the Torah states, "In the beginning, God created the heaven and the earth," there is room for but one conclusion: God is not the heaven and the earth. God is the Creator; the heaven and the earth are included among the created beings.

Immanence in Judaism

Some streams in Judaism prefer not to sever completely God from the world. We find rabbinic statements that speak of a divine presence in the world. This, for example, is what follows from the midrash that asks why God revealed Himself to Moses in a small and lowly bush:

> A certain gentile once asked Rabbi Yehoshua ben Korcha: Why did the Holy One, blessed be He, see fit to speak with Moses from a burning bush? He said to him: Had it been from a burning carob tree, or from a burning sycamore, you would have asked me the same thing. But to send you out empty-handed is impossible; why out of a burning bush? To teach you that there is no place void of the *Shekhina*, not even a bush.
>
> (Exodus Rabba 2)

The idea of God's immanence is found many times in the writings of the kabbalists and of those who came under kabbalistic influence. The kabbalistic world often inclines to the idea of immanence. We cite an example from the writings of Rabbi Abraham Isaac Kook:

> It is natural that the common perception, the understanding of God stemming from the monotheistic idea, which is also the more well-known perception, should sometimes cause sadness and weakness of spirit, as a result of the feebleness entering man's spirit when he imagines that he, being a weak and limited being, is so distant from the divine perfection which illuminates with the light of the majesty of its greatness…
>
> (*Orot ha-Kodesh*, vol. 1, p. 399)

Rabbi Kook emphasizes here the emotionally problematic nature of a purely transcendental approach. The idea of God's absolute detachment from the world can lead man to a certain weakness of spirit and a feeling of distance and alienation. Some have emphasized the metaphysical difficulty posed by this idea: God being infinite, how can there be anything outside Him? By saying that God is not to be found in the world, we are, as it were, imposing limits on Him. Let us see the alternative proposed by Rabbi Kook:

> Less wearisome to man than this perception is the monotheistic perception which inclines to pantheistic explanation, when it is refined from its dross. This stands out in the rational dimension of the new *Chassidut* which asserts that there is nothing outside God.
>
> (Ibid.)

The kabbalists promoted what Rabbi Kook calls a "monotheistic perception which inclines to pantheistic explanation." What precisely does this compromise mean? Rabbi Kook's disciple, Rabbi David Hakohen, known as the Nazir, explains:

> The negative doctrine of pantheism [i.e., that all is God], after being purified of its disease and refined of its dross, should be elevated and renamed "panentheism" [i.e., all in God], the main idea of which is the divine life force of the world, that He gives life to all, while remaining apart from and above all.
>
> (Hakohen, *Kol ha-Nevu'a*, p. 163)

According to the Nazir, the kabbalistic approach rejects Spinoza's identification of God with nature. God is not the same thing as nature, but He embraces nature. That is to say, God includes nature, but also exists over and beyond nature. The Sages have already alluded to this idea: "He is the place of the world, but the world is not His place" (Genesis Rabba 68). The Nazir explains that the primary intention here is not to identify every molecule in nature as a part of God. We are dealing with the "divine life force of the world"; the energy and forces that move the world are divine powers. Thus, the clear distinction that Judaism makes between God and His world is retained.

An approach of extreme immanence, like that espoused by Chabad, for example, poses educational dangers. Rabbi Chayyim Volozhiner noted these dangers in his *Nefesh ha-Chayyim*. R. Chayyim argues: If everything is God, then why is it forbidden to reflect on words of Torah in soiled places? And he adds: If even a pig is God, then why is it forbidden to eat pig? The Chassidic masters were surely capable of offering theoretical answers to these questions, but from an educational perspective there is a problem here. R. Chayyim concludes that from God's perspective, everything is God, but from our perspective, a distinction must be made between different times, places, and the like. The position he proposes is complex and not entirely clear, and the question remains whether he has overcome the problems that he himself raised.

Jewish thought presents a wide spectrum of views on the question of God's presence in the world. The common denominator in all of these views is the rejection of pantheism, the basis of which is found in the opening verse of the Torah. Within these bounds, we find a wide variety of positions.

Rabbi Joseph B. Soloveitchik presents a unique and original position. He discusses the frustration experienced by a man who is unable to commune with God through nature or to discern God in the spiritual moments he occasionally experiences. For this reason, another type of faith is needed – a revelation of God who comes down into this world, reveals Himself to man, and commands him. Why is man unable to find God? Is it because God is not found in nature?

> Why does man not find his Maker when he seeks and searches after Him?…The cause of man's frustration in this area is sin, which separates man from his Maker. Were it not for sin, man

> would reveal the Creator in creation without any disappointment.
>
> (*U-Vikashtem mi-Sham*, pp. 140–141)

Man fails to reach God. Why does this gap exist? Rabbi Soloveitchik answers: Because of sin. He seems to be referring to the limitations and deficiencies of the human personality. Since man is imperfect, because of his wild desires and evil inclinations, we cannot experience the fullness of God's presence. But Rabbi Soloveitchik explains the meaning of the distance between God and man:

> Indeed, now also the Holy One, blessed be He, is the place of the world, and there is no place empty of Him. This presence, however, is not visible or open to experience. The Holy One, blessed be He, sees, but remains unseen. He descends into the world in a pillar of cloud, but man is unable to penetrate into the cloud. When man begins to draw near to God, because he hears the voice of God walking across the expanses of the world and the fullness thereof, God distances Himself from him.
>
> (Ibid.)

Rabbi Soloveitchik makes an interesting distinction: on the metaphysical level, God is present in the universe; on the existential plane, it is very difficult to experience His presence. This position, which does not necessarily reflect the entirety of Rabbi Soloveitchik's thought, advocates immanence from a metaphysical perspective, and transcendence from an existential perspective. Rabbi Soloveitchik's point here pertains to a distressing question regarding immanence and pantheism: man does not experience God's immanence. The answer offered by Rabbi Soloveitchik provides us with a new perspective on our entire discussion: Over and beyond the issue of metaphysical truth, it is perhaps even more important to understand what it is that we are experiencing.

Providence

Creation and Providence

Maimonides argued that our belief in the creation of the world *ex nihilo* is critical, for without it our belief in God's dominion over the world would collapse. It is only the belief in God's creation of the world *ex nihilo* that leads us to the recognition of God's dominion over the world. For this reason we must reject Aristotle's position claiming that the world has always existed.

> The belief in eternity the way Aristotle sees it – that is, the belief according to which the world exists in virtue of necessity, that no nature changes at all, and that the customary course of events cannot be modified with regard to anything – destroys the law in its principle, necessarily gives the lie to every miracle, and reduces to inanity all the hopes and threats that the Law holds out.
>
> (*Guide of the Perplexed* II, 25)

God's involvement in the world finds expression in every chapter of the book of Genesis. In Maimonides' eyes, a necessary condition for such involvement is the tenet that God created the world and therefore can change its laws and interfere with them. We refer to God's dominion over the world as *hashgacha* – "providence." What is providence? How is it expressed? We shall attempt to answer these questions in the discussion that follows.

What Is Providence?

The term "providence" as used in Jewish thought refers to God's dominion over the world. Providence includes God's knowledge of what is taking place in the world, as well as His ability to intervene and change what is happening.

The idea of providence can be divided into the concepts of general providence and individual providence. General providence refers to the establishment of the laws of nature; individual providence refers to God's constant intervention in worldly events.

When a computer programmer markets a certain program, it is he who decides how the program will work in specific situations; this is akin to general providence. From time to time the programmer may offer support and updating by way of the Internet; this is similar to individual providence. The notion of individual providence raises many difficult questions, some of which we shall deal with below.

The Scope of Individual Providence

The classic and most comprehensive discussion of the nature and scope of providence is found in Maimonides' *Guide of the Perplexed*. We shall cite here some passages selected from part III, chapter 17 of the *Guide*, and add our comments.

> The opinions of people about providence are five in all. All of them are ancient; I mean that they are opinions that were heard at the time of the prophets, since the true Law has appeared that has illuminated all this darkness.
>
> The first opinion is professed by those who hold that there is no providence at all with regard to anything whatever in all that exists; that everything in it, the heavens and the things other than they, has happened by chance and in accordance with the way things were predisposed; and that there is no one who orders, governs, or is concerned with anything. This is the opinion of Epicurus.

The first opinion discussed by Maimonides is held by thinkers who totally reject the notion of providence. This does not necessarily mean that they do not believe in God. During the period of the Enlightenment, there was a religious-philosophical belief system called "deism," according to which God created the world and set it in motion, but since then has taken no interest in what happens in the world. As believing Jews we cannot accept this view. The belief that God rules the world and watches over it is one of the cardinal beliefs of our faith. Anyone who reads Scripture understands how fundamental to it is God's intervention in the world.

Scripture describes God as directing and controlling history. Our religious life looks different on account of this belief. The Greek philosopher Epicurus, who lived in the fourth century B.C.E., rejected this doctrine. The Sages viewed his position with such disfavor that his name, in the form *epikoros*, became synonymous with total heresy. Plato also said things that were unacceptable to the Sages; nevertheless, the Sages said, "Know how to answer *epikoros* [i.e., the heretic]" (*Ethics of the Fathers* 2:19), and not "Know how to answer Plato."

We shall skip over the second opinion, that of Aristotle, because it is so outdated by our modern knowledge, that it is no longer relevant.[1]

> The third opinion...being the opinion of those who hold that in all that exists there is nothing either among universal or particular things that is in any respect due to chance, for everything comes about through will, purpose, and governance. Now it is clear that everything that is governed is also known. This is the opinion of an Islamic sect, the Ash'ariya. Great incongruities are bound up with this opinion, and those who hold it are burdened with them and obliged to accept them.

1. Maimonides himself summarizes this position: "God's providence ends at the sphere of the moon."

> Thus they agree with Aristotle regarding the equality he established between the fall of a leaf and the death of a human individual. They say: This is so; but the wind does not blow by chance, for God sets it in motion; and it is not the wind that causes the leaves to fall, for every leaf falls through an ordinance and a decree of God; and it is He who causes them to fall now in this particular place; it is not possible that the time of their falling should be postponed or retarded; nor is it possible that they should fall in another place than this, for all this has been everlastingly decreed. In consequence of this opinion, they are obliged to think that every motion and rest of animals has been decreed, and that man has in no way the ability to do or not to do a thing.... They bear the burden of all these incongruities for the sake of the integrity of this opinion. They go so far as to hold that if we see someone who was born blind or a leper, although we are unable to say that he might have deserved this because of a previous sin of his, we should say: "He [i.e., God] has willed this."

Maimonides presents us with two diametrically opposing positions on providence. After discussing the view that totally rejects the idea of providence, he refers to those who take providence to the opposite extreme. The Ash'ariya (Asharites) were an Islamic philosophical sect that had great influence on the Muslim world.

In general, Islam is marked by a tendency to magnify God's might, at times to the point of nullifying man. The Ash'ariya gave this tendency a philosophical basis. They argued that there is no such thing as natural law; everything is governed by providence. Every movement in the world occurs through the direct will of God. "Natural laws" are a fiction: they merely reflect the way God customarily runs the world. Generally speaking, God arranges things such that objects released in the air fall down; He could, however, decide that in certain situations they would rise. Thus there is no "law of gravity," but rather a "custom of gravity."

In their desire to strengthen God's absolute control of the world, the Ash'ariya went so far as to deny man's capacity to exercise free will. In their view, if man had free will, God's rule over the world would be diminished. And furthermore, they argued, God is not subject to the laws of morality; He can do good or evil as He pleases. Thus the whole idea of "good" is wrong and distorted.

None of this is directly related to the matter at hand; we wish only to show how all these ideas flow from the same attitude and approach. Surely, one could adopt the Ash'ariya view on providence without accepting their position on free will or the question of God and morality. There is, in fact, another Islamic sect which took this path.

> The fourth opinion is the opinion of those who hold that man has the ability to act of his own accord; it is for this reason, according to them, that the commandments, prohibitions, rewards, and punishments figuring in the Law are well ordered. They hold that all of God's acts are consequent upon wisdom, that injustice is not permissible for Him, and that He does not punish a man who does good. The Mutazila also hold this opinion.... They also believe that He, may He be exalted, has knowledge of the falling of this particular leaf and of the creeping of this particular ant, and that His providence watches over all beings.

Maimonides himself opposes this view, and proposes another understanding of divine providence:

> As for my own belief with regard to this fundamental principle, I mean divine providence, it is as I shall set forth to you.... For I for one believe that in this lowly world – I mean that which is beneath the sphere of the moon – divine providence watches only over individuals belonging to the human species, and that in this species alone all the circumstances of the individuals and the good and evil that befall them are consequent upon

> their deserts, just as it says: "For all His ways are judgment" (Deuteronomy 32:4). But regarding all the other animals and, all the more, the plants and other things, my opinion is that of Aristotle. For I do not by any means believe that this particular leaf has fallen because of a providence watching over it; nor that this spider has devoured this fly because God has now decreed and willed something concerning individuals; nor that the spittle spat by Zaid has moved till it came down in one particular place upon a gnat and killed it by a divine decree and judgment…. For all this is, in my opinion, due to pure chance, just as Aristotle holds.

Maimonides maintains that some things happen in the world as a result of pure chance; that is to say, some things in the world are subject to natural law, and not to God's direct intervention. He argues that individual providence exists – but only for man, and not for the rest of the world. Maimonides' distinction is not arbitrary, for it is based on principle. Providence reaches man in a special manner:

> In my view, as I consider the matter, divine providence is consequent upon the divine overflow; and the species with which this intellectual overflow is united, so that it has been endowed with intellect, and so that everything disclosed to a being endowed with intellect is disclosed to it, is the one accompanied by divine providence, which appraises all its actions from the point of view of reward and punishment. If, as he [Aristotle] states, the foundering of a ship and the drowning of those who were in it, and the falling down of a roof upon those who were in the house, are due to pure chance, the fact that the people in the ship went on board and that the people in the house were sitting in it is, in our opinion, not due to chance, but to divine will in accordance with the deserts of those people as determined in His judgments, the rule of which cannot be attained by our intellects.

Maimonides explains that we are not dealing here with an arbitrary limitation imposed on the objects of providence, but with a different type of providence. According to Maimonides, our intellect and the knowledge we accumulate result from a divine overflow. Accompanying the intellect comes God's providence. God does not intervene in everything that happens in the world. He only intervenes in human affairs, guiding individuals to act in the correct manner if they are deserving. If a righteous man is about to board a rickety ship, God will not prevent the ship from sinking, but He will bring the righteous man to understand that he should not embark on the voyage. According to Maimonides, the external world operates on "automatic pilot"; God, however, intervenes in man's internal world.

In the chapter that follows (III, 18), Maimonides argues that even among human beings there are different levels of providence. Since providence depends upon intellect, the more developed a man's intellect, the more divine providence will he receive.

Maimonides continues with an explanation of what brought him to this opinion:

> I was impelled to adopt this belief by the fact that I have never found in any prophetic book a text stating that God has a providence watching over any individual animal, but only over individual humans....
>
> Do not think that this opinion may be refuted in opposition to me by means of the dictum: "He gives the beast its food," and so on (Psalms 147:9).... For all these texts refer to providence watching over the species and not to individual providence. It is as if they described His bounty, may He be exalted, which prepares for every species the food necessary for it and the matter for its subsistence. This is clear and manifest.
>
> (*Guide of the Perplexed* III, 17)

Maimonides' understanding of providence is far from representative of the consensus of Jewish thought. Many thinkers disagreed with Maimonides and greatly expanded the scope of divine providence.

Let us consider, for example, the words of Rabbi Chayyim Moshe Luzzatto (Ramchal) in his discussion of the trait of trust in God:

> Man could even sit idle and his allotted portion would still be provided, were it not for the primeval penalty imposed upon all men: "By the sweat of your brow you shall eat bread" (Genesis 3:19). It is because of this decree that man must put forth some effort for the sake of his sustenance, for thus did the supreme King ordain. This is like a tax which must be paid by every member of the human species; there is no escape.... It is not that the exertion brings about results, however, but rather that the exertion is indispensable. Once a person has exerted himself, however, he has fulfilled his duty, and then there is room for heaven's blessing to rest upon him.
>
> (*Mesilat Yesharim*, chap. 21)

Ramchal mentions a new and very important concept: striving (*Hishtadlut*). The idea of striving refers to the obligation to make efforts on behalf of our sustenance even if we know that in truth our reward comes from God, and is not necessarily dependent upon our own efforts. Ramchal severs the connection between effort and result: he argues that one's sustenance is determined not by natural laws but by divine providence. Our obligation to exert ourselves for our sustenance is a decree imposed upon us by God. A person who makes no effort to sustain himself violates God's decree, and will therefore not receive of God's bounty.

The connection between effort and sustenance is indirect. If a person is lazy and fails to get up in the morning to irrigate his field, he will forfeit his livelihood, as a punishment of God. Maimonides, on the other hand, would say that he will forfeit his livelihood because the laws of nature are such that plants will grow only when watered.

Those who hold the same view as Ramchal arrive at interesting conclusions. According to this view, for example, there is no reason for a person to change vocations if he is unable to support himself in his chosen profession. As long as a person makes the minimal effort required of him, he will receive the same sustenance no matter where he turns.

> So if you find your traits and nature luring you to a profession that you are physically suited for and can live with, then make it your own and endure the bitter and the sweet of it. Do not resent it if your livelihood is occasionally withheld from you. Trust instead that God will provide you with sustenance your whole life long. Also have it in mind that you are immersing yourself in God's *mitzvot* as you work hard and become emotionally involved in whatever profession you have chosen. Because it is God who has commanded you to engage in a profession.... Do not believe that your livelihood comes to you one way rather than another: trust God alone for your livelihood, and know that all ways of earning it are one and the same to Him, and that He can sustain you through whatever means He cares to, any way He wants.
>
> (Bachya ibn Pekuda, *Duties of the Heart*, *Sha'ar ha-Bitachon*, chap. 3)

There is room for a variety of intermediate positions on this point. One might argue, for example, that while we are generally subject to the laws of nature, God intervenes in exceptional cases of people who are especially deserving of reward or punishment.[2] Even in Maimonides' writings there are hints of a position more balanced than the one represented by the aforementioned citations.[3]

2. Nachmanides' position, which we shall discuss below, is one such intermediate position.
3. See, for example, *Guide of the Perplexed* III, 51.

Manner of Providence

We now move on to another issue: the manner of divine providence. What do we mean by this? In order to clarify the subject of our discussion, it is worthwhile to examine the instructive words of Nachmanides, in his commentary to *Bechukotai*, on the many blessings promised to the Jewish people:

> We have already explained that all these blessings are miracles. It is not natural that rain should fall, and that we should enjoy rest from our enemies, and that fear should enter their hearts so that a hundred flee from five, because we observe the statutes and the *mitzvot*; or that it should all be the opposite because we sow during the seventh year. Although these are hidden miracles, because the world appears to be following its natural course with respect to them, they are nevertheless known [as miracles], because they occur constantly in the entire land. For if one righteous man lives, God having removed his illness, and he lives out his days, this might also happen to certain wicked people. But if an entire land and an entire people always have rain falling in its season, and plentitude, security, peace, health, strength, and defeat of the enemies, in a manner unlike anything else in the world, everyone knows that God did this....
>
> The rule is that when Israel is perfect, and great in numbers, their affairs are not governed at all by nature, nor are their bodies, nor their land, neither collectively nor individually, for God blesses their bread and their water, and removes illness from their midst, to the point that they do not require doctors, and do not have to observe any of the rules of medicine, as it says: "For I am the Lord who heals you" (Exodus 15:26). And thus did the righteous ones act during the period of prophesy, so that even if they sinned and therefore took ill, they did not turn to doctors, but only to the prophets....
>
> The Torah does not base its laws upon miracles, as it says: "For the poor shall never cease out of the land" (Deuteronomy

> 15:11), knowing that such will be the case. But when a man's ways are pleasing to God, he need have nothing to do with doctors.
>
> (Nachmanides, commentary to Leviticus 26:11)

In this passage Nachmanides establishes his classic distinction between divine providence through open miracles and hidden providence. Nachmanides offers a brilliant analysis: he argues that even the hidden providence of God is miraculous. If more rain falls because we have observed the *mitzvot*, this is a miracle, because rain is not affected by *mitzvot* but by barometric pressure. In Nachmanides' eyes, therefore, all the blessings and curses, and essentially all of God's providence in this world, fall into the category of "hidden miracles." The difference between open and hidden miracles is solely an issue of public relations: open miracles are clear and evident to all; hidden miracles, as the name implies, are hidden. We also see in Nachmanides' commentary an intermediate position regarding the scope of individual providence: the world generally operates according to the laws of nature, but at certain times and regarding certain people, God intervenes and directly oversees what is happening.[4]

Nachmanides emphasized that even nature is a miracle. Others went in the opposite direction, arguing that even miracles are part of nature. Various midrashic passages teach us that all

4. In certain places, however, Nachmanides implies that there is no nature whatsoever: "A person has no share in the Torah of Moses Rabbenu unless he believes that everything that happens to us is a miracle; nothing is governed by nature or the natural course of the world, whether regarding the collective or the individual" (commentary to Exodus 13:16; and similarly in "Torat ha-Shem Temima," in *Kitvei ha-Nachmanides*, ed. Chavel, [Jerusalem, 5723], p. 153). This is not the implication of his statement on *Parashat Bechukotai*, which we cited above; and on *Parashat Eikev* he explicitly writes otherwise: "Know that miracles are only performed for good or for bad, for absolutely righteous men or for absolutely wicked men. But average people are governed by the natural course of the world, for good or for bad" (Nachmanides, Deuteronomy 11:13; and similarly on Genesis 18:19).

of the miracles were already planted in the universe at the time of creation:

> Rabbi Yochanan said: The Holy One, blessed be He, made a stipulation with the sea that it would divide before Israel; thus it is written: "And the sea returned to its strength (*le-etano*)" (Exodus 14:27), in accordance with its agreement (*li-tena'o*). Rabbi Yirmiya ben Elazar said: Not with the sea alone did God make a stipulation, but with everything that was created in the six days of creation.... I commanded the sea to divide, and the heavens and the earth to be silent before Moses.... I commanded the sun and the moon to stand still before Yehoshua. (Genesis Rabba 5:5)

Maimonides understood the profound significance of this midrash:

> It was willed during the six days of creation that all things would always act in accordance with their nature, as it is stated: "That which has been is that which shall be...and there is nothing new under the sun" (Ecclesiastes 1:9). The Sages were forced to say therefore, regarding all the miracles that seem to be outside nature, that they occurred and shall occur as was impressed upon them during the six days of creation, when it was impressed in their nature that something new would come into being. And when that something new came into being at the appropriate time, it seemed as if it were happening then, but that is not so. (Introduction to *Ethics of the Fathers*, chap. 8)[5]

Maimonides emphasizes the importance of an independent

---

5. Rabbi Yehuda Halevi expressed himself similarly in his *Sefer ha-Kuzari* III, 73. Ramchal, however, understood that the midrash cited by Maimonides does not mean that there are never any changes in nature. "For it certainly changes at all times." Rather it means that all created beings, at the time of their creation, know about their future destiny (*Derekh ha-Shem* II, chaps. 5–6).

nature operating in accordance with its own laws. He maintains that even miracles are part of nature, and therefore every miracle that was to occur until the end of time was already planted in the world's nature during the six days of creation. Just as there is a law of nature that the sea rises whenever the tide is high, so, too, there is a law of nature that the sea parts whenever the people of Israel leave Egypt. This is not a continuing divine intervention, but a natural law like all other such laws.

Maimonides' approach is just the opposite of Nachmanides'. It limits the miraculous dimension of nature and magnifies its regularity. Why did Maimonides strive to intensify the permanence and fixedness of nature? The answer to this question follows from what he writes elsewhere:

> The thing that is changed is changed because of a deficiency in it that must be made good or because of some excess that is not needed and must be gotten rid of. Since the works of the deity are absolutely perfect, there is no possibility of an excess or a deficiency in them. Accordingly they are, of necessity, permanently established as they are, for there is no possibility of something calling for a change in them.
>
> (*Guide of the Perplexed* II, 28)

According to Maimonides, if there was any need for God's constant involvement in nature, this would indicate that God did not, as it were, create nature in the best possible way.

Rabbi Naftali Tzvi Berlin (Netziv) limits God's intervention in nature from another direction. He deals not with the open miracles, but with the hidden ones. Netziv relates to individual providence, the recompense that God pays each of us for our actions. He argues that this involves natural law and not constant divine intervention by way of hidden miracles.

> Know that reward and punishment for *mitzvot* do not constitute a royal decree, which depends on the king's will and intent

> at all times to do as his heart pleases. Rather, they are like a doctor warning a person about certain foods that will cause him harm. [The injury] does not depend on his [the doctor's] will; he merely informs him [the person] what was done in the creation of nature. Similarly, in regard to the commandments and prohibitions, it was established by the Creator, may He be blessed, that reward and punishment depend upon their observance and violation.... The Holy One, blessed be He, does nothing more; rather, the commandments do their part and the prohibitions do their part, as the verse says: "The good and evil do not come out of the mouth of the Most High" (Lamentations 3:38). This is like the reward and punishment of a doctor; he does not impose a punishment when he knows that a person has disregarded his warning, but instead [the patient] is punished by himself; and it is not like punishment by a king.
>
> (*Ha'amek Davar*, Leviticus 26:3)

Since Netziv hangs the hidden miracles – but not the revealed ones – on the fixed laws of nature, he does not speak of exceptional events, like the splitting of the sea, but of a fixed principle of recompense. Netziv squarely disagrees with Nachmanides, who claims that the observance of *mitzvot* and the commission of sins have no natural consequences. According to Netziv, just as there are physical laws of nature, so, too, there are spiritual laws of nature. Whenever one commits a sin, one automatically and naturally receives a punishment.

The Meaning of Individual Providence

Let us conclude with an idea expressed by Rabbi Yehuda Halevi. Rabbi Yehuda Halevi explains the benefit and importance of individual providence, which finds expression in hidden miracles:

> [The Holy Land's] fertility or barrenness, its happiness or misfortune, depend upon the divine influence your conduct

> will merit, while the rest of the world continues on its natural course. For if the divine presence is among you, you will perceive by the fertility of your country, by the regularity with which your rainfalls appear in their due seasons, by your victories over your enemies in spite of your inferior numbers, that your affairs are not managed by simple laws of nature, but by the divine will. You will also see that drought, death, and wild beasts pursue you as a result of disobedience, although the whole world lives in peace. This shows you that your concerns are arranged by a higher power than mere nature.
>
> (*Kuzari* I, 109)

Rabbi Yehuda Halevi's intent in this section is to demonstrate that divine providence proves the veracity of the Torah. But we see another important principle here: divine providence in itself is a goal, for it gives expression to our clinging to the divine. Even the punishments that God inflicts upon us have value and meaning, for they demonstrate that God is close and present among us. It is like a mother who punishes her son, thereby demonstrating her love for him and her desire to be close to him. As King David said in the book of Psalms: "Your rod and your staff they comfort me" (Psalms 23:4). *Metzudat David* offers the following comment on this verse:

> "Your rod and your staff they comfort me" – that You beat me with a rod of affliction, and then once again You support me, these are the things that comfort me, for I see thereby that You have not abandoned me to chance.
>
> (*Metzudat David*, Psalms 23:4)

Proof for the explanation provided by *Metzudat David* may be adduced from Scripture. Consider God's description of his relationship with King Solomon:

> I will be his father, and he will be My son. If he commits iniquity, I will chasten him with the rod of men, and with such plagues as befall the sons of man.
>
> (II Samuel 7:14)

God relates to Solomon as a father relates to his son – and for that very reason He chastens him with the rod.

Torah and Science

The opening chapter of Genesis describes the creation of the universe. In this chapter we shall examine the degree to which this description should be viewed as an exact scientific account of the events. This question arises wherever there is a clash between the plain sense of Scripture and modern scientific findings.

Many people are troubled by the real or imagined contradictions between the Torah and science. In this chapter we treat some of the principal approaches that have been proposed to deal with these questions. The discussion will focus on the tension between the plain sense of the Torah and the natural sciences (and, to a certain degree, history) with respect to the credibility of the factual assertions in the Torah.

Obviously, this is only one small element of the wider question of the conflict between the Torah and science. Truth be told, this conflict is no longer a "hot topic." Over the course of the twentieth century, religious thinkers successfully formulated satisfying answers to these questions, so that believing Jews, generally speaking, no longer find them disconcerting. Nonetheless, we are dealing here with an important issue that deserves careful treatment, not only because these questions can still at times be unsettling, but also because the answers can teach us some basic principles of both the Torah and science.

Skepticism About Scientific Claims

The first approach to this issue tries to raise doubts about the certainty of the claims of science. There are extremists who scornfully reject science outright. But it is difficult to identify with them, because in our daily lives we rely on science; to give only one small example, we use a microwave oven without fear that it will explode. Science may not offer absolute certainty, but there is a world of difference between baseless theories and accepted scientific positions that are close to certain. It is difficult to accept the argument that science has no reliable foundation whatsoever.

Then there is the argument that acknowledges science's ability to explain the present but not its ability to reconstruct the past. The Lubavitcher Rebbe, Rabbi Menachem Mendel Schneersohn, argued that attempts to reconstruct the past are not scientific because the hypotheses cannot be tested in a laboratory.

> We must distinguish between empirical or experimental science dealing with, and confined to, describing and classifying observable phenomena, and speculative "science," dealing with unknown phenomena, sometimes phenomena that cannot be duplicated in the laboratory.

Therefore, he maintained, as long as we are unable to conduct a laboratory experiment that reconstructs the precise conditions of the universe in the ancient past, any conjecture about life at that time is frivolous speculation.

> One cannot exclude the possibility that dinosaurs existed 5,722 years ago, and became fossilized under terrific natural cataclysms in the course of a few years rather than in millions of years, since we have no conceivable measurements or criteria of calculations under those unknown conditions.
>
> (*Iggerot Kodesh*)[6]

6. The citations from the Lubavitcher Rebbe are taken from Prof. Shalom

Another approach to the limitations of science is based on a philosophical position concerning the nature of science. Certain philosophers of science maintain that science does not pretend to tell us what is actually happening in the universe; it merely offers a parallel model that generates results identical to those found in the real world. This position finds support in what Maimonides says about astronomy (*Guide of the Perplexed* II, chap. 11). Many modern scientists and philosophers endorse this view, including the important philosopher and mathematician, Bertrand Russell.[7]

As Russell observers, no one has ever *seen* an atom. We assume the existence of atoms as an abstract logical construct that allows us to make certain calculations regarding the universe. The world behaves as if it were made up of atoms, but it is impossible to know whether they actually exist. Basing themselves on this proposition, some argue that one cannot speak of a contradiction between science and religion, because science does not pretend to tell us what is really happening in the universe.[8]

This argument is somewhat exaggerated. Even if we say that an atom or an electron is merely an abstraction, it is difficult to put forward the same argument about the age of the universe. Moreover, science may not be able to unequivocally confirm a particular proposition about the real world, but it stands to reason that it can at least rule out certain theories about the universe.

The Lubavitcher Rebbe proposed an additional argument, different in its details, but also giving expression to the limits of science:

> Even assuming that the period of time which the Torah allows for the age of the world is definitely too short for fossilization (although I do not see how one can be so categorical), we can still readily accept the possibility that God created ready fossils,

---

Rosenberg's *Torah u-Mada* [Jerusalem 5748].

7. Bertrand Russell, *Mysticism and Logic*, p. 123.

8. See, for example, Pierre Duhem, *The Structure of Physical Theory*, p. 176.

> bones, or skeletons (for reasons best known to Him), just as He could create ready living organisms, a complete man, and such ready products as oil, coal, or diamonds, without any evolutionary process.
>
> (*Iggerot Kodesh*)

The Lubavitcher Rebbe suggests that God may have created the world with dinosaur bones already buried in its depths. It is difficult to refute such an argument, but it leaves a bad taste in the mouth as a description of the way God operates in the world.[9]

Interpreting the Assertions of Religion

A second approach takes the opposite stance. Instead of questioning the validity of the assertions of science, this view reexamines our understanding of the pronouncements of religion. The Torah is certainly absolute truth. But have we really understood the Torah properly?

A classic example of this approach may be found in what Maimonides says about the eternity of the world. Aristotle maintained that the world is eternal, that is, it was never created. Maimonides was in doubt about this issue. In discussing it, he explores the question of how to deal with the plain sense of the biblical passages.

> Know that our shunning the affirmation of the eternity of the world is not due to a text figuring in the Torah according to which the world has been produced in time. For the texts indicating that the world has been produced in time are not more

9. A similar argument was put forward by the English naturalist Philip Henry Gosse in 1857 in his *Omphalos: An Attempt to Untie the Geological Knot*. Gosse argued that God created the first man with a navel (*omphalos* in Greek) despite the fact that he had never been in a woman's womb. So, too, God created the world with fossils despite the fact that dinosaurs and other primeval animals had never existed. Regarding Gosse and his book, see S.J.G. Gould, *The Flamingo's Smile*, Norton. 1985.

> numerous than those indicating that the deity is a body. Nor are the gates of figurative interpretation shut in our faces or impossible of access to us regarding the subject of the creation of the world in time. For we could interpret them as figurative, as we have done when denying His corporeality. Perhaps this would even be much easier to do: we should be very well able to give a figurative interpretation of those texts and to affirm as true the eternity of the world, just as we have given a figurative interpretation of those other texts and have denied that He, may He be exalted, is a body.
>
> (*Guide of the Perplexed* II, chap. 25)

Maimonides states that he would have no problem interpreting Scripture in other than a literal sense if our scientific or philosophical knowledge required it. The fact is that the Torah speaks of God's "anger" literally as His "burning nose," and yet we do not infer from this that God has a nose. Maimonides explains that it is not because of the plain sense of the text that he does not accept the eternity of the world, but because there is no philosophical proof for the assumption, and because from a religious perspective Aristotle's position is problematic.

We find another example in Nachmanides' comments about the rainbow. According to the plain sense of Scripture, Nachmanides says, God created the rainbow only after the Flood. Since science tells us that a rainbow is a natural phenomenon, he continues, we must understand that the Torah means to say that the natural phenomenon of the rainbow, which had existed since creation, was endowed with new meaning after the Flood (commentary to Genesis 9:12).

Many in our generation have followed this path, attempting to reinterpret the biblical verses so that they fit modern science. One of the first to do so was Rabbi Israel Lipschutz, author of the *Tiferet Yisrael* commentary to the Mishna:

> In 1807, in Siberia, in the northernmost tip of the world, under the dreadful ice that is always there, an enormous elephant was found, about three or four times as big as those found today, the bones of which are now housed in a museum in St. Petersburg.... And we already knew of the bones of a gigantic animal found in the depths of the ground in America near the city of Baltimore, seventeen feet long, and eleven feet tall from its forefeet to its shoulders, and nine feet from its hind feet to its back. The bones of this animal were also found in the depths of the ground in Europe, scattered about one here and one there, and they called this species of animal "mammoth."...
>
> From all this it is clear that everything the kabbalists have told us for hundreds of years – that the world had already once existed and was then destroyed, and then it was reestablished four more times, and that each time the world appeared in a more perfect state than before – now in our time it has all become clear in truth and righteousness. And would you believe, my brothers, that this wonderful secret is clearly written in the first section of our holy Torah.
>
> (*Derush Or ha-Chayyim*)[10]

Rabbi Lipschutz cites the bones of the dinosaurs and the mammoth as proof that the creation story should not be understood literally. The bones are remnants of ancient worlds predating our own that God created and then destroyed.[11]

We can cite another example from a book written by a physicist, Prof. Nathan Aviezer. He claims that "any attempt to connect the Torah's description with science must be based on the assumption that the term *yom* [lit. day] means a 'stage' or 'period' in the development of the universe, and not a time period of twenty-four

10. Printed in *Mishnayot Yakhin u-Bo'az*, following tractate *Sanhedrin*.
11. It was primarily for kabbalistic reasons that Rabbi Lipschutz was attracted to the idea of the repeated creation and destruction of the world; the scientific consideration is brought only as additional support.

hours." Prof. Aviezer is aware of the fact that the Sages understood that the "day" in Genesis need not necessarily be identified with our "day." It is on this assumption that he bases his interpretation of the chapters dealing with the creation:

> The view adopted in the present book is that the six days of creation do not refer to a time interval of 144 hours, but rather to six specific phases in the development of the universe-from the initial creation to the appearance of man.
>
> (Aviezer, *In the Beginning*, Hoboken, NJ, 2001, p. 2)

According to Aviezer, the verses should not be taken literally. The word "day" should not be understood as a unit of time twenty-four hours long, but as a stage in the development of the universe.

Distinguishing Between the Two Realms

A third approach makes no attempt to reinterpret the Torah or to raise doubts about the validity of science. It argues that the Torah and science are concerned with two entirely different realms. Science generates facts; religion teaches us values and commandments. Therefore, *a priori*, there can be no clash between them. When science tries to teach values, it is overstepping its boundaries; and when religion seems to be teaching facts, there must be a misunderstanding.

Galileo, in the seventeenth century, raised a similar argument. When he announced that he had demonstrated the truth of Copernicus' view that the earth revolves around the sun, and not the reverse, his opponents countered that according to the plain sense of Scripture, it is the earth that is at rest and the sun that moves (e.g., "Sun, stand still upon Giv'on"; Joshua 10:12). Galileo responded that Scripture teaches us nothing about scientific matters:

> Take into consideration, O theologians, who wish to connect matters of faith to scientific questions. You expose yourselves to the danger that in the end anyone who believes that the sun

> moves will be declared a heretic; in the end, that is, when it will be proven in scientific or logical manner that the earth moves and the sun stands in its place.
>
> (Galileo, *Dialogue of the Two Chief World Systems*)

Galileo is warning his opponents: If you don't sever the connection between science and religion, the day will come that my theory will be proven correct, and then you will be burned at the stake. The sole solution lies in a recognition that we are dealing with two entirely different realms.

In the Jewish world, Rabbi Samuel David Luzzatto raised a similar argument:

> The enlightened will understand that it is not the Torah's intention to teach us the natural sciences, and that the Torah was given only to direct man along the path of righteousness and judgment, and to establish in his heart the belief in the unity of God and in providence.... It is, therefore, inappropriate for a Torah-minded person to interpret Scripture not in its plain sense in order to make it agree to the natural sciences. It is also inappropriate for a scholar to deny the divine origins of the Torah if he finds among its stories statements that do not agree with scientific scholarship.... God wanted to inform man of the unity of the world and the unity of the human species. It is the general intention of the creation story to teach these two principles.
>
> (Shadal, Commentary to Genesis 1:1)[12]

Rabbi Abraham Isaac Kook said much the same thing:

> Even if it were to become clear to us that the world came into being by way of the evolution of the species, still there would be no contradiction, for our count follows the plain sense of

12. See also the introduction to his commentary.

> the biblical verses, which is far more relevant to us than knowledge about the past, which carries little value for us. Without question, the Torah concealed much about creation, speaking in allusions and parables. For everyone knows that the creation story is included among the secrets of the Torah, and if everything followed the plain sense [of the verses], what secret would there be here?...The main thing is what arises from the entire story – knowing God and [living] a truly moral life. God, who provides in measure even the spirit that falls upon the prophets, arranged that when these great ideas entered these images, man could draw from them, with great effort, whatever is most beneficial and elevating in them.
>
> (*Iggerot Ra'ayah* 1, letter 91, p. 105)

According to Rabbi Kook, there is no need to be upset by the theory of evolution even if it seems to contradict the plain sense of Scripture. The Torah's account of creation does not pretend to teach us science, but is a source of spiritual ideas. That is why God did not formulate the Torah with scientific precision, but in a manner that allows most easily for the inculcation of such spiritual ideas.

Rabbi Kook tells us that the Torah contains factual information about the creation of the world, but it is hidden and esoteric. The important element in the creation story is its fundamental ethical message, and what is this primary message? We have seen Luzzatto's suggestion on the topic. The ethical message of the story of creation might also be that God rules over nature and should not be identified with it (negation of pantheism).

Elsewhere, Rabbi Kook adds the following:

> I find myself obligated to arouse your pure spirit about the ideas put forward by recent studies, which for the most part contradict the plain sense of the words of the Torah. My opinion on this matter is that anyone with straightforward thinking should know that while there are no proven truths in any of

> these new studies, we are under no obligation to refute or oppose them. For it is not at all the essence of the Torah to teach us simple facts or events that once transpired. The main thing is the content, the inner meaning.
>
> (*Iggerot Ra'ayah* 1, letter 134, p. 164)[13]

In the continuation of the passage, Rav Kook establishes an important educational-religious principle that also has ramifications beyond the narrow topic of science and religion:

> Here is a great principle in the war of ideas: Whenever any idea comes and contradicts something in the Torah, the first thing we must do is not to refute it, but to build the palace of Torah above it. In that way we are elevated, and through that elevation the ideas reveal themselves, so that afterward, when we are free of all pressure, we can fight with full confidence.
>
> (Ibid.)

This rule was not observed by the Catholic Church, which fiercely fought against Galileo and was eventually defeated. It is preferable to demonstrate from the outset that even if the exceptional opinion turns out to be correct, the Torah will not suffer as a result.

According to the position presented here, there is no conflict between the Torah and science, for the Torah does not pretend to provide us with scientific information. This position is relevant not only to the apparent contradictions between the Torah and the natural sciences, but also to the contradictions between the plain sense of Scripture and our knowledge of history, in the spirit of what the Sages said: "Job never existed and was never created, but rather he is a parable" (*Bava Batra* 15a).

Similarly, much ink has been spilled over the camels that are mentioned in Scripture. The book of Genesis describes our

13. See also the similar position of the Maharal, *Be'er ha-Gola, be'er shishi* (Jerusalem, 1984), p. 112.

patriarchs riding camels. Scholars and rabbis have been arguing for decades about whether camels had already been domesticated in the patriarchal period. According to the position presented here, the question is totally irrelevant. Perhaps the patriarchs never really rode on camels, but on donkeys or on oxen or on winged horses, or perhaps they traveled on foot. Who cares? God, for various reasons connected to the Torah's influence upon the generation in which it was given and upon later generations, preferred to write that the patriarchs rode on camels. Within Scripture's internal historical system, this is not an anachronistic failing. The comparison with real history is out of place, for we are talking about two entirely different systems that do not presume to parallel each other.

Y. Rosenson brings another relevant example: the rejection by biblical scholars of the account of the collapse of the walls of Jericho because archaeology has been unable to verify it. Scripture's objective, argues Rosenson, is not to give a detailed historical description of Jericho's fortifications, but is to portray a nomadic people standing outside a settled and fortified city, and to describe their experiences and feelings.

> From this perspective, it is not the "archaeological" presence of the wall that is important, and it makes no difference whether we are dealing with an actual wall or with a city that was protected in some other manner. The point is that the wall symbolizes the significant urban settlement that faced the nomadic people.
>
> (Rosenson, *Al Atar* 7 [2000], p. 144)[14]

We are not dealing here with a "lie," God forbid, just as the

14. In his important article, Rosenson stresses a point that differs slightly from the focus of our discussion. He relates primarily to the tension between the historical and literary aspects of Scripture. The two discussions, however, touch upon each other and are intimately connected.

creation story in Genesis is not a "lie," even according to Rabbi Kook, who maintains that it may not correspond precisely to the events that actually took place. The Torah does not claim to mirror historical reality with any degree of exactitude; it expects its students to read it after they have already mastered its historical background.

According to those who advocate this approach, God never meant to give us the impression that the biblical stories reflect historical reality. If both the author and the reader understand that the Torah does not reflect historical reality, there is no room to talk of a "lie." The key point is that the Torah and science, including historical science, are two separate realms, with entirely different objectives, and thus there cannot be any contradiction between them.

Of course, there are limits to this approach, and it cannot be applied to all the stories in Scripture, for every believing Orthodox Jew believes that the Sinaitic experience took place in reality, and was not merely a parable. But saying that in Jericho there was only a fence and not a wall will not undermine the foundations of our belief.

Prof. Mordecai Breuer, in a famous article, applies this approach to the world of the Sages. Breuer argues that we should not be troubled by the discrepancies between rabbinic chronology and the generally accepted scientific chronology. Our holy Sages were not historians, and never aspired to provide us with true and precise historical information:

> The purpose of the historical assertions of the Sages is not to provide us with historical and chronological information, but only to open our eyes so that they may see God's providence over the ways of the world and the nations.
>
> (Breuer, "*Hora'at ha-Historiya ve-Emunat Chakhamim*," *Shema'atin* 36–37 [1973], p. 54)[15]

15. See Rabbi Jacob Medan's sharp critique, "Mavo le-Ma'amaro shel Ch. Chefetz,"

Prof. Yeshayahu Leibowitz took this approach to the extreme. Whereas Rabbi Kook argued that the Torah's aim is to teach us not facts but spiritual lessons, Leibowitz went even further, arguing that the Torah's objective is far narrower: to teach us the *mitzvot*. In his view, the demarcation between the realms of science and religion is much sharper.[16]

It is important to understand that the total demarcation between science and religion affects not only our understanding of the nature of religion, but also our understanding of the nature of science. Just as religion does not deal with simple factual pronouncements, so, too, science does not deal with moral, ethical, or spiritual assertions:

> Over the course of the generations, scientists have argued that there is no connection between science and morality.... What is better – man or a bacterium? Clearly, this question is meaningless in the eyes of science. The bacterium that causes tuberculosis is no better nor any worse than man. Science is incapable of asking: Is this "good" or "bad"?
>
> (Aharon Katzir, *Be-Kur ha-Mahapekha ha-Mada'it*, p. 59)

Megadim 14 (5751), pp. 69–71. See also in this context Rabbi Yitzchak Hutner, *Pachad Yitzchak, Iggerot u-Khetavim*, pp. 50–52, whose position is similar to that of Prof. Breuer.

16. Yeshayahu Leibowitz, *Yahadut, Am Yehudi u-Medinat Yisra'el*, p. 342.

The Image of God

"In the Image"

On the final day of creation, the Torah tells us,

> God said, Let us make man in Our image, after Our likeness; and let them have dominion over the fish of the sea, and over the birds of the air, and over the cattle, and over all the earth, and over every creeping thing that creeps on the earth. So God created mankind in His own image, in the image of God (*be-tzelem Elohim*) He created him; male and female He created them.
>
> (Genesis 1:26–27)

The Sages teach us that it is the image of God in man that obligates us to honor man. It is also what gives value and meaning to human existence, as was already expressed in the famous words of Rabbi Akiva:

> He used to say: Beloved is man, for he was created in the image of God; an extra love is made known to him that he was created in God's image. As it is stated: "For God made man in His own image."
>
> (*Ethics of the Fathers* 3:14)

Several of our Sages diminish the significance of the expression *betzelem Elohim*. Yonatan ben Uziel renders *betzelem Elohim* as *betzalma Hashem* and not *betzalma de-Hashem*. Some infer from this that according to Targum Yonatan, the verse means: "In a [special] image, God created man." According to this interpretation, the words *tzelem* and *Elohim* are not joined grammatically. Ibn Ezra mentions this interpretation (but rejects it):

> Some say…"So God created mankind in his own image" – that the [possesive] *vav* [in the word *betzalmo*] relates to "mankind." And they explain *betzelem Elohim* – that the word *Elohim* is attached to *asa*, as if the verse said that God fashioned man in an image.
>
> (Ibn Ezra)

Others accepted the concept of *tzelem Elohim*, but understood these words as referring not to the image of God, but to the image of the angels. This is the interpretation suggested by Ibn Ezra. But how then do they explain the verse: "And God created man *betzalmo* [in H/his image]"? Rashbam adopted the interpretation that *tzelem Elohim* refers to the image of the angels, and maintains, as we saw earlier, that the verse refers to the image of man. That is to say, man was created in an image unique to him (like the interpretation attributed to Yonatan), namely, the image of the angels.

Rabbi Yehuda Halevi interpreted the verse the same way:

> A prophet's eye is more penetrating than speculation. His sight reaches directly up to the heavenly host, he sees the host of heaven – the spiritual beings which are near God and others – in human form. They are alluded to in the verse "Let us make mankind in Our image, after Our likeness."…God created man in the form of His angels and servants, which are near Him, not in place, but in rank.
>
> (*Kuzari* IV, 3)

According to these authorities, the expression *tzelem Elohim* does not mean "the image of God," but the image of the angels and the other spiritual beings in heaven. Many others, however, have understood the verse as referring here to the image of God Himself. Following on this understanding, we can clarify what "the image of God" means by asking what bestows such great importance upon man among all the created beings.

Reason

Some have suggested that man's intellect and reason comprise the image of God in him. Rashi, for instance, explained *betzalmenu* as "in our type," and *kidemutenu* as "with the power to comprehend and to discern."

This approach is most commonly attributed to Maimonides, whose rationalistic teachings stress the importance of man's intellect:

> Now man possesses as his proprium something in him that is very strange in that it is not found in anything else that exists under the sphere of the moon, namely, intellectual apprehension. In the exercise of this, neither sense, nor any part of the body, nor any of the extremities are used; and therefore this apprehension was likened unto the apprehension of the deity, which does not require an instrument, although in reality it is not like the latter apprehension, but only appears so to the first stirrings of opinion.
>
> It is because of this something, I mean because of the divine intellect conjoined with man, that it is said of man that he is "in the image of God" and "after His likeness," not that God, may He be exalted, is a body and possesses a shape.
>
> (*Guide of the Perplexed* I, 1)

And similarly he writes in his *Mishne Torah*:

> The vital principle of all flesh is the form which God has given it. The superior intelligence in the human soul is the specific form of the man who is perfect in his intellect. The Torah refers to this form in the text, "Let us make man in Our image, after Our likeness." This means that man is to have a form that knows and apprehends idealistic beings that are devoid of matter, such as angels, which are forms without substance, so that man is like the angels.
>
> (*Hilkhot Yesodei ha-Torah* 4:8)[1]

According to Maimonides, the intellect is man's crown, that which makes him unique and distinguishes him from all other living things. It is the key to the worship of God:

> For it is not logical that man's major purpose is to eat or to drink or to engage in copulation or to build a house or to be a king, because these are all passing occurrences and do not add to his essence. Moreover, he shares all these activities with other types of living creatures.... For he is not different from other types of animals except in his reason. He is a rational living being. The word "rational" means the attainment of rational concepts. The greatest of rational concepts is the understanding of the Oneness of the Creator, blessed and praised be He, and all that pertains to this divine matter.
>
> (Introduction to Commentary to the Mishna)

> One only loves God with the knowledge with which one knows Him. According to the knowledge will be the love. If the former be little or much, so will the latter be little or much. A person ought therefore to devote himself to the understanding and

1. The matter requires clarification, which is beyond the present scope, for it would appear from this that the expression "in Our image," even according to Maimonides, refers to the image of the angels, and not the image of God Himself.

> comprehension of those sciences and studies that will inform him concerning his Maker, as far as it lies in human faculties to understand and comprehend.
>
> (*Hilkhot Teshuva* 10:6)

The identification of the image of God with the intellect is familiar to us primarily because of Maimonides. But due to the influence of Greek philosophy, this idea was accepted by many Jewish thinkers who grappled with philosophical issues. The first to propose this identification seems to have been Philo, who lived in Hellenistic Alexandria during the Second Temple period and was the first thinker to combine Greek thought and Judaism:

> It is in respect of the mind, the sovereign element of the soul, that the word "image" is used.... For the human mind evidently occupies a position in men precisely answering to that which the great Ruler occupies in all the world: It is invisible while itself seeing all things, and while comprehending the substances of others, it is as to its own substance unperceived.
>
> (*On the Creation* 69)

Philo views the intellect as "the image of God," not because God is also endowed with intellect, as Maimonides argues, but because the intellect's status in the human body is similar to God's in the world. His basic position, however, is the same as Maimonides'.

Free Will

Rabbi Meir Simcha ha-Kohen of Dvinsk, author of *Meshekh Chokhma*, suggests another way to understand the essence of the image of God in man:

> The image of God refers to man's ability to choose freely without his nature coercing him, to act out of free will and intellect.... It is this alone that we know, that free will results from divine constriction, that God, may He be blessed, leaves room

> for His creatures to act in the manner of their choosing.... He therefore said to Himself, "Let us make man in Our image"; that is to say, the Torah speaks in the language of men, for He said, "Let us leave room for man to choose, that he not be forced in his actions and obligated in his thoughts, and that he have the free will to do good or evil as he desires, and that he be able to do things against his nature and against what is regarded as upright in the eyes of God."
>
> (*Meshekh Chokhma*)

Rabbi Meir Simcha views free will as a wonderful gift, the image of God in man.[2] It should be noted that there are some who disagree with this idea. When we discuss the sin committed in the Garden of Eden, we will see that Nachmanides maintains that man did *not* have free will before his primal sin, and even argues that we will return to that state in the messianic period. For Nachmanides, free will plays a far less significant role in the definition and essence of man, and in a certain sense it may even be viewed as a negative phenomenon. Rabbi Meir Simcha, a man of the modern world, understood and appreciated the great significance of free will. Everything in the natural world is subject to the laws of causality. Every activity, every action, and every movement stems necessarily from a prior network of causes.

The belief in free will asserts that man is not subject to the laws of causality, or, at the very least, that he can overcome them. According to this belief, in the very same situation, under the same circumstances, without anything being changed, man can choose between two different avenues of action. What causes him to choose one and not the other? This paradox is difficult to understand, but critical, nevertheless, for our religious belief.

The difficulty of explaining free will was already noted by

2. Compare with the words of Pico della Mirandola, *Oration on the Dignity of Man*.

Rabbi Yitzchak Isaac Chaver, a disciple of a disciple of the Vilna Gaon:

> Now the matter of how free will works is difficult to understand with human reason.... For without a doubt the two forces of the will for good and for evil are exactly equal, for if not there would be no choice. For the one that is stronger and greater will decide [the matter], and if so, free will and reward and punishment are removed. Now then, if the two of them are exactly equal, how does one of them rise up, and in what manner does it overcome the other? This matter is impossible to comprehend, because it is beyond human comprehension.
>
> (*Si'ach Yitzchak, Likkutim*, p. 286)

The one who understood the importance of free will for our religious world was, of course, Maimonides.

> Every man is given free will. If one desires to turn toward the good way and be righteous, he has the power to do so. If one wishes to turn toward the evil way and be wicked, he is at liberty to do so. And thus it is written in the Torah: "Behold, the man is become as one of us, to know good and evil" (Genesis 3:22), which means that the human species had become unique in the world, there being no other species like it in the following respect, namely, that man, of himself and by the exercise of his own intelligence and reason, knows what is good and what is evil, and there is none who can prevent him from doing that which is good or that which is evil.[3] And since this is so [there is reason to fear] "lest he put forth his hand, etc."
>
> Let not the notion, expressed by foolish gentiles and most of the senseless folk among Israelites, pass through your mind

3. Maimonides understands the verse as follows: "Behold, the man is become like one" – unique in his world; "knowing by himself (*mimenu*) good and evil" – deciding by himself and on his own between good and evil.

> that at the beginning of a person's existence, the Almighty decrees that he is to be either righteous or wicked. This is not so. Every human being may become righteous like Moses or wicked like Jeroboam; wise or foolish, merciful or cruel, niggardly or generous, and so with all other qualities. There is no one that coerces him or decrees what he is to do, or draws him to either of two ways; but every person turns, spontaneously and of his own volition, to the way he desires.
>
> (*Hilkhot Teshuva* 5:1–2)

Maimonides explains the significance of free will at great length, emphasizing that it is one of the fundamental tenets of our faith.[4] Were it not for free will, man would fall into despair and renounce all responsibility for his fate. Maimonides' primary objection is to fatalism – the notion that God determines man's destiny in each and every matter. In the fatalist view, Maimonides points out, there is no reason to command or admonish man, nor to promise reward or punishment; in any event, we have no control over our conduct.

Rabbi Chasdai Crescas, in his *Or Hashem*, argues that free will can be denied from another direction: the causal forces of nature. In this view, God does not directly determine every particular event, but whatever happens is automatically determined by the natural causes that govern the world. Today we speak primarily about psychological determinism. An individual must act in a certain manner because of his nature or personal history. This approach leaves room for Torah and *mitzvot*, as well as reward and punishment, for all these may serve as additional psychological factors pushing a person to do good. Nonetheless, in this view man does not have free will. It should be noted that Rabbi Meir

4. Maimonides (in the eighth chapter of *Shemona Perakim*) also expanded the scope of free will, arguing that the saying "Everything is in the hands of heaven except for the fear of heaven" excludes from free will only those things that depend on natural law, e.g., whether a person is tall or short, whether or not it will rain, and the like.

Simcha rejects this approach as well. He speaks of divine contraction (*tzimtzum*), but later adds that man is free to act "*against his nature* and against what is regarded as upright in the eyes of God." God has no control over man – "everything is in the hand of heaven, except for the fear of heaven" – but neither has nature control over man.

Our struggle today is primarily with the second type of denial of free will. Many schools of psychology (psychoanalysis, behaviorism, certain physiological-neurological approaches) deny the possibility of free will and turn man into a machine driven by impulses and urges. This approach frees us of responsibility for our actions. It is precisely for this reason that it is important to remember the significance the Sages attach to free will. Against the backdrop of the psychology of our period, and in appreciation of the importance of free will, one of the leading representatives of the Musar movement in our generation, Rabbi Shlomo Wolbe, the author of *Alei Shur*, emphasizes that free will should not be regarded as a given, but as a noble virtue to which man must aspire. He concedes that under ordinary circumstances, much as the psychologists claim, people do not exploit their free will, but nonetheless every human being is capable of attaining a state of free will and must see this as a challenge:

> How often do we invoke our power of choice? Personal disposition, education, habit, and interests maintain almost absolute rule over us from childhood to old age. A person can go through life without ever having to invoke the power of choice!...It is clear from this that free choice is not at all part of man's daily spiritual bread. It is one of the noble virtues that man must labor to attain.
>
> (*Alei Shur*, pp. 155–156)

Domination over the Universe

Rabbenu Sa'adya Gaon, in his translation of the Torah, renders *betzalmo* as "He created him as a ruler." Interestingly, Rabbenu

Sa'adya's suggestion is supported by the verse itself, for after God says, "Let us make man in Our image, after Our likeness," He immediately continues: "And let them have dominion over the fish of the sea, and over the birds of the air, etc." Thus, the image of God is associated with domination.

Rabbi Chayyim Volozhiner, like Rabbenu Sa'adya Gaon, speaks of the "image of God" as embodied in man's strength and dominion, but he takes this idea in a mystical direction, referring to dominion over the upper worlds rather than dominion in this world.

> This is "So God created mankind in His own image, in the image of God.... For in the image of God made He man..." For just as He, blessed be His name, is *Elohim*, possessor of the powers that exist in all the worlds, He who arranges and leads them at every moment according to His will, so, too, He, blessed be He, gave man dominion, that he be the one who opens and closes thousands of ten-thousands powers and worlds...in accordance with the supernal root of his actions, words, and thoughts, as if he were in possession of those powers.
>
> (*Nefesh ha-Chayyim*, *sha'ar* 1, chap. 3)

Creativity

Rabbi Joseph B. Soloveitchik proposes a different approach, which may be seen as a continuation of the previous understanding. He sees the image of God in man as residing in man's creative powers. Dominion over the world, according to Rabbi Soloveitchik, is merely one aspect of human creativity.

> There is no doubt that the term "image of God" in the first account refers to man's inner charismatic endowment as a creative being. Man's likeness to God expresses itself in man's striving and ability to become a creator. Adam the first, who was fashioned in the image of God, was blessed with great

> drive for creative activity and immeasurable resources for the realization of this goal.
>
> (*The Lonely Man of Faith*, p. 11)

Rabbi Soloveitchik sees in man's creative activity a fulfillment of *imitatio Dei*. The classic midrashim demand of us to imitate God by assuming His moral attributes. Rabbi Soloveitchik unhesitatingly broadens the canvas and demands that we imitate God in the creative sphere as well.

> The Torah describes the creation at length in order to teach us a very important lesson – "to walk in all His ways" – and to instruct man to imitate his Creator and be himself a creator. A person should not shake his head saying that this demand of man is impossible, for he cannot imitate his Creator in creativity.... The Torah, nevertheless, demands of man and commands him to tirelessly exert himself to cling to the traits of the Holy One, blessed be He, and be a creator.
>
> (*Yemei Zikaron*, p. 86)

Rabbi Soloveitchik's words here certainly include physical creation – the construction of bridges and railroads, technological development – but primarily he is concerned with spiritual creation: Torah study and moral perfection. He regards creativity and innovation as a supreme value, the very image of God in man. The creative enterprise contains a dimension of creation *ex nihilo*: the development of something that never existed before. In this context, Rabbi Soloveitchik speaks of God as having not entirely completed the creation of the world, and thus of leaving room for man to create and perfect.

Morality

Still other Jewish thinkers identify the image of God in man with man's innate morality.

> The power of giving is a divine power, one of the traits of the Creator of all things, may He be blessed, who shows compassion, is beneficent, and gives, without receiving anything in exchange.... In this way He made man, as it is written: "God created mankind in His own image," so that he would be able to show compassion, be beneficent, and give.
>
> (Dessler, *Mikhtav mei-Eliyahu* I, p. 32)

Rabbi Dessler explains that the image of God in man is his moral inclination. This assertion may be understood in two ways: It may refer to man's free will. Man's natural inclination is to act for his own benefit, to advance his own interests. He has the capacity, however, to overcome his nature and choose what is good and moral. But Rabbi Dessler may be trying to make a different point: God implanted in man, alongside his natural inclination to look out for his own personal interests, a natural inclination to do good without receiving anything in return.

The Body

Maimonides emphasized that the idea of the "image of God" surely does not refer to God's physical image. Rabbi Samson Raphael Hirsch, however, in a surprising and unusual comment, argues that what is under discussion here is man's physical image:

> "So God created man in His image..." Man's physical frame is worthy of God and appropriate for his godly mission. Thus, the Torah teaches us to recognize and value the godlike dignity of the body. Indeed, the Torah does not come to sanctify the spirit, but first and foremost, to sanctify the body. This is the foundation of all human morality: Man's body, with all its urges and forces, was created in the image of God. And it falls upon man to sanctify his body in a manner commensurate with his godly mission.
>
> (Commentary to Genesis 1:27)

Rabbi Hirsch's comment is seemly and fitting. Rashi (following the Sages) alludes to the same idea in his well-known explanation of the verse "For he that is hanged is accursed of God" (Deuteronomy 21:23). Rabbi Hirsch, however, seems to go too far when he asserts that this is what is meant by "the image of God" found in man. Maimonides' position on this is more persuasive. In any event, note that Rabbi Hirsch is careful not to say, God forbid, that man's body is similar to that of God, so to say. He says that the human body is called the "image of God" because it is "worthy of God" and fills "a godlike mission." Exactly what he means by these expressions is uncertain.

Divine Spark

The last opinion on the meaning of "image of God" is different in essence from all the other opinions we have thus far surveyed. This position holds that the image of God in man is not a trait or quality that lends itself to identification and classification, but rather a divine spark that lies hidden deep within the human soul. We find this view stated in the Zohar:

> In what way is man similar to Him? Rabbi Avahu said: In his soul, which is holy and will never be consumed, for it was taken from Him, from His power and His strength. It is not like his body, which was taken from the ground, and will be consumed, and will return to the dust as it was.
>
> (Zohar *Chadash*, Genesis 28b)

Maharal adds the following explanation:

> This is the meaning of the verse "Let us make man in Our image, after Our likeness," for splendor clings to his face and a divine spark clings to him. This is the "image of God." It is in this way that man is unique among all creatures, in the splendor and light of the image. This light is not at all a physical

> light, but rather is the divine light and splendor that clings to man, and about which it is stated: "For in the image of God made He man."
>
> (*Derekh ha-Chayyim* 3:14)

Nachmanides mentions a similar idea in his commentary to the verse "And He breathed into his nostrils the breath of life" (Genesis 2:7):

> "And He breathed into his nostrils the breath of life." This verse alludes for us to the preeminence of the soul, its foundation and its mystery, for it mentions the full divine name. And it says that He breathed into his nostrils the breath of life, to inform us that it did not come to him from the elements, as was intimated concerning the soul of moving things,[5] nor was it an evolvement from the Separate Intelligences. Rather, it was the spirit of the great God, from whose mouth came intelligence and understanding. For one who breathes into the nostrils of another person gives him something of his own soul.
>
> (Commentary to Genesis 2:7)

Nachmanides explains that when God breathed the breath of life into man, He transferred to him of His divine essence, "for one who breathes into the nostrils of another person gives him something of his own soul." Nachmanides does not connect this to the "image of God," but he makes the same point: God implanted within man something of His own essence. Man contains a divine spark, an element of the divine spirit.

Fact or Mission?

In conclusion, let us take a look at what Rabbi Joseph Soloveitchik has said. His observation is connected to what was cited earlier

---

5. That is, the souls of animals, whose primary activity is movement (following Chavel).

from the *Alei Shor.* The image of God, however we understand it, is not only a fact but a mission, too, and we must be fit to assume this status.

> Judaism considered the *imago* element to be not a gratuitous grant bestowed upon man but rather a challenge to be met by man; not as an endowment fashioned by God but rather as a mission to be implemented.... Perhaps the central norm in our ethical system is related to *Imago Dei*, to be like God, reflect His image.... It is up to man to either realize or shake off the *Imago Dei*.
>
> (*Family Redeemed*, p. 7)

Rabbi Soloveitchik connects the idea of "image of God" to the commandment to be like God. When we fulfill the *mitzva* of "walking in His ways," we realize the divine image within us.

The Torah and the Ancient Near East

Traces of Ancient Legends in Scripture

Traditional biblical commentators as well as academic scholars have noted the problematic nature of the description of the creation of the fifth day:

> And God said, Let the waters swarm abundantly with moving creatures that have life, and let birds fly above the earth in the open firmament of heaven. And God created the great *Taninim*, and every living creature that moves, which the waters brought forth abundantly, after their kind, and every winged bird after its kind; and God saw that it was good.
>
> (Genesis 1:20–21)

The reference to the "great *Taninim*" poses a serious exegetical difficulty. The verse does not specify all the species of animals created on that day; why then were the great *Taninim* singled out for special mention? And furthermore, aside from verse 1, the term *beri'a* ("creation") is used solely in connection with the creation of man and the creation of the great *Taninim*; what is so special about these animals?

Several of our commentators have discussed the uniqueness of the *Taninim*. We begin with Rashi:

> "The *Taninim*" – the large fishes that are in the sea. And according to the statement of the Agada it means here the Leviathan and its consort, which the Holy One, blessed be He, created male and female. He killed the female, however, and preserved it in salt for the benefit of the righteous in the time to come, for had they been permitted to be fruitful and multiply, the world could not have endured because of them.

Rashi offers two explanations. According to the first explanation, we are dealing here with a whole category of creatures. According to the second explanation, we are dealing here with a specific animal, and there is a special reason that it was singled out from among all others.

Nachmanides focuses on the second question raised above, namely, why the term *beri'a* is used here:

> Because of the great size of these creatures, because some are many miles long.... For this reason, Scripture attributes their creation to God, because He brought them into being out of nothing from the beginning, as I have explained the term *beri'a* [creation]. Scripture does the same regarding man owing to his superiority, thus teaching us that he was also brought into being out of nothing with his intelligence and reason.

Seforno suggests a different answer:

> The generative potential which was present in the water (as endowed by God) was not sufficient to bring forth the first *Taninim* without seed, until [God] created at that time sufficient potential [power] to do so.

According to Seforno, it was generally the water or the earth that brought forth the various creatures in compliance with God's command. The *Taninim*, however, which appear to have been especially huge creatures, required God's personal involvement, because the water was not sufficiently powerful to create them.

One of the leading biblical scholars of recent generations, Prof. M.D. Cassuto, adduced this verse in support of his basic approach to the Torah.

> [The Torah] intended to sound a protest, as it were, against concepts that were current among the Gentiles, and to a certain extent even among the Israelites, but which were not in accord with its own spirit. In Egypt, in Mesopotamia, all sorts of legends used to be recounted about the battles of the great gods against the sea dragon and similar monsters. The Ugaritic epics mention among the enemies of Baal, along with the god Mot – his chief foe – and the lord of the sea, a number of different monsters like the Dragon, Leviathan the Fleeing Serpent, the Twisting Serpent, and similar creatures. In Israelitic circles, the tradition concerning the sea monsters and their confederates assumed an aspect in keeping with the spirit of Israel. No longer do divine forces oppose the supreme godhead, but, following the same principle as in the case of the lord of the sea, Scripture depicts them as creatures in revolt against their Maker.
>
> It voices its protest in its own quiet manner, relating: "So God created the great sea monsters." It is as though the Torah said, in effect: Far be it from any one to suppose that the sea monsters were mythological beings opposed to God or in revolt against Him; they were as natural as the rest of the creatures, and were formed in their proper time and in their proper place by the word of the Creator, in order that they might fulfill His will like the other created beings.
>
> (Cassuto, *From Adam to Noah*, pp. 49–51)

According to Cassuto, the Torah speaks of the *Taninim* (and, it may be added, uses the term *beri'a*) in order to fight against an idolatrous idea that was prevalent at the time. Against the common ancient belief that the *Taninim* were divine sea monsters that fought against the Creator, the Torah emphasizes that they were animals created by God, as were all of the world's other animals. Cassuto explains the verses describing the gathering of the waters into one place on the third day of creation in the same spirit. The Torah is rejecting the notion that the sea – or the "angel of the sea" – fought against God as an equal.

To sum up Cassuto's position, the Torah does not totally reject the ancient mythological tradition but instead modifies it. "New ideas were attached to it in consonance with the conscience and ethos of the Hebrew people" (Cassuto, *Biblical and Oriental Studies*, vol. 2, p. 98). Thus the Torah uses the *Tannin* and Leviathan as symbols of the forces of evil against which God contends. The Torah eradicates the idolatrous meaning of these myths and turns them into symbols of the war against the forces of evil and suffering.

What is the source of Cassuto's claim that the Torah continues to use these ancient Canaanite symbols? He adduces many verses and midrashim that relate to these myths. Here are several striking examples:

> On that day the Lord with His sore and great and strong sword shall punish Leviathan the flying serpent, and Leviathan that crooked serpent; and He shall slay the *Tannin* that is in the sea.
>
> (Isaiah 27:1)

> Awake, awake, put on strength, O arm of the Lord; awake, as in the ancient days, in the generations of old. Are you not it that has cut *Rahav* in pieces, and wounded the *Tannin*?
>
> (Isaiah 51:9–10)

> You divided the sea by Your strength; You broke the heads of the sea monsters in the waters. You crushed the heads of Leviathan; you gave him for food to the desert people.
>
> (Psalms 74:13–14)

Many other verses and midrashim describe God's struggle with the angel of the sea, as well as His encounters with the *Tannim* and the Leviathan. We shall suffice with one example:

> At the time when the Holy One, blessed be He, wanted to create the world, He said to the patron-angel of the sea: "Open your mouth and swallow up all the waters of the world." [The angel] said to Him: "Master of the Universe! It is enough if I can manage [to swallow] my own [seawater]." Immediately [God] kicked him and killed him, as it says: "He split the sea with His might and with His understanding He smote *Rahav*" (Job 26:12).
>
> (*Bava Batra* 74b)

Basing himself on various scriptural proof-texts, Cassuto further argues that the Torah usually brings these descriptions in the context of a moral or national war. The sea monsters symbolize both the enemies of good and the enemies of Israel, whom God fights and defeats. Cassuto's argument can be summarized as follows: The Torah does not ignore the Canaanite civilization that preceded it. On the one hand, the Torah fights against the idolatry that pervaded the Canaanite culture. On the other hand, it exploits the symbols of that culture for its own purposes. A study of the similarities and differences between the Torah and Canaanite literature can offer some very instructive insights on the uniqueness of the Torah's outlook.[1]

The Laws: Meaning of the Similarity, Significance of the Differences

The similarity between the Torah and various ancient Near Eastern

1. Cassuto assumes that Scripture adopted the myths of the ancient Near Eastern peoples and altered them to suit its own needs. It may just as well be that the Near Eastern myths are rooted in the traditions of the forefathers of the Jewish people but were distorted by foreign nations.

writings goes beyond the myths with which the Torah is forced to contend. It is also found in a far more problematic area: the laws of the Torah. In the nineteenth century, scholars began to take note of the similarity between the laws of the Torah and the legal codes that governed the ancient Near East. The similarity was considered so striking that many adduced it as proof that the Torah was the work of human hands, written against the backdrop of contemporary compilations of laws. Traditional believing Jews vigorously rejected this entire avenue of scholarship. But the arguments of these scholars remain in force, and we must confront them.

In the twentieth century, an approach developed within traditional Judaism that was willing to accept the proposed similarity. How is this possible? How can we possibly find a resemblance between the eternal laws of God and the transient laws of man?

Rabbi Abraham Isaac Kook argues that there are no intellectual grounds for fearing the study of the ancient Near East and worrying that it will undermine the foundations of our faith. It is not at all surprising, he observes, to find laws that closely resemble those in our Torah.

> Is it not well known that among the ancients there were those who recognized God, prophets and spiritual giants, such as Metushelach, Chanokh, Shem and Eber, and the like? Is it possible that they had no effect on the members of their generations? Even though their achievements do not compare with those of Abraham our father, how could their influence have left no impression whatsoever upon their generations? Surely [their teachings] must have resembled those that are found in the Torah!
>
> (*Eder ha-Yakar*, p. 42)

Rabbi Kook continues with an explanation of another aspect of the similarity between the laws of the Torah and the laws of the nations of the ancient Near East:

> As for the similarity regarding practices, surely already in the days of Maimonides, and before him in the words of the Sages, it was well known that prophecy operates upon man's nature. For man's natural inclinations must be uplifted through divine guidance, for the *mitzvot* were only given for the purpose of refining men through them. Therefore, anything that found a place in the nation and the world prior to the giving of the Torah, as long as it had a moral foundation and could be elevated to an eternal moral height, was retained in God's Torah.
>
> (Ibid.)

Rabbi Kook argues that our religious beliefs have not been undermined by the discoveries of Assyriology. It is possible to reconcile the similarity between the Torah and ancient Near Eastern law with our belief in a divinely revealed Torah. He proposes two explanations for this similarity.

First, firmly believing in the natural goodness of man's heart, Rabbi Kook states that the ancient codes may very well have embraced righteousness and justice. If we believe in the "good cultural consciousness that is found in the depths of human nature," there is reason to assume that human laws, even those that are not based on the Torah, will contain elements of truth, justice, and righteousness, and therefore resemble the laws of the Torah. Moreover, the Torah itself tells us that there were spiritual giants in those ancient nations, and it is reasonable to think that they left their mark on their respective generations. Rabbi Kook resolves the tension between divine revelation and its historical context by asserting that the historical context also has religious value, and thus that history gives expression to a certain type of divine revelation.

Second, as for the practical details – that is to say, specific laws – it is reasonable to assume that the Torah wished to retain, to the extent possible, any laws observed prior to the giving of the Torah that did not involve injustice or heresy. When the earlier laws had a moral foundation, the Torah did not want to deviate from them to any great extent, in order to facilitate acceptance by the Jewish people. Rabbi Kook bases this position on that of Maimonides.

Maimonides applies the same approach most strikingly in his explanation of the reasons for the sacrifices. According to Maimonides, in order to ensure that the Jewish people would accept the Torah and act in accordance with its laws, it was impossible for the Torah to dramatically deviate from the accepted customs of the period. God, therefore, commanded the people of Israel to worship Him through sacrifices:

> For a sudden transition from one opposite to another is impossible. And therefore man, given his nature, was not capable of suddenly abandoning everything he was accustomed to…. And as at that time the way of life generally accepted and customary in the whole world, and the universal service upon which we were brought up, consisted in offering various species of living beings in the temples in which images were set up, in worshipping the latter, and in burning incense before them…His wisdom, may He be exalted, and His gracious ruse, which is manifest in regard to all His creatures, did not require that He give us a Law prescribing the rejection, abandonment, and abolition of all these kinds of worship. For one could not then have imagined the acceptance of [such a Law], considering the nature of man, which always likes that to which it is accustomed.
>
> (*Guide of the Perplexed* III, 32)

According to Maimonides, the Torah adopted the sacrificial service because this type of worship was widely observed, and weaning the Jewish people from it would have been difficult. Using the same logic, one may say that the Torah adopted other laws from the laws of the gentiles, provided that they did not contain a moral or spiritual defect.

Rabbi Kook accounts for the similarity between the laws of the Torah and the ancient Near Eastern codes by pointing to the truth and justice embodied in the codes. He also calls attention to the social-educational factor that would not allow for any significant deviation from them.

In recent generations, rabbinic authorities as well as academicians have argued that there is much to be learned from a comparison of the Torah's laws to those of the ancient Near East. Such a comparison does not simply demonstrate the similarities; it also emphasizes the differences. It is precisely the similarities that often highlight the points where the Torah deviates from its ancient parallels. Reflecting upon these points can be very instructive about the values underlying the laws of the Torah. In the present chapter we shall examine the similarities and differences between the laws of the Torah and the codes of the ancient Near East, focusing on the common values that underlie them.[2]

Between Man and God, Between Man and His Fellow

We will focus our discussion on *Parashat Mishpatim*. What stands out, first of all, is the intermingling of commandments pertaining to the relationship between man and God and commandments pertaining to the relationship between man and his fellow. No similar phenomenon exists in the ancient Near Eastern codes; they all view the laws of God and the laws of man as entirely separate spheres. This approach has significant implications.

---

2. Our discussion of the relationship between the laws of the Torah and the ancient Near Eastern codes is based primarily on the following articles: M. Sabato, "Yesodot Hagutiyim be-Farashat Mishpatim," *Alon Shevut Bogrim*, 11 (1998); M. Zer-Kavod, "Ma Bein Mishpetei ha-Torah le-Vein Chukkei Hammurabi?" *Sefer Zeidel – Kiryat Sefer*, 1962; M. Korngreen, "Hashva'at Hukkei ha-Avdut she-be-Torat Moses im Chukkei ha-Bavlim, ha-Asshurim, ve-ha-Chittim," *Sefer Karl – Kiryat Sefer*, 1990.

The citations of the ancient Near Eastern laws are based on Abraham Levanon, *Kevatzei Chukkim shel ha-Amim be-Mizrach ha-Kadmon*.

The Torah sets a fixed punishment for adultery, both for the man and for the woman:

> If a girl that is a virgin be betrothed to a husband, and a man finds her in the city, and lies with her; then you shall bring them both out to the gate of that city, and you shall stone them with stones that they die; the girl, because she cried not being in the city; and the man, because he has humbled his neighbor's wife: so you shall put away evil from among you. But if a man finds a betrothed girl in the field, and the man forces her, and lies with her: then only the man that lay with her shall die: but to the girl you shall do nothing.
>
> (Deuteronomy 22:23–26)

Compare this with what is stated in the ancient Near Eastern codes:

> If a man seizes a woman in the mountain, it is the man's offense; he shall die. But if he seizes her in the house, it is the woman's offense; the woman shall die. If the man finds them and then slays them, there shall be no punishment for him. If he brings them to the gate of the king, and says: My wife shall not be put to death, and he then pardons the wife, he must also pardon the adulterer.
>
> (*Hittite Laws* 197–198)

The similarity is striking; "mountain" here is comparable to "field," and "house" to "city." The difference, however, is equally remarkable: According to the Hittite laws, the husband is given a certain amount of discretion, and there is no absolute, objective law. The husband's authority is also emphasized in the Middle Assyrian laws and the laws of Hammurabi:

> If a man lies with a married woman, in the temple chamber or on the street, knowing that she is a married woman, they

> shall do to the adulterer as the husband commands be done to his wife.
>
> (*Middle Assyrian Laws* 14)

> If a man's wife be caught lying with another man, both shall be tied and thrown into the water. But if the husband wishes to pardon his wife, the king, if he so desires, may also pardon his subject.
>
> (*Code of Hammurabi* 129)

According to these ancient codes, the husband may pardon his adulterous wife. We find another difference between the laws of the Torah and those of the ancient Near Eastern peoples with respect to the death penalty. In the Torah it is explicitly stated:

> You shall take no ransom for the life of a murderer, who is guilty of death; but he shall surely be put to death.
>
> (Numbers 35:31)

In contrast, according to the Assyrian laws, the blood avenger may choose to receive monetary compensation in place of the murderer's execution:

> If a man or a woman breaks into another man's house and strikes a man or a woman, the murderer shall be turned over to the closest relative, and the blood avenger may decide whether the murderer should be put to death, or whether he should be allowed to live, and his property confiscated.
>
> (*Middle Assyrian Laws* 10)

In light of what is found in the Assyrian code, we better understand why the Torah saw a need to emphasize that a ransom may not be taken for the life of a murderer (we do not find a similar admonition not to take a ransom for the life of a Sabbath desecrator!).

The differences between the laws of the Torah and the Assyrian laws outlined above stem from the fact that the ancient Near Eastern codes see the adulterer and the murderer as sinning against the husband or against the murder victim and his family, respectively. Thus, the injured party can pardon the criminal or convert his punishment into a monetary ransom.[3] According to the Torah, on the other hand, the criminal does not simply cause injury to another man, but he also violates the laws of God, and therefore it is not in man's power to pardon him.

The same principle is illustrated when Joseph tells Potiphar's wife that if he lies with her, he will have sinned against God (Genesis 39:9), and not only against her husband. Similarly, God says to Abimelech: "For I also withheld you from sinning against me: therefore I did not permit you to touch her" (Genesis 20:6). The point is made even more apparent by the Torah's rationale for executing a murderer: "Whoever sheds man's blood, by man shall his blood be shed, for in the image of God made He man" (Genesis 9:6). Even the laws pertaining to the relationship between man and his fellow are laws pertaining to God.

Slaves

An interesting law in the Torah states that when a slave refuses to be liberated by his master, his ear is pierced.

> And if the servant shall plainly say, I love my master, my wife, and my children; I will not go out free: then his master shall bring him to the judges; he shall also bring him to the door, or to the doorpost; and his master shall pierce his ear through with an awl; and he shall serve him forever.
>
> (Exodus 21:5–6)

3. Even in the Middle Ages, it was still generally only the victim's family who could bring the killer to justice, and it was impossible to pardon the killer without their consent. See Marc Bloch, *Feudal Society*.

In contrast, the Code of Hammurabi states the exact opposite:

> If a slave says to his master: "You are not my master," if they convict him, his master shall cut off his ear.
>
> (*Code of Hammurabi* 282)

As in the Torah, so in the Code of Hammurabi, a pierced ear symbolizes slavery. In the Torah, however, the piercing is done at the request of the slave, a request which the Torah frowns upon. In the Code of Hammurabi, on the other hand, it is the master who demands that his slave's ear be pierced in order to crush him and ensure his eternal enslavement.

The Torah further states:

> You shall not deliver to his master the servant who is escaped from his master to you.
>
> (Deuteronomy 23:16)

The Sages circumscribed this law (*Gittin* 45a) but its fundamental conceptual significance remains in place. Compare this to what is stated in the Code of Hammurabi:

> If anyone receives into his house a runaway male or female slave of the court, or of a freedman, and does not bring him out at the public proclamation of the major domus, the master of the house shall be put to death.
>
> (*Code of Hammurabi* 16)

The Torah sanctifies freedom, not slavery. The value the Torah attaches to freedom is infinitely greater than what is found in the codes of the nations that were Israel's neighbors.

An Ox That Killed a Man

There is a remarkable similarity between the Torah and the ancient Near Eastern codes with respect to the laws governing an ox that caused injury. Compare, for example, the Torah's laws and the Eshnunna laws regarding an ox that gored another ox:

> And if one man's ox hurts another's, that he die; then they shall sell the live ox, and divide the money of it; and the dead ox also they shall divide.
>
> (Exodus 21:35)

> If an ox gores another man's ox, and it dies, the two owners of the oxen shall divide the money of the live ox, and they shall also divide the money of the dead ox.
>
> (*Eshnunna Laws* 53)

The linguistic similarity resulted from the stylistic decisions of the translator. Clearly, however, we are dealing here with a similarity in regard to substance as well as style. In light of the amazing parallelism between laws of an ox that gored another ox, the difference between the Torah and the Eshnunna laws with respect to an ox that killed a man is all the more striking:

> If an ox gores a man or a woman, that they die; then the ox shall be surely stoned, and his flesh shall not be eaten; but the owner of the ox shall be acquitted. But if the ox was wont to gore with his horn in time past, and his owner had been warned, yet he had not kept him in, but it killed a man or a woman, the ox shall be stoned, and its owner also shall be put to death.
>
> (Exodus 21:28–29)

> If the ox was known to be wont to gore, and the authorities brought the matter to the attention of the owner, and he did not cut off its horns, and it gored a man and he died, the owner of the ox shall pay two-thirds of a mina.
>
> (*Eshnunna Laws* 54)

The Eshnunna Laws recognize the difference between an ox

that was not known to be a gorer and an ox that was known to be a gorer. Nonetheless, they are lenient with regard to an ox that killed a man, even when it was known to be a gorer. Similarly, we find in the Code of Hammurabi:

> If an ox, while passing on the street, gored a man and killed him, the case is not a matter fit for a legal claim. If an ox be a goring ox, and it was shown that he is a gorer, and he did not cut his horns, or fasten the ox up, and the ox gored a free-born man and killed him, the owner shall pay one-half a mina in money.
>
> (*Code of Hammurabi* 250–251)

According to the Code of Hammurabi, if an ox that was not known to be a gorer killed a man, its owner was totally exempt from liability, and if the ox was known to be a gorer, its owner was only liable for monetary payment. According to the Torah, in contrast, the ox was stoned in both cases, and if it was a known gorer, "its owner also shall be put to death." While it is true that the Halakha only requires the owner to pay a fine, and does not execute him, the Torah clearly intends to emphasize the value of human life, for which there is no compensation or substitution.

Hurting a Pregnant Woman

We will now compare the Torah and the ancient Near Eastern codes in regard to injuries during pregnancy. The Torah says:

> If men strive, and hurt a woman with child, so that her fruit depart from her, and yet no further harm ensue: he shall be surely punished, according as the woman's husband will lay upon him; and he shall pay as the judges determine.[4] But if any harm ensue, then you shall give life for life.
>
> (Exodus 21:22–23)

---

4. Even if we understand that the ransom depends on the woman's husband, it is still different from the laws of the nations that we saw earlier, for there it

The Code of Hammurabi, on the other hand, states:

> If a man strikes the daughter of a man,[5] so that her fruit depart from her, he shall pay ten silver shekels for her fruit. And if the woman dies, the assailant's daughter shall surely die.
>
> (*Code of Hammurabi*, 209–210)

According to the Code of Hammurabi, a daughter can be put to death for her father's offense. Children are viewed as their fathers' property, and not as independent human beings of unlimited value. This idea repeats itself in many other ancient Babylonian laws. For example:

> If a builder built a house for another person, but the construction was not sound, so that as a result the house that he had built collapsed, causing the death of the owner of the house, the builder shall surely die. And if he caused the death of the son of the owner of the house, they shall put the son of the builder to death.
>
> (*Code of Hammurabi* 229–230)

All this stands in sharp contrast to the Torah, which quite specifically declares that children are not put to death for their fathers' transgressions:

> Fathers shall not be put to death for children, neither shall children be put to death for fathers; every man shall be put to death for his own sin.
>
> (Deuteronomy 24:16)

---

is not the amount of compensation that is decided by the victim's family but the death penalty.

5. That is, the daughter of another upper-class man. The term "daughter of a man" and the law itself imply that we are dealing here with a young woman who presumably had never had a child.

The following strange and inexplicable verse is found in the Torah in the context of the laws pertaining to an ox that killed a man:

> Whether he has gored a son or gored a daughter, according to this judgment shall it be done to him.
>
> (Exodus 21:31)

Why should the law be different for killing a son or a daughter? Maybe it was necessary to emphasize that children's lives are not worth less than those of adults, and therefore the punishment for killing children is not less severe. Cassuto suggests just the opposite: the Torah is excluding the accepted law of the ancient Near East that one's own child is put to death if one is found liable for the death of another man's child.

Theft

The Torah does not impose the death penalty for stealing. The only mention of death in connection with stealing is in the case of a break-in, and even in that situation, killing the thief is only allowed in self-defense, that is, in the course of the robbery.

> If a thief be found breaking in, and be smitten that he die, no blood shall be shed on his account. If the sun be risen upon him, blood shall be shed on his account. He should make full restitution; if he have nothing, then he shall be sold for his theft.
>
> (Exodus 22:1–2)

The Code of Hammurabi also deals with break-ins:

> If anyone breaks a hole into a house, and is caught, he shall be put to death before that hole and be buried.
>
> (*Code of Hammurabi* 21)

Thus, in the Babylonian code, the death penalty is imposed on anyone caught breaking into another person's house, whereas the Torah limits the allowance to kill the thief to self-defense during the course of the burglary. The Code of Hammurabi also imposes the death penalty for other kinds of theft besides break-ins. The penalty is death, for instance, in cases where the thief is unable to pay an indemnity.

> If anyone steals cattle or sheep, or an ass, or a pig or a goat, if it belongs to a temple or to the royal court, the thief shall pay thirty-fold; if they belonged to a free man of the king he shall pay tenfold; if the thief has nothing with which to pay he shall be put to death.
>
> (*Code of Hammurabi* 8)[6]

The Torah rules explicitly against this, as we have seen: "If he has nothing, then he shall be sold for his theft" (Exodus 22:2).

Seizing a Pawn

The Torah strictly limits the creditor's right to seize a pawn:

> No man shall take the nether or upper millstone for a pledge; for he takes a man's life for a pledge.
>
> (Deuteronomy 24:6)

> If you at all take your neighbor's garment for a pledge, you shall deliver it to him by sundown. For that is his only covering, it is his garment for his skin; in what shall he sleep? And it shall come to pass, when he cries to Me, that I will hear; for I am gracious.
>
> (Exodus 22:25–26)

6. In the Code of Hammurabi, the punishment for theft is dependent on the class of the person from whom the property was stolen: one who steals from the king is subject to a more severe penalty than one who steals from a free man.

The Torah prohibits taking the nether or upper millstone as a pledge because one would "be taking a man's life for a pledge." In contrast, the Code of Hammurabi permits the creditor to take the debtor himself as a pledge.

> If anyone has a claim for corn or money upon another and imprisons him; if the prisoner dies in prison a natural death, the case shall go no further. If the prisoner dies in prison from blows or maltreatment, the master of the prisoner shall convict the merchant before the judge. If he was a freeborn man, the son of the merchant shall be put to death; if it was a slave, he shall pay one-third of a mina of gold, and all that the master of the prisoner gave he shall forfeit.
>
> (*Code of Hammurabi* 115–116)

How different is the spirit of the Torah from that of the Code of Hammurabi!

The comparisons we have drawn between the Torah and the legal codes of the ancient Near East are precisely what strengthens our recognition of the moral intensity and uniqueness of the Torah.

> And what nation is there so great, that has statutes and judgments so righteous as all this Torah, which I set before you this day?
>
> (Deuteronomy 4:8)

Man's Place in the World

Why Was Man Created Last?

The first chapter of the book of Genesis raises an issue that is central to our entire outlook: man's place in the world. By this we mean man's rank vis-à-vis the rest of creation: is man the ultimate end and pinnacle of creation, or is he just another creature, in no way essentially superior to all others? According to chapter 1 of Genesis, man was created last. Does this imply elevated rank, or perhaps, on the contrary, insignificance?

> Man was created last.... Why was he created last? So that he would not become haughty. He is told: A gnat preceded you in the act of creation.... Another explanation: So that he would immediately begin his meal. They drew an analogy. To what may this be compared? To a king who built a palace, dedicated it, and prepared a meal, and then afterward invited guests.
>
> (Tosefta, *Sanhedrin* 8:7–9)

Thus the fact that man was created last lends itself to two interpretations. It may point to man's insignificance: he was created only after all the other creatures had already been fashioned. Alternatively, perhaps it indicates man's elevated rank: he is the final end of creation, and so was only created after everything else was ready to serve him.

Midrash Genesis Rabba raises this question in a slightly different form:

> As Resh Lakish said: "And the spirit of God hovered over the surface of the water" (Genesis 1:2) – this is the spirit of the messianic king.... If man merits, he is told: You preceded the ministering angels; and if not, he is told: A fly preceded you, a gnat preceded you, a snail preceded you.
>
> (Genesis Rabba 8:1)

This midrash sees the chronological order of creation as a criterion for establishing the relative value of created beings. The midrash notes, however, that the spirit of man was created first, before the rest of creation. Thus, if man makes good use of his soul and spirit, he is first among all created beings; but if his life focuses on his body, he is reminded that his body was created last.

The tension regarding man's rank in creation finds expression in a well-known passage from Psalms:

> When I behold Your heavens, the work of Your fingers, the moon and the stars, which You have ordained; what is man, that You are mindful of him? And the son of man, that You visit him? Yet You have made him a little lower than the angels, and You crown him with glory and honor. You make him to have dominion over the works of Your hands; You have put all things under his feet.
>
> (Psalms 8:4–7)

What, then, is man? "What is man, that You are mindful of him," or perhaps "You have made him a little lower than the angels"?

Man as King

Our early authorities discussed at length the question of man's place in creation. The commonly accepted view elevates man and magnifies his significance:

> Rabbi Nechemya says: From where do we know that man is equal in importance to all of creation? For it says (Genesis 5:1): "This is the book of the generations of man [in the day that God created mankind, in the likeness of God He fashioned him]," and below it says (Genesis 2:4): "These are the generations of the heaven and of the earth when they were created, [in the day that the Lord God fashioned the earth and the heavens]." Just as there creation and fashioning, here, too, creation and fashioning.
>
> (*Ethics of the Fathers de-Rabbi Natan* 31)

Rabbenu Sa'adya Gaon takes the same position, and adduces a cosmological argument in its favor:

> When we see that the creatures are many in number, nevertheless we need not be confused in regard to which of them constitutes the goal of creation. For there exists a natural criterion by means of which we can determine which one of all the creatures is the end.... Habit and nature place whatever is most highly prized in the center of things which are themselves not so highly prized.... When, therefore, we see that this situation appertains to many things and then find the earth in the center of heaven with the heavenly spheres surrounding it on all sides, it becomes clear to us that the thing which was the subject of creation must be on the earth.[1] Upon further investigation of all its parts, we note that the earth and water are both inanimate, whereas we find that the beasts are irrational. Hence only man is left, which gives us the certainty that he must unquestionably have been the intended purpose of creation. When we examine the Scriptures, we likewise find in them a statement by

1. Rabbenu Sa'adya Gaon's position may help us understand why Galileo's view that the earth is not at the center of the universe was considered so strange and problematic to the people of his generation (besides the fact that it seems to contradict Scripture).

> God to the effect that "I, even I, have made the earth, and created man upon it" (Isaiah 45:12). In fact, at the very beginning of the Torah God listed all the classes of creation. Then, when He had completed them all, He said: "Let us make man" (Genesis 1:26), like a person who builds a palace and, after having furnished and decorated it, brings its owner into it.
>
> (*Book of Doctrines and Beliefs* IV)

Rabbenu Sa'adya argues not only that man is the most distinguished element of creation, but also that he is the ultimate goal of creation. That is to say, everything else was created around him for the purpose of serving him and being of benefit to him. Maharal writes in a similar vein:[2]

> Just as the sun reigns, so is man a king, for everything is subject to him. Man's royalty expresses itself in his bringing perfection to all earthly creatures, for everything was created in order to serve man and minister to him. In this way he is the form for all earthly creatures, bringing perfection to everything, like a king, who perfects everything.
>
> (*Tiferet Yisra'el*, chap. 4)

Many thinkers among the nations of the world also affirm man's greatness and his uniqueness in creation. We shall cite here the words of the chorus in the Greek play *Antigone* by Sophocles:

> Wonders are many, and none is more wonderful than man; the power that crosses the white sea, driven by the stormy southwind, making a path under surges that threaten to engulf him; and Earth, the eldest of the gods, the immortal, the unwearied, doth he wear.... And the light-hearted race of birds, and the tribes of savage beasts, and the sea-brood of the deep, he snares

2. Compare also the words of Ramchal in his *Mesilat Yesharim*, "The world was created to be used by man" (chap. 1).

> in the meshes of his woven toils, he leads captive, man excellent in wit.... And speech, and wind-swift thought, and all the moods that mould a state, hath he taught himself.
>
> (*Antigone*, first choral ode)

In the Middle Ages, the prevailing attitude was entirely different. Medieval Christian thinkers spoke about the worthlessness and insignificance of man. The Renaissance, the period of the revival of European thought, was characterized first and foremost by a recognition of the value of man and his elevated rank within creation. Here is what the fifteenth-century philosopher Pico della Mirandola wrote in a work that shows Jewish and especially kabbalistic influence:

> At long last, however, I feel that I have come to some understanding of why man is the most fortunate of living things and, consequently, deserving of all admiration; of what may be the condition in the hierarchy of beings assigned to him, which draws upon him the envy, not of the brutes alone, but of the astral beings and of the very intelligences which dwell beyond the confines of the world....
>
> [And so God said to man:] We have given you, O Adam, no visage proper to yourself, nor endowment properly your own, in order that whatever place, whatever form, whatever gifts you may, with premeditation, select, these same you may have and possess through your own judgment and decision. The nature of all other creatures is defined and restricted within laws which We have laid down; you, by contrast, impeded by no such restrictions, may, by your own free will, to whose custody We have assigned you, trace for yourself the lineaments of your own nature.
>
> (*Oration on the Dignity of Man*)

Pico sees the unique value of man in his free will, which distinguishes him from all other creatures, earthly and celestial. Unlike the rest of creation, man is not defined and limited by particular patterns of behavior, and this is his greatness.

In the modern period (at least until, very recently, the post-modern period), the greatness of man's power has been widely recognized. Modern thinkers tend to associate man's greatness with his rapid development of technology.

Maimonides' Position: Man Is Not the Purpose of Creation

Maimonides disagrees with Rabbenu Sa'adya's position that man is the final end and pinnacle of creation. Maimonides opens with the assertion that were it true, God forbid, that the world has no Creator, it would be irrelevant to ask about the final end of creation (for an end assumes intentional initiative). However, even according to our faith regarding the creation of the world, it is inappropriate to speak of a single grand end for the entire world, and all the more so is it inappropriate to speak of man as being the final end of the entire creation.

> It is accordingly clear that, according to the doctrine of eternity,[3] the question of ultimate finality for being as a whole does not arise. On the other hand, it is sometimes thought that, according to our opinion and our doctrine of the production in time of the world as a whole after nonexistence, this question is obligatory – I mean that it is obligatory to seek out the finality of all that exists. It is likewise thought that the finality of all that exists is solely the existence of the human species so that it should worship God, and that all that has been made has been made for it alone so that even the heavenly spheres only revolve in order to be useful to it and to bring into existence that which is necessary for it. Some passages in the books of the prophets, if taken according to their external sense, give

3. According to the doctrine that the world was never created but has always existed.

strong support to this thought.... However, if this opinion is carefully examined, as opinions ought to be carefully examined by intelligent men, the flaw in it becomes clear.... Even if the universe exists for the sake of man, and the final end of man is, as has been said, to worship God, a question remains to be asked regarding the final end of his worship. For He, may He be exalted, would not acquire greater perfection if He were worshipped by all that He has created!...Necessarily and obligatorily the argument must end with the answer being given that the final end is: God has wished it so, or: His wisdom has required this to be so. And this is the correct answer....

For this reason, to my mind, the correct view according to the beliefs of the Law – a view that corresponds likewise to the speculative views – is as follows: It should not be believed that all the beings exist for the sake of the existence of man. On the contrary, all the other beings too have been intended for their own sakes and not for the sake of something else.... Just as He has willed that the human species should come to exist, He also has willed that the spheres and their stars should come to exist....

If you consider the book which guides all those who seek guidance toward what is correct and therefore is called the Torah, the notion that we have in view will become manifest to you from the commencement of the account of creation till the end. For with reference to none of them is the statement made in any way that it exists for the sake of some other thing. He only says that He brought every part of the world into existence and that its existence confirmed to its purpose. This is the meaning of his saying: "And God saw that it was good" (Genesis 1)....

Hence be not misled in your soul to think that the spheres and the angels have been brought into existence for our sake. For it has explained to us what we are worth: "Behold, the nations are as a drop of a bucket" (Isaiah 40:15). Consider accordingly your substance and that of the spheres, the stars, and the

> separate intellects; then the truth will become manifest to you, and you will know that man and nothing else is the most perfect and the most noble thing that has been generated from this [inferior] matter; but that if his being is compared to that of the spheres and all the more to that of the separate beings, it is very, very contemptible.
>
> (*Guide of the Perplexed* III, 13)

Maimonides raises several important points. He argues that man is not the final end of creation, for there are beings in the universe greater than him.[4] What he says here is connected to his general philosophy and metaphysics, according to which there exist separate intellects and spheres that are greater than man. While man is, indeed, the noblest and most important creature on earth, he is not so in the entire universe. Maimonides connects this to another point, namely, that it is inappropriate to speak of a single overall end of the world as a hierarchical system, for in the final analysis it is not at all clear why God wants the entire world. This being the case, it is reasonable to assume that every creature has its own end, which is unknown to us.[5] Maimonides finds support for this in the account of the creation. Scripture, he observes, does not connect any created being to another. Nowhere does it say that the trees were expressly created for the benefit of man. Rather, each species came into existence separately on a particular day, and about each one it was stated "that it was good," without any reference to the benefit that something else may derive from it.

When Maimonides says that man is the noblest of the material creations, his words are very different from those of Maharal, who spoke about man being the noblest creation among the

4. Douglas Adams, in his series *A Hitchhiker's Guide to the Galaxy*, spins a story in which those who truly control the world are white mice who experiment on human beings but allow them to believe that it is they (the human beings) who are performing the experiments.

5. This is an important lesson in general: it is not always necessary to put forward all-embracing metaphysical principles; local explanations often suffice.

"earthly" creatures. According to Maimonides, the separate intellects and the spheres are not mystical creatures from some other world; they are part of the physics of this world, and they, too, are superior to man. Furthermore, and again in contrast to Maharal, Maimonides maintains that even those creatures that are more lowly than man were not created in order to serve him. Every creature has its own ends.

Malbim: Negation of Maimonides' Position

Malbim devoted his commentary on the eighth chapter of Psalms ("You have made him a little lower than the angels") to proving that man is the choicest of created beings. He argues against "the philosophers," including Maimonides, who see man as merely one of many creatures. Let us illustrate his position with the following passage:

> Here he will judge those who are high and argue with the philosophers who greatly diminish the value of man, to the extent that they regard it as madness that we should say that man is the finest creature and that he is God's inheritance in His world. And they come with arguments that on first glance seem to be decisive proofs. For if we look upon the multitude of immense stars that circle tiny earth, the dwelling place of man, it being merely a tiny speck in comparison with them and like a drop in the bucket in the midst of powerful river waters.... However, the community of believers who are at one with the Torah's counsel and ways cannot deny that it is God's faithful testimony that the stars were all created for the sake of the earth, as it is written: "And God set them in the firmament of heaven to give light upon the earth" (Genesis 1:17). And that which issued forth from the earth was all created only for man, who was created last.
>
> (Malbim, Psalms 8)

The Educational Significance of Man's Greatness

Standing in extreme opposition to Maimonides is Rabbi Chayyim Volozhiner, author of *Nefesh ha-Chayyim*. Rabbi Chayyim argues not only that man is the focus of this world, but that he is also the focus of the celestial worlds.

> This, too, should cause the heart of a member of the holy nation to tremble, for he embraces in his form all the forces and all the worlds....
>
> This being the case, when a person strays and contemplates an impure thought in his heart, such as adultery, he brings a harlot, the symbol of jealousy, into the celestial Holy of Holies in the holy heavenly worlds, God forbid....
>
> For man, through the soul of life within him, becomes the living soul of a multitude of innumerable worlds. For just as all the behaviors and motions of the body follow from the force of the soul within him, so is man the force and living soul of infinite heavenly and mundane worlds, all of them conducted by him....
>
> For He, blessed be His name, after having created all the worlds, created man at the end of Creation, a marvelous creation, an ingathering force, which includes all the bright and marvelous lights and the worlds and the heavenly temples that preceded it.... all of them contributed part of their essence for his formation.
>
> (*Nefesh ha-Chayyim*, *sha'ar* 1, chaps. 4–6)

Rabbi Chayyim goes beyond Maharal and Rabbenu Sa'adya Gaon. He argues that man is the crowing jewel not only of all earthly creatures, but also of the celestial beings: man is raised above the celestial worlds and influences them. Rabbi Chayyim's position has an important educational ramification: The more glory, importance, and authority are bestowed upon man, the more responsibility may be imposed upon him. Rabbi Chayyim argues that it is precisely because man recognizes his power that he must understand that he can do much good but also much evil, and therefore must be all the more careful.

The same educational point was emphasized by some of the leading authorities of the Musar movement:

> All conduct of life, whether material life or moral life, whether the life of the community or that of the individual, is based on the measure of man's recognition of his own worth. A person of low self-esteem treats himself lightly and treats life itself lightly, to the point that he is liable at times to expose himself to dangers, without any regard, even for the most trivial of matters. Not so a person who enjoys high self-esteem; he values and cherishes life, and with all his strength he strives to elevate himself, and to elevate all of life along with him.
>
> (Natan Zevi Finkel, *Or ha-Tzafun* 1, p. 270)

Rav Kook connects this question to developments in the study of cosmology.[6]

> How much truth and song appears before us in the vision of the centrality of the human soul in relation to all of existence. This vision does not fall away because of the revelation of the broad and infinite dimensions of the cosmos, of the worlds of the stars, of the constant formation of the mists. On the contrary, this song is magnified and glorified by eternity and size.
>
> In vain do the short-sighted think that in the aftermath of the discovery of the dimensions of the cosmos, the centrality of the spirit of man is voided. They want to say that this has caused a diminishment of the value of religion, even though religion has been strong even in the hearts of those who never accepted the centrality of man, like Maimonides and his followers. This being so, the argument is null from the very outset.

6. Malbim in his commentary to *Psalms* 8 also makes reference to these developments.

> But even in the depths of the esoteric [i.e., kabbalistic] idea, which finds an important place in the life of religion, especially in recent generations when it has spread widely – there, too, no harm has been suffered, but rather the vision has been glorified. Moral responsibility has grown in proportion to existence of this sort.
>
> (*Orot ha-Kodesh* III, 357)[7]

We have already seen how Rabbenu Sa'adya Gaon connects man's centrality in creation with the centrality of the earth in the celestial system. Rabbi Kook argues that the fact that the earth, as we now know, is not the center of the universe has no bearing on the question of man's worth. On the contrary, the larger the universe, the more responsibility is imposed upon man.

Rabbi Soloveitchik relates to the psychological tension in the consciousness of *homo religiosus*, who feels important and lofty, but, all too often, at the same time also feels low and insignificant. Rabbi Soloveitchik notes that Halakha provides an unequivocal answer to this question and tension:

> One verse declares, "When I behold Thy heavens, the work of Thy fingers, the moon and the stars which Thou hast established; what is man, that Thou art mindful of him, and the son of man, that Thou thinkest of him" (Psalms 8:4–5), while the other verse declares, "Yet Thou hast made him but a little lower than the angels, and hast crowned him with glory and honor. Thou hast made him to have dominion over the works of Thy hand; Thou hast put all things under his feet" (Psalms 8:6–7). And *homo religiosus* has yet to find the third harmonizing verse.
>
> However, halakhic man has found the third verse – the Halakhah. He, too, suffers from this dualism, from this deep

7. See also *Ma'amarei ha-Ra'aya* I, p. 110.

> spiritual split, but he mends the split through the concept of Halakhah and law....
>
> If "man hath no pre-eminence above a beast; for all is vanity," then what is the nature of the Day of Atonement? What is the meaning of pardon and forgiveness? What is the purpose of the sacrificial service of the day? The private, intimate encounter between the high priest and his Creator in the holy of holies? What is the whole nature of the holiness of the day, that holiness which bestows atonement upon us? Why should we be confronted at all with the concept of sin and iniquity on the one side and the obligation to repent on the other? Indeed, the Halakhah set man at the very center of the world, and the Day of Atonement attests to this.... Indeed, I am the one creature in this world who reflects the image of Divine Presence. Do I not study the Torah, the cherished plaything [see Psalms 119:77] of the Holy One, blessed be He? The angels themselves long to learn Torah from me: Am I not at this very moment reaching out to my lover and beloved?...
>
> In the blinking of an eye the lowliest of creatures turns into the noblest of creatures, whom the Holy One, blessed be He, elected at the very inception and recognized as worthy of standing before Him. Standing before God! What self-esteem is present here!
>
> (*Halakhic Man*, pp. 66–70)

We stated earlier that power gives rise to a sense of responsibility. Rabbi Soloveitchik points here to the opposite process: Responsibility gives rise to a sense of power. Halakhic man is commanded by God; a mission has been imposed upon him; he has responsibility. The recognition that God has commanded him, that God has given him a defined mission to execute – this recognition gives man a sense of power. He is not some passing creature, but an agent of God. From here stems man's centrality in creation.

Equality

Man Was Created Alone

According to the Sages, the creation story teaches us a fundamental principle, one that may be termed "humanistic," namely, the principle of equality.[1]

> Therefore man was created alone, to teach you that whoever destroys a single soul in Israel, Scripture regards him as if he destroyed the entire world. And whoever saves a single soul in Israel, Scripture regards him as if he preserved the entire world. And for the sake of peace among people, so that one person should not say to his fellow: "My father is greater than your father."
>
> (Mishna, *Sanhedrin* 4:5)

It is from the Torah's account of creation that the Sages derived the principle of equality: Man was created alone, so that no one would be able to boast that he descends from ancestry more noble than his fellow's. We are all children of the same father. As was pointed out above in Chapter 3, many Jewish thinkers have argued that the creation story need not be understood according to its plain sense, and that Jews can accept the theory of evolution

1. The discussion in this chapter does not deal with the status of women, which is treated below in Chapter 11.

and other scientific hypotheses. According to these thinkers, the objective of the creation story is not to provide a scientific description of how the universe came into being, but to teach us certain moral and spiritual principles. From this perspective, the Sages' question should be formulated in a slightly different way: not "Why did God create man alone?" (for if we accept the theory of evolution, man was not created alone), but "Why did God state in the Torah that man was created alone?" The explanations offered by the Sages provide an adequate answer to this question.

One of the ideas found in the Mishna is formulated in a slightly different manner in the Tosefta:

> Man was created alone. And why was man created alone? So that the righteous could not say: "We are the children of a righteous man," and so that the wicked could not say: "We are the children of a wicked man."
>
> (Tosefta, *Sanhedrin* 8:4)

On the one hand, the Tosefta's formulation is sharper than the one found in the Mishna. On the other hand, the Mishna emphasizes the boastful pride of one who sets himself above others, whereas the Tosefta comes to deny the same argument when voiced by one who perceives himself as descended from inferior stock. Either way, the principle is essentially the same.

Jews and Gentiles

As we all know, however, the matter is not so simple. Although the Mishna and the Tosefta emphasize the basic equality of all men, many have argued that Jews enjoy a certain qualitative genetic superiority over all other peoples. The most prominent representative of this school of thought is Rabbi Yehuda Halevi. He argues that the fact that all of mankind descends from one father does not mean that all peoples are equal. The superior qualities of Adam were passed on only to the patriarchs of the Jewish people.

> Adam had this choice essence, for he was perfection itself without exception.... He left many children, of whom the only one capable of taking his place was Abel, because he alone was like him. After he was slain by Cain through jealousy of this privilege, it passed to his brother Seth, who also was like Adam. He, therefore, became the choice essence and heart of man, while the others were like husks. The choice essence of Seth passed to his son Enosh.... Abraham represented the choice essence of Eber, being his disciple, and for this reason he was called "Ivri." Eber represented the choice essence of Shem, the latter that of Noah.... The choice essence of Abraham passed among his sons to Isaac.... The choice essence of Isaac passed to Jacob...
>
> (*Kuzari* 1, 95)

> At first the divine influence rested on one person in a family, who was the heart of his brethren and the essence of his father. It was he in whom this divine light was concentrated, all the others being like husks which had no share in it. The sons of Jacob were, however, distinguished from other people by godly qualities, which made them, so to speak, an angelic caste. Each of them endeavored to attain the degree of prophecy, and many of them succeeded in so doing.
>
> (Ibid. 1, 103)

According to Rabbi Yehuda Halevi, there is a fundamental genetic difference between Jews and gentiles. The "divine essence" which includes the potential for prophecy, is unique to the Jewish people. This perception leads Halevi to make a distinction between descendants of the original Israelites and those who join the Jewish people through conversion:

> Any gentile who joins us shares our good fortune, without, however, being quite equal to us.
>
> (Ibid. 1, 27)

> God allows the convert who treads this path, as well as his progeny, to approach Him very closely. Those, however, who become Jews do not take equal rank with born Israelites, who are specially privileged to attain to prophecy, while the former can only achieve something by learning from them, and can only become pious and learned, but never prophets.
>
> (Ibid. I, 115)[2]

In the introduction to his Hebrew edition of *Sefer Kuzari* (pp. 30–31), Yehuda Kaufman Even-Shmuel cites some of the objections raised by the *maskilim* against this position. Saul Israel Horowitz, for instance, dismissed it as "Crude human mythology: My father is greater than your father, my land is unlike your land, theory of racial superiority, chosen people." Even-Shmuel counters that Rabbi Yehuda Halevi sees the Jewish people as the chosen nation not in the sense that they should lord over other peoples, but rather that they are responsible for other peoples and are bound by special obligations. The objections, however, still stand: Even if Halevi never meant to enslave the other nations, he still proclaims the essential superiority of the Jewish people.

Maimonides presents an entirely different perspective:

> Says Moses the son of Rabbi Maimon, one of the exiles of Jerusalem living in Spain: We have received the questions of our master and teacher Obadiah, the enlightened and understanding one, true convert, may God reward him for his deeds, and may he receive full compensation from the Lord, God of Israel, under whose wings he has sought refuge. You have asked about the blessings and prayers that you recite when you are alone or when you pray with a congregation, should you say "Our God,

2. Rabbi Yehuda Muscato, author of the *Kol Yehuda* commentary to the *Kuzari*, noted that according to the Sages, the prophet Obadiah was a convert to Judaism, which implies that even converts can merit prophecy. Regarding R. Yehuda Halevi, he said: "I fear for him that he has sinned in turning away from the position of the Sages."

> and the God of our fathers," and "who has sanctified us with his *mitzvot*, and commanded"...
>
> You must say them all in the proper manner, and make no changes. Just as any native member of Israel blesses and prays, so should you, whether you pray alone or you serve as prayer leader. The principle is that it was the patriarch Abraham who taught the entire people and made them wise, informing them of the true religion and the unity of the Holy One, blessed be He.... Therefore, whoever converts until the end of all the generations, and whoever declares the unity of God's name as it is written in the Torah, is a disciple of the patriarch Abraham, may he rest in peace; they are all members of his household. It was he who restored them to the good way; just as he restored the people of his generation through his words and teachings, so, too, did he restore all those who would convert in the future by way of the testament he left for his sons and the members of his household. Thus, the patriarch Abraham, may he rest in peace, is the father of his fitting descendants who walk in his path, and father to his disciples and all the converts. Therefore, you should say, "Our God and the God of our fathers," for Abraham, may He rest in peace, is your father.... Since you have entered under the wings of the *Shekhina* and have accompanied it, there is no difference between you and us. And all of the miracles that had been performed on our behalf are as if they had been performed for us and for you.
>
> (Maimonides, *Responsa*, no. 293)

Maimonides' position is absolutely clear: "There is no difference between you and us." As opposed to Rabbi Yehuda Halevi, who views the Jewish people as genetically unique, Maimonides emphasizes the cultural factor: the patriarch Abraham is the father both of his physical descendants and of everyone who walks in his path. The uniqueness of the Jewish people is not genetic, but cultural and behavioral. Therefore, anyone can convert and join the Jewish people and enjoy full equality with born Israelites.

Maimonides' approach is reflected in his attitude toward the possibility of prophecy among non-Jews:

> The fact that we do not believe in the prophecy of Omar and Zhayyid[3] is not because they are not of Israel, as the masses think, so that we have to learn this from "a prophet from among you, from your brothers." For Job, Eliphaz, Bildad, Zophar, and Elihu are all regarded by us as prophets, even though they were not of Israel. And similarly Hananiah ben Azur was a cursed false prophet, even though he was from Israel.
>
> (*Epistle to Yemen*)

Kohanim, Israelites, and Torah Scholars

One of the central motifs running through the book of Genesis is the denial of the special rights of the firstborn son. Time and again a firstborn son is set aside in favor of his more successful younger brother. This theme teaches us that a person's rank is determined not by inborn qualities, but by the personal decisions he makes over the course of his life.

Within Jewish society, however, there is room to speak about the genetic superiority of a particular caste. We refer, of course, to the priesthood. All *kohanim* trace their ancestry to a single family, upon whom was imposed an important and venerable role. It may, therefore, be suggested that they enjoy fundamental genetic superiority over the rest of the Jewish people.

In this context, however, let us examine the laws applying to the Nazirite. *Parashat Naso* records the three special regulations that apply to a Nazirite. He may not drink wine, he may not defile himself through contact with a corpse, and he may not cut his hair. The three special laws pertaining to a Nazirite convey a profound spiritual message.

There is a surprising parallelism between the laws of the

3. Equivalent to the English "Tom, Dick, and Harry," and referring to the prophecy of a non-Jew.

Nazirite and the laws of the High Priest. The Nazirite may not defile himself through contact with a corpse, not even when the deceased is a close relative. The same applies to the High Priest (Leviticus 21:1). Defilement through contact with a corpse contradicts holiness and closeness to God. An ordinary *kohen* is forbidden to defile himself for strangers, but is required to defile himself for a relative; the High Priest and the Nazirite were warned not to do so, for they enjoy a higher level of holiness.[4]

The Nazirite may not drink wine; the same applies to the High Priest. Immediately following the sin of Nadab and Abihu, Aaron and his sons were warned not to drink wine when they come to serve God. "Do not drink wine or strong drink, you, nor your sons with you, when you enter the Tent of Meeting, lest you die" (Leviticus 10:9). Drunkenness blurs man's personality and clouds his thought. A person standing before God must be at the peak of his powers and concentration. Thus, the *kohanim* were warned not to drink wine when engaged in the divine service, and the Nazirite, who sanctifies his life to God, was commanded to distance himself from wine and from grape derivatives.

The third commandment given to the Nazirite is that he may not cut his hair. Do we also find here a parallel law applying to the High Priest? Let us examine the relevant verses. The Torah states: "All the days of the vow of his separation there shall no razor come on his head; until the days are fulfilled, during which he separates himself to the Lord, he shall be holy (*kadosh hu*), and shall let the locks of the hair of his head grow" (Numbers 6:5). Rashi explains that the words *kadosh hu* refer not to the Nazirite but to his hair, so that the verse should be translated, "it shall be holy." The hair that is allowed to grow wild is, in the end, offered to God, together with the peace offering brought by the Nazirite, and so it is considered to be holy from the very outset. Regarding the Nazirite, the verse states: "Because the crown of his God is upon his head"

4. Maimonides noted the similarity between the High Priest and the Nazirite on this point (*Guide of the Perplexed* III, 48).

(Numbers 6:7). The plain sense of the verse seems to be that the hair growing on the Nazirite's head is the crown of his God. This is not merely a metaphor; it is a concrete description of the hair growing on the Nazirite's head. Ibn Ezra (Numbers 6:7), in fact, suggests that the word *nazir* is derived from *nezer* ("crown"). According to this, the parallelism between the High Priest and the Nazirite is perfect: The crown of hair on the Nazirite's head parallels the *tzitz* on the head of the High Priest, which is also referred to as a "holy crown" (Exodus 29:6).

This parallelism carries a very important spiritual message: Anyone can elevate himself to the High Priest's level of holiness; no special ancestry is necessary.[5] Everyone bears the responsibility of developing himself and rising to the highest possible spiritual level. Noble ancestry does not suffice, and base ancestry is no excuse. The sons of Eli the High Priest were wicked, whereas Abraham was the son of Terah the idol worshipper, but nevertheless he became a spiritual giant. The Torah section dealing with the Nazirite teaches us that anyone can reach any goal, provided that he wants it enough.

Only *kohanim* may serve in the Temple, and only the High Priest may enter the Holy of Holies. The Torah may well have thought it preferable that a fixed caste of people should train themselves from early childhood for a life of holiness and purity. Anyone can reach the level of supreme holiness. Statistically, however, this goal is more easily reached by those who have trained themselves to do so from their earliest years, and in the Temple we take no chances. We are not dealing here with genetic preference or with strict preference based on social class, because non-*kohanim* have an alternative route to holiness – Naziriteship.

The Second Temple period was characterized by the struggle between the Sages, who represented this egalitarian approach, and the noble priestly families, who inclined, for the most part, to the

5. Nor is a special social-educational background necessary. We shall deal with this issue below.

Sadducees, believing in the sanctity of their ancestry and in their own special status. Many of the midrashim and stories related by the Sages can best be understood against this backdrop:

> Abba Saul the son of Botnit said in the name of Abba Yosef the son of Chanin: Woe to me, on account of the house of Boethius, woe to me on account of their curses. Woe to me on account of the house of Chanin, woe to me on account of their charms. Woe to me on account of the house of Katros, woe to me on account of their quills. Woe to me on account of the house of Yishma'el the son of Pi'akhi, woe to me on account of their fists. For they are High Priests, their sons are treasurers, their sons-in-law are trustees, and their slaves beat the people with sticks.
>
> (*Pesachim* 57a)[6]

> A man is given priority over a woman to save his life and to restore his lost property, and a woman is given priority over a man regarding clothing and ransoming her from captivity.... A *kohen* is given priority over a Levite, a Levite over an Israelite, an Israelite over a *mamzer*, a *mamzer* over a *netin*, a *netin* over a convert, and a convert over an emancipated slave. When? When they are all equal. But if a *mamzer* is a Torah scholar and the High Priest is an ignoramus, the *mamzer* who is a Torah scholar is given priority over the High Priest who is an ignoramus.
>
> (*Horayot* 3:7–8)

> From where do we know that a gentile who engages in Torah study is regarded like a High Priest? The verse states: "Which if a man do, he shall live in them" (Leviticus 18:5). It does not say "*kohanim*, and Levites and Israelites," but rather "a man."

6. This appears to have been a popular song against the noble priestly houses, which was adopted by the Sages.

> Thus, you learn that even a gentile who engages in Torah study is regarded like a High Priest.
>
> (*Bava Kama* 38a)

According to the Sages, a Torah authority is more important than a High Priest. Elsewhere (*Yoma* 71b), it is related that a certain High Priest took offense when the people showed greater respect to Shema'aya and Avtalyon, who were the descendants of converts, than to him. Thus, when the two sages came to greet him, he said: "Let the sons of the nations come in peace," to which they answered: "Let the sons of the nations come in peace, those who act in the manner of Aaron, and let the son of Aaron not come in peace, he who does not act in the manner of Aaron."

While the question about the gap between Jews and gentiles remains open, the Sages' position on the various components of Jewish society is emphatically clear: the priestly tribe is in no way superior to the rest of the people. What is important is acting "in the manner of Aaron," and not inheriting his genes.

The Non-Jewish Position

In the distant past, non-Jewish thinkers rejected the idea of absolute equality. Aristotle vigorously argued that certain people are destined from birth to be slaves and are essentially different from free men:

> For that some should rule and others be ruled is a thing not only necessary, but expedient; from the hour of their birth, some are marked out for subjection, others for rule.
>
> (*Politics*, 1, chap. 5)

Today, however, the idea of innate equality is one of the cornerstones of Western thought. The philosophers of the Enlightenment asserted this idea repeatedly.

> Nature hath made men so equal in the faculties of body and mind as that, though there be found one man sometimes manifestly stronger in body or of quicker mind than another, yet when all is reckoned together the difference between man and man is not so considerable as that one man can thereupon claim to himself any benefit to which another may not pretend as well as he.
>
> (Hobbes, *Leviathan*, chap. 13)

The underlying assumption is that in regard to the essentials, the things that define humanity, all men are equal. We shall cite a number of fundamental historical proclamations that emphasize this point:

> Men are born and remain free and equal in rights. Social distinctions may be founded only upon the general good.
>
> (*Declaration of the Rights of Man*, 1789)

> We hold these truths to be self-evident, that all men are created equal, that they are endowed by their Creator with certain unalienable Rights, that among these are Life, Liberty and the pursuit of Happiness.
>
> (*Declaration of Independence*, 1776)

> All human beings are born free and equal in dignity and rights. They are endowed with reason and conscience and should act towards one another in a spirit of brotherhood.
>
> Everyone is entitled to all the rights and freedoms set forth in this Declaration, without distinction of any kind, such as race, color, sex, language, religion, political or other opinion, national or social origin, property, birth or other status.
>
> (*Universal Declaration of Human Rights*, 1948)

Social Equality

The French Declaration of the Rights of Man and the Citizen cited above raises an additional question. The authors of the declaration recognized that even if there are no essential inborn differences between men, there are differences between them with respect to social class. The declaration suffices with the demand that "social distinctions may be founded only upon the general good." Are social distinctions really necessary, or is this also an area where we should aspire to equality?

On this point, there are, of course, many different opinions. The Communists aspired to create a world absolutely free of social distinctions:

> Political power, properly so called, is merely the organized power of one class for oppressing another. In place of the old bourgeois society, with its classes and class antagonisms, we shall have an association in which the free development of each is the condition for the free development of all.
>
> (Marx, *Communist Manifesto*, chap. 2)

Others felt that class distinctions are necessary in order to create a class of leaders who are trained from early childhood for leadership and values. Power would remain in the hands of a class specially qualified and trained to exercise it in a fitting manner. This position was expressed by the English thinker Edmund Burke, who came out against the French Revolution on exactly these grounds:

> The power of perpetuating our property in our families is one of the most valuable and interesting circumstances belonging to it, and that which tends the most to the perpetuation of society itself.... With us [i.e., the English] the House of Peers is formed upon this principle.... Some decent, regulated preeminence, some preference (not exclusive appropriation) given to birth is neither unnatural, nor unjust, nor impolitic.
>
> (*Reflections on the Revolution in France*, vol. III)

Just as Marx was an extremist in his rejection of social classes, so, too, Burke was an extremist in his insistence of the need for them.

What is Judaism's position on this question? We spoke earlier about the essential inborn and genetic equality between *kohanim* and ordinary Israelites. Nonetheless, there is no question but that *kohanim* enjoy special standing within the Jewish people. The Sages recognized this, for they stipulated that if a *kohen* and an ordinary Israelite are equal in Torah, priority is given to the *kohen*.[7] This does not reflect any inborn, genetic difference; it acknowledges the social reality that the various classes are assigned different roles. Although the Sages restricted the priestly advantage, they clearly recognized it. Some Jewish thinkers, however, disagree.

> True divine service does not require priests. If the Law of Moses left room for *kohanim* and Levites, it was only because in the ancient period people were unable fully to grasp that divine service is possible without priests.
>
> Proof may be adduced that the priesthood does not reflect the true intentions of the Torah: For the [divine] service was originally supposed to be performed by the firstborns, and it was only because Israel sinned with the [Golden] Calf that the service was removed from the firstborns and given to the Levites.
>
> In other words, if Israel had truly remained on a high level, they would not have needed special Levites. Each family would have worshipped God in accordance with its own understanding. When they bowed down to the [Golden] Calf,

7. And furthermore, the Sages asserted, for example, that it is shameful for the daughter of a priest to marry an ignorant Israelite, but praiseworthy for her to marry an Israelite who is a Torah scholar (*Pesachim* 49a; Maimonides, *Hilkhot Issurei Bi'a* 21:31).

> the children of Israel demonstrated that they too were strongly attracted to the forms of worship common in their day. There was no alternative; it became necessary to create a class of *kohanim* and Levites.
>
> This notwithstanding, it was attempted to the extent possible to ensure that the *kohanim* and the Levites would not achieve domination over the Jewish people.
>
> (Zeitlin, *Alef Bet shel ha-Yahadut*, p. 83)

Rabbi Hillel Zeitlin argues that the priesthood is an institution of second choice; ideally there should be no class distinctions whatsoever. It would appear, however, that Zeitlin has overstated his case. While the *Rishonim* disagree as to whether the *kohanim* were chosen before or after the sin of the Golden Calf, the plain sense of Scripture surely follows Nachmanides' understanding that the *kohanim* had already been chosen (in *Parashat Teruma-Tetzave*) before the sin, and it was only the status of the Levites that changed in its aftermath. Furthermore, since the firstborns were originally supposed to perform the divine service, they actually constitute a distinct class. Zeitlin sees the firstborns as family representatives, but practically speaking, if they had been charged with the service over the years, a special class of firstborns would have come into being, who would have raised themselves over everyone else (though less so than did the *kohanim*). In Rabbi Zeitlin's view, it is not at all clear why from the outset God designated certain people to perform His service. Social divisions are necessary so that each class can gain expertise in its assigned role. It is true, however, that the Torah tries to minimize the divisions, and also to emphasize that spiritual ascent is barred to no one (as we saw with respect to the laws of the Nazirite).

With respect to slavery, as was mentioned above, Aristotle maintained that there was an inborn, "metaphysical" distinction between slave and freeman. Judaism did not simply reject this view, it even tried to minimize the social distinctions between the two classes. All of the Torah's laws regarding slavery are meant to narrow the gap between freeman and slave.

Judaism, however, does not stand for absolute social equality. It was Korah who called for total equality:

> And they gathered themselves together against Moses and against Aaron, and said to them, You take too much upon you, seeing that all the congregation are holy, every one of them, and the Lord is among them; why then do you raise yourselves up above the congregation of the Lord?
>
> (Numbers 16:3)

The episode of Korah is meant to show the people of Israel that the *kohanim* and Levites were chosen to perform the divine service, and thus, that whereas the entire congregation is holy, some are holier than others. The Sages picturesquely illustrate Korah's complaint:

> Korah jumped up and asked Moses: "If a cloak is entirely of blue, what is the law as regards its being exempted from the obligation of *tzitzit*?" Moses answered him: "It is subject to the laws of *tzitzit*." Korah retorted: "A cloak that is entirely composed of blue cannot free itself from the obligation, yet the four blue threads do free it!" "If," he asked again, "a house is full of scriptural books, what is the law as regards its being exempt from the obligation of *mezuza*?" He answered him: "It is under obligation of having a *mezuza*." "The whole Torah," he [Korah] argued, "which contains two hundred and seventy-five sections, cannot exempt the house, yet the one section in the *mezuza* exempts it!"
>
> (Numbers Rabba 18:3)[8]

8. The Jerusalem Talmud, *Sanhedrin* 10, brings another argument that does not immediately fit in with our explanation: If a person has a spot of leprosy the size of a barley grain, he is ritually unclean, but if the leprosy spreads over his entire body, he is ritually clean.

The midrash tells us that Korah's fundamental argument was based on misguided imagery. The people of Israel, he said, are comparable to a cloak that is entirely blue, and therefore should not require *tzitzit*! The answer, however, is that even a cloak that is entirely blue requires *tzitzit*.

Rav Kook draws a connection between Korah's fallacy and present-day differences regarding the equality of nations:

> The call going out to all the nations who are immersed in all the filth of uncleanness, in all the depths of wickedness and ignorance, in the most frightening abysses of darkness: "You are all holy, you are all children of God, there are no differences between peoples, there is no holy and chosen people, every person is equally holy" – this is the Korah element in man, the new Cain element from which man suffers.
>
> (*Orot*, pp. 32–33)

Rav Kook's concern here is not the genetic difference between Israel and the nations, but the cultural and spiritual difference. He connects the call for absolute equality not only to Korah, but also to Cain, who wished to rise to Abel's level without investing hard work and significantly changing his personality. The Torah rejects such an approach.

The social structure described in the Torah is not marked by absolute equality. As explained above, the Sages' glorification of Torah scholars was based on an understanding that the *kohanim* are not endowed with an inborn genetic superiority over the rest of the Jewish people. The very act of glorification, however, reflects the social superiority of the Torah scholar over the ignoramus! It is important to emphasize that Torah scholars do not constitute a closed social caste similar to the priesthood, for theoretically, anyone can join their ranks. We are still dealing, however, with a social advantage enjoyed by certain people and not by others. The Sages recognized this advantage, but tried to minimize it.

> A pearl in the mouth of the mouths of the Rabbis of Yavne: I am a creature, and my [unlearned] friend is a creature. My work is in the city and his work is in the field. I rise early to my work, and he rises early to his work. Just as he does not distinguish himself by doing my work, so I do not distinguish myself by doing his work. And perhaps you will say: I am able to study extensively, whereas he would only be able to study minimally. We have learned: Both the one who does much and the one who does a little [are equally rewarded], provided that each directs his heart toward heaven.
>
> (*Berakhot* 17a)

Before concluding this section, let us cite another statement by Rabbi Yehuda Halevi. In a recently discovered letter, he perceives the world as totally hierarchical:

> Not every living thing is human. And not every human being is a Jew. And not every Jew is a *kohen*. And not every *kohen* is Moses or Aaron. And not every place is Canaan. And not all of Canaan is a gate to heaven. And not all gates to heaven are Jerusalem. And not all days are fixed times. And not all fixed times are Sabbaths. And not all Sabbaths are Yom Kippur. And not all divine service involves offerings. And not all offerings are whole-burnt offerings. And not every whole-burnt offering is brought inside.
>
> (*Shalem* 7, p. 44)

Rabbi Yehuda Halevi wrote this letter to explain his intention to emigrate to the Land of Israel.

What Next?

Our era is unquestionably characterized by total acceptance of the idea of equality. The general consensus is in favor of equality for women, blacks, homosexuals, and all other minorities. Some believe that the next step will be a demand for equality for children, based, perhaps, on the notion that compulsory education infringes upon the principle of equality, and represents an antiquated and non-egalitarian outlook.

> Today changes are taking place in the social and legal status of children.... The circle of those benefiting from the protection of these principles is expanding, so that today it includes as self-evident women and ethnic and racial minorities. In the last generation, its application has expanded further, so that it has begun to include sexual minorities and children as well.
> (Aviram, *Chinukh be-Idan Ha-Siach ha-Postmoderni*, p. 111)

In this context, we should keep in mind the instructive words of Rabbi Kalonymus Kalmish Shapiro, the Admor of Piaszena, who saw the possibility of great harm in the blurring of the hierarchy of adults and children:

> Why in previous generations was every type of education effective, the students of every teacher and the sons of every father, almost every one of them, becoming [faithful] servants of God, which is not the case now? The primary and simple answer is that the youths have begun to consider themselves adults before their time.... This folly has caused our youths to regard themselves as adults in knowledge and will, when their knowledge is still upside-down and their will unripe and bitter.... This has become so widespread that we are sometimes astonished to see really small children, in whom independent spirit and false courage have sprouted forth, regard themselves as adults.
> (*Chovat ha-Talmidim*, pp. 15–16)

Judaism has established a graded social structure. Even if our Sages attempted to mitigate the differences and contrasts between the classes, in no way whatsoever did they call for a totally classless society. There is no reason for us to align ourselves with the prevalent mood and automatically support sweeping social equality.

The Individual and Society

The Words of the Sages

> And the Lord God said, It is not good that the man should be alone; I will make him a help to match him.
>
> (Genesis 2:18)

The preceding verse constitutes a fitting introduction to our discussion of the relationship between man and society, between individual and community.

The fundamental question is: Which of the two is of higher rank? Does the individual enjoy primacy over society, which is no more than a mass of separate individuals; or does society take precedence over the individual, who is just one small element of the community that surrounds him?

We know that Judaism assigns great importance to the community. Many religious rites can only be performed in a communal context. The quorum of ten that is required for prayer teaches us the vital importance of society and now community for religious life. God turns to the people of Israel and commands them as a single entity, "And there Israel camped before the mountain" (Exodus 19:2). In the Hebrew, the word translated as "camped" (*vayichan*) is in the singular tense.

On the other hand, many familiar sources emphasize the

value of the individual. Here, too, the starting point is the second chapter of Genesis:

> Therefore, man was created alone – to teach you that whoever destroys a single soul in Israel, Scripture regards him as if he destroyed the entire world. And whoever saves a single soul in Israel, Scripture regards him as if he preserved the entire world. And for the sake of peace among people, so that one person should not say to his fellow: "My father was greater than your father." And so that the heretics should not say: "There are many powers in heaven." And to tell the greatness of the Holy One, blessed be He, for man mints many coins with a single mold, and they are all similar to one another. But the King, the King of kings, the Holy One, blessed be He, stamped every man with the mold of the first man. And not one is similar to his fellow. Therefore, each and every person must say: "For my sake, the world was created."
>
> (Mishna, *Sanhedrin* 37a)

The assertion that every human being must say, "For my sake, the world was created," underscores the importance of the individual. In an earlier chapter, we discussed the fact that man was created alone in connection with the value of equality. We now raise this point a second time in a different context: the status of the individual vis-à-vis society. In light of the fact that man was created alone (at least according to the description in Chapter 2), it is difficult to argue that the individual is merely an element of society with no independent significance.

As we mentioned earlier, the Torah was given to the entire Jewish people. Rabbi Chayyim ibn Attar, author of *Or ha-Chayyim*, emphasizes the point that the Jewish people received the Torah as a community:

> Here Scripture joined the entirety [of Israel] in the fulfillment of the Torah, demonstrating how the Israelites can confer merit

> one upon the other. The Torah in its entirety is only capable of fulfillment by means of the entire Jewish nation. Every individual Jew is charged with the duty to perform those commandments which he is able to fulfill, all conferring merit one upon the other. The verse may allude to this when it states: "You shall love your neighbor as yourself" (Leviticus 19:18) – i.e., you shall love your fellow Jew as he is part of yourself. For his well-being will benefit you, and through him you can achieve perfection; thus, he is not another person, but you yourself and like one of your parts. In this we have found pleasure, for God has commanded us with 613 *mitzvot*, but there is no one who can fulfill them all. Here is your proof: *kohen*, Levite, and Israelite, and women. There are positive precepts that apply to *kohanim* but not to Israelites, and there are *mitzvot* that apply to Israelites but not to *kohanim*. And similarly regarding Levites, and so, too, women. How can the individual fulfill them so that he may perfect his 248 organs and the 365 tendons which correspond to them? Rather, there is no question but that the Torah is only capable of fulfillment by means of the entire Jewish nation, each individual conferring merit upon the other.
>
> (*Or ha-Chayyim*, Exodus 39:32)

The six hundred and thirteen commandments correspond to the traditional number of man's organs and tendons. No single individual can fulfill all the *mitzvot* on his own; the perfection of his body is, therefore, dependent upon his working together with his co-religionists. The object of the Torah is the entirety of the people of Israel as a single entity.

Nachmanides points out, however, that the members of the Jewish people are bound by the Torah's *mitzvot* as individuals, and not only as members of the Jewish community.

> All of the [Ten] Commandments are formulated in the singular – "the Lord your God, who brought you out [*hotzeitikha*, in the singular]" (Exodus 20:2) – rather than, as He said at the

> beginning: "You [*atem*, in the plural] have seen" (ibid. 19:4), "if you [*tishme'u*, in the plural] will hearken" (ibid.). In this way He warns that every individual is liable to punishment for [transgressing] the commandments, for He speaks to each one individually, and commands each one separately. They should not think that He will judge according to the majority, and that the individual will be saved along with the rest.
>
> (Commentary to Exodus 20:2)

Nachmanides notes that the Ten Commandments were formulated in the singular in order to emphasize that each individual is independently bound by the *mitzvot*, and that everyone is individually judged for his actions.

There is a certain tension in Jewish thought between individualism and collectivism, between the belief in the primacy of the individual and the view that exalts society. Maimonides, following Aristotle (whose position will be cited below), argues that man is a political creature. He does not claim, however, that the individual is merely an element of society, but only that man cannot live without society.[1] According to Maimonides, man lives in society not by choice, but of necessity; not based on the calculation that in this way he can improve his life, but because he is forced to do so, having no other alternative.

> The first perfection consists in being healthy and in the very best bodily state, and this is only possible through his finding the things necessary for him whenever he seeks them. These are his food and all the other things needed for the governance of his body, such as a shelter, bathing, and so forth. This cannot be achieved in any way by one isolated individual. For an

1. Maimonides recognized the superiority of the man who has reached perfection to the common people around him. But even the most perfect of men is in need of society, as it follows from what Maimonides says in the introduction to his commentary to the Mishna.

> individual can only attain all this through a political association, it being already known that man is political by nature.
>
> (*Guide of the Perplexed* III, 27)[2]

Maimonides maintains that man's material needs can only be satisfied through the cooperative efforts of many individuals. Rabbi Kook went further. He, too, does not denigrate the value of the individual, but he stresses the individual Jew's dependence upon the Jewish people:

> The relationship between the Jewish people and its individual members is different from the relationship between any other national group and its constituents. All other national groups only bestow upon their individual members the external aspect of their essence. But the essence itself each person draws from the all-inclusive soul, from the soul of God, without the intermediation of the group.... This is not the case regarding Israel. The soul of the individual is drawn from...the community, the community bestowing a soul upon the individuals. One who considers severing himself from the people must sever his soul from the source of its vitality. Therefore, each individual Jew is greatly in need of the community. He will always offer his life so that he will not be torn from the people, because his soul and self-perfection require that of him.
>
> (*Orot*, p. 144)

It is important to note that Rabbi Kook is not presenting a universal theory. What he says pertains exclusively to the Jewish people. He explicitly differentiates the collective of the Jewish people from the collectives of other nations:

> The state does not constitute man's greatest joy. This applies to an ordinary state...which is not the case regarding a state

2. A similar idea is found in Maimonides' *Guide* I, 40.

> founded on an ideal, which has implanted in its very existence the most sublime ideal content, which is truly the individual's greatest joy. This state is truly the highest on the scale of happiness. And this is the case with our state, the state of Israel.
>
> (Ibid., p. 160)

Rabbi Joseph B. Soloveitchik, in his usual manner, stresses the continuing dialectic of Jewish thought, pointing out the complexity of the issue, which has no simple resolution.

> Judaism has always viewed man from this dual perspective. It sees every person as an independent individual and also as part of a community, a limb of the body of Israel. Jewish thinkers have conducted an ongoing dialectic on this subject throughout the ages.... Even the greatness of an individual like Moses is dependent upon the community. It would seem that the community and the individual are placed in balance with each other and are interdependent....
>
> Never is the individual's worth belittled when measured against the whole community; and never is the community undermined because of any individual or individuals. Each has its own position of strength.
>
> (*On Repentance*, pp. 114–115)

Rabbi Soloveitchik's formulation does not resolve the difficulty with which we have been grappling: What is the relationship between the individual and the community? Which of the two is more important? Put otherwise, when should we focus on the one, and when on the other? Rabbi Soloveitchik himself seems to attach greater importance to the individual. The great majority of his writings relate to lonely man's encounter with God, as is apparent even in the titles of his major works: *Halakhic Man* and *The Lonely Man of Faith*. Considerable latitude, however, is left for practical wisdom to choose its path in real life, while taking diverse circumstances into account.

Individual Versus Society in Non-Jewish Thought

It was not only Jewish sages who occupied themselves with the relationship between individual and society. Non-Jewish thinkers also dealt with this issue at great length. In fact, as we mentioned above, Maimonides' position was based upon Aristotle. Let us now examine Aristotle's actual words:

> Hence it is evident that the state is a creation of nature, and that man is by nature a political animal. And he who by nature and not by mere accident is without a state, is either above humanity, or below it.... Thus the state is by nature clearly prior to the family and to the individual, since the whole is of necessity prior to the part; for example, if the whole body be destroyed, there will be no foot or hand.
>
> (*Politics* 1, chap. 2)

As this passage demonstrates, it was Aristotle who coined the expression that "man is a political animal." According to Aristotle, man by his very nature is destined to live in society. The collective note is far more pronounced in Aristotle than in Maimonides. Whereas Maimonides suffices with the assertion that man needs society in order to satisfy his basic needs, Aristotle declares that the state by its very nature is prior to the individual, just as the whole is prior to the part. Individuals are merely the limbs of society. This is an organic notion of society – a notion that sees the whole of society as a single organism. In a subsequent passage of the same work, Aristotle elaborates on his statement that a man without a state "is either above humanity, or below it": "But he who is unable to live in society, or who has no need because he is sufficient for himself, must be either a beast or a god: he is no part of a state" (ibid.)

During the Enlightenment of the eighteenth century, philosophers and social thinkers developed the idea of the "social contract," a construct that makes the individual superior to society. According to this outlook, society is an aggregation of individuals who have entered into a contract (generally unconsciously) with one another that enables each of them to acquire more resources for his own preservation. While it was recognized that human beings may also organize themselves into communities for emotional reasons – out of loneliness, say – proponents of the social contract emphasized the economic-utilitarian dimension. The most prominent proponent of this theory was Jean-Jacques Rousseau:

> I suppose men to have reached the point at which the obstacles in the way of their preservation in the state of nature show their power of resistance to be greater than the resources at the disposal of each individual for his maintenance in that state. That primitive condition can then subsist no longer.... But, as men cannot engender new forces, but only unite and direct existing ones, they have no other means of preserving themselves than the formation, by aggregation, of a sum of forces great enough to overcome the resistance.... This sum of forces can arise only where several persons come together.... The problem is to find a form of association which will defend and protect with the whole common force the person and goods of each associate, and in which each, while uniting himself with all, may still obey himself alone, and remain as free as before. This is the fundamental problem of which the Social Contract provides the solution.... Although they have perhaps never been formally set forth, they are everywhere the same and everywhere tacitly admitted and recognized, until, on the violation of the social compact, each regains his original rights and resumes his natural liberty, while losing the conventional liberty in favor of which he renounced it.
>
> (*The Social Contract*, chap. 6)

Rousseau's outlook is individualistic, elevating the individual over society. Man enjoys essential (though not necessarily historical) priority over society; the individual comes before the community. The practical ramifications of such an attitude are revolutionary, for they endow the individual with the right to dismantle society when the social contract is breached. This approach gave rise to our democratic world. It was an essential element in the spirit that led to the French Revolution.

An individualistic approach of this type leads to certain conclusions regarding the individual's conduct in society and society's attitude toward the individual:

> The only purpose for which power can be rightfully exercised over any member of a civilized community, against his will, is to prevent harm to others. His own good, either physical or moral, is not a sufficient warrant. He cannot rightfully be compelled to do or forbear because it will be better for him to do so, because it will make him happier, because, in the opinions of others, to do so would be wise, or even right.
>
> (Mill, *On Liberty*, chap. 1)

The more we emphasize the individual and view society as a collectivity, the more we will limit society's right to control its individual members and fashion their lives. Mill's individualistic outlook led him to conclude that society has no right to prevent a person from acting in a certain manner unless his conduct interferes with the rights of others.[3]

In the first third of the nineteenth century, Georg Wilhelm Friedrich Hegel proposed an entirely different approach. Karl Popper claims that Hegel's ideas were meant to justify the Prussian state of his day as the ultimate development of history. We shall not go into Hegel's complex philosophical views, and instead limit ourselves to a single citation that illustrates the importance he attaches to the collective in contradistinction to the individual.

---

3. This is, of course, a very wide topic, which we can only touch upon in the present framework.

> If the state is confused with civil society, and if its specific end is laid down as the security and protection of property and personal freedom, then the interest of the individuals as such becomes the ultimate end of their association, and it follows that membership of the state is something optional. But the state's relation to the individual is quite different from this. Since the state is mind objectified, it is only as one of its members that the individual himself has objectivity, genuine individuality, and an ethical life. Unification pure and simple is the true content and aim of the individual, and the individual's destiny is the living of a universal life.
>
> (Hegel, *Philosophy of Right*, sec. 258)

In contrast to the idea of the social contract, there are other approaches that see society, the nation, or the state as an organic unity that goes beyond the sum of the individuals of whom it is constituted. Society is not derived from individuals. Just the opposite is true; individuals are derived from society. The fundamental unit is society, it being a whole entity. This attitude reached its most perverted expression in the fascism of the twenties and thirties of the twentieth century. We shall cite here the words of the leader of Italian fascism, Benito Mussolini:

> In the Fascist conception of history, man is man only by virtue of the spiritual process to which he contributes as a member of the family, the social group, the nation, and in function of history to which all nations bring their contribution. Hence the great value of tradition in records, in language, in customs, in the rules of social life. Outside history man is a nonentity. Fascism is therefore opposed to all individualistic abstractions based on eighteenth-century materialism.
>
> Anti-individualistic, the Fascist conception of life stresses the importance of the State and accepts the individual only in so far as his interests coincide with those of the State, which stands for the conscience and the universal will of man as a

> historic entity.... The Fascist conception of the State is all-embracing; outside of it no human or spiritual values can exist, much less have value.
>
> (Mussolini, *The Doctrine of Fascism*)

It is unnecessary to explain how this differs from Judaism's approach.

In the first half of the twentieth century, radical collective ideas received wide expression. Fascism, Nazism, and Communism are all totalitarian ideologies with an extreme collective emphasis. In the middle of the twentieth century, perhaps in reaction to these ideologies, a radical ideology of individualism began to thrive in Western civilization. On the philosophical level this approach was represented by existentialism, but its primary expression was on the cultural level. To this day, Western culture inclines toward individualism.

Today, however, the collective is emphasized once again by post-modernism. The school of thought known as post-modernism mocks the modernistic claim that the individual can attain personal salvation. According to post-modernistic thinkers, man is the product of his environment, society, and community, and he cannot escape their contours. A historian's ideas, for instance, will always reflect the thought patterns and interests of his social group.

Two Types of Community

Many biblical commentators and thinkers have noted the contradictions between the descriptions of the creation found in the first and second chapters of the book of Genesis. Rabbi Joseph B. Soloveitchik, in his *The Lonely Man of Faith*, holds that the two chapters describe different types of man; God intentionally describes the creation twice, each time presenting a different human type. In this view, the two chapters concomitantly describe two different types of society and community.

Rabbi Soloveitchik sees the relationship between Adam and

Eve as the archetype of social relations between individuals. Chapter 1 of Genesis describes practical-technological man, who does not experience existential loneliness. The community that he establishes is merely utilitarian. It is a "natural" community, born spontaneously and without effort out of man's need for collective living and promoting his interests. This community is founded not on shared values, but on mutual interests. Typical of this attitude is the theory of the social contract, which, as explained above, describes the community and society as products of joint interests.

This is the community of Adam the first in Chapter 1. Rabbi Soloveitchik here criticizes the theory of the social contract, but in a footnote he says that he has similar reservations about the theory of organic society. The nature of organic society, he observes, is also, first and foremost, utilitarian. Its proponents emphasize that society is essential for proper human functioning.

In contrast to these communities, Rabbi Soloveitchik presents the community of Adam the second, the Adam of Chapter 2. This is a man with a clear spiritual inclination. He is a profound man, sensitive to his uniqueness and feeling his loneliness. In Chapter 2, Adam is created alone – without a woman at his side. This is because the man described in this chapter is fundamentally a lonely man. He succeeds in forming a community only after exerting great effort, just as Adam had to sacrifice a rib in order to acquire the companionship of Eve. Rabbi Soloveitchik describes the difference between the two communities as follows:

> Adam the second must quest for a different kind of community.... His quest is for a new kind of fellowship which one finds in the existential community. There, not only hands are joined, but experiences as well; there, one hears not only the rhythmic sound of the production line, but also the rhythmic beats of hearts.
>
> (*The Lonely Man of Faith*, pp. 27–28)

Adam the second is a profound man, and therefore also a

lonely man. The community he establishes, therefore, is existentially far more significant. It is also more demanding: in order to benefit from social relations, one must also sacrifice. The partnership that Adam creates with Eve, which is the archetype for the community he creates, is profound and meaningful. Spiritually sensitive people create more meaningful social connections. Rabbi Soloveitchik argues that such a community is connected to religious life as well, for without devotion to God, it is impossible to maintain a deep and meaningful social unity.

What is the relationship between religious profundity and emotional profundity in social life? One may argue that there is no direct connection; but just as a profound person needs God, so, too, he needs a partner and mate. But it may also be argued that standing before God teaches man the extent to which he is in need of a partner, and also teaches him to sacrifice. Man learns to reveal himself before God, and only afterward is he able to reveal himself also before his fellow man, and thus achieve true partnership.

Let us compare this to what the historian and sociologist Jacob Katz has written. In Katz's view, religion has an important social function. This function, however, is only fulfilled when man devotes his entire self, body and soul, to God, and does not relate to religion merely as a means of achieving social goals.

> At the climax of Jewish public devotions, on Rosh Hashana and Yom Kippur, when the likelihood is greatest that the individual will turn his thoughts away from his selfish motives and social ambitions, he is likely to be absorbed almost completely in his society-congregation.... The internal cohesiveness of the Jewish community was undoubtedly nourished by the depth of the religious experience of the ever-recurring ritual.... Only where religion lives on its own independent resources – man facing God – is it unconsciously and paradoxically also transformed into an all-important social preservative.
>
> (Katz, *Tradition and Crisis*, pp. 181–182)

When a person comes to synagogue for social purposes, he sets himself in the center, seeking pleasure and benefit. When he comes to synagogue to *pray*, his standing before God teaches him how fragile he really is, how much he is need of society, and how a true society requires sacrificial gestures.

The Sin of the Tree of Knowledge

"Original Sin"?

How significant a factor in our consciousness is Adam's sin of eating from the Tree of Knowledge? Christianity teaches that Adam's "original sin" in the Garden of Eden turned all of mankind into sinners who are guilty from birth. In Judaism, however, man's first sin plays a far less central role.

Here is the Jewish position on this issue as summarized by Moses Mendelssohn:

> Straightforward reason knows nothing about the legacy of original sin. Nor does the Old Testament have any knowledge about it. Adam sinned and died, and his descendants sin and die. But his sin did not cause them to die to goodness,[1] nor to fall into the hands of Satan.
>
> (Mendelssohn, *Jerusalem*)

Rabbi Samson Raphael Hirsch said much the same thing:

> Based on what happened in the Garden of Eden, they [i.e., Christianity] fabricated a lie that undermines the moral future of man. From here they derived the dogma of original sin, on

1. In other words, they did not lose their connection to goodness.

> the foundation of which a spiritual edifice was constructed, against which a Jew must protest in his very being.... The belief that sin has become implanted in man, that he has lost his ability to be good, that he is forced to sin – against this belief Judaism vehemently objects.
>
> (Hirsch, Commentary to Genesis 3:19)

Adam's sin in the Garden of Eden is much less significant in Judaism than in Christianity.

Rabbi Abraham Isaac Kook emphasizes the spiritual significance of the sin without referring to any of the particulars. His conclusion is the antithesis of the Christian understanding. As he explains, the most important message of the story of what happened in the Garden of Eden is the idea that man can rise to an exceedingly exalted level and also fall to abysmal depths. The very idea of the Garden of Eden, according to Rabbi Kook, serves as proof against the Christian approach, which sees this world as a prison. Man started out in an earthly paradise, and eventually he will be restored to it (*Iggerot ha-Ra'aya* 1, pp. 163–164).

Rabbi Kook's explication of the account of Adam's sin gives rise not to pessimism, but to optimism. We learn from the story that at the outset of human history, man was of high rank and happy, and from this it follows that we have the ability to correct the sin and return to our original eminence.

As Rabbi Kook shows us, even if we reject the Christian idea of "original sin," we must nonetheless consider the multiple aspects of the sin of eating from the Tree of Knowledge in order to fully appreciate its moral lessons.

Essence of the Sin

The rest of this chapter will deal with the following question: What was the Tree of Knowledge, and what was Adam's sin? We are dealing here with a symbolic event that conveys some profound messages; but the Sages disagree about the nature of these messages. What was the sin of eating from the Tree of Knowledge? What exactly was the Tree of Knowledge? What are the eternal lessons that may be learned from this story?

Sexual Desire

One of the simplest explanations was offered by Rabbi Abraham ibn Ezra:

> The Tree of Knowledge gave rise to sexual desire, and it is for this reason that the man and his wife covered their private parts.... When Adam ate from the Tree of Knowledge, he "knew his wife," this knowledge being a euphemism for sexual relations. This is called ["knowing"] on account of the Tree of Knowledge. When a youth "knows good and evil," then his sexual desire begins.
>
> (Ibn Ezra, commentary to Genesis 3:6)

Enslavement to the Evil Impulse

The idea proposed by Ibn Ezra was further developed by Rabbi Samson Raphael Hirsch:

> As long as they were worthy of the divine image in both spirit and body, they remained pure and holy in spirit and body.... Man's pure body, the materiality that accepted the yoke of morality – is no less holy than the spirit.... But when man became subjected to his passions, when he no longer strove to raise his sensuousness to the realm of the holy, but just the opposite, his sensuousness dragged his sanctity down to its realm – he was immediately ashamed of the nakedness of his body.
>
> (Commentary to Genesis 2:25)

Rabbi Hirsch understands that man has been a sensual being from his very creation. But as long as he exercised control over his bodily passions, he had no reason to feel shame. When he sinned by eating of the Tree of Knowledge, man became enslaved to his sensuousness.[2] According to Rabbi Hirsch, the tree did not have any special desire-arousing properties. But since the tree had been forbidden to man by divine decree, eating from it involved the sin of submitting to the evil impulse.

Violating God's Command

Benno Jacob emphasizes the idea of violating God's command:

> The tree was the touchstone of good and evil, the permissible and forbidden, life and death, irrespective of the content of the precept. On the contrary, by not being influnced by any practical calculations of the benefits of the precept, by directing his will to obeying the author of the command, man would be tested.... the fruit of the tree was not harmful or deadly but, on the contrary, good to eat.
>
> (in Leibowitz, *New Studies in* Genesis, p. 24)

Benno Jacob, who had Reform inclinations, offers an explanation that is strikingly "mitnagdish." He emphasizes obedience to God's will and establishes that the obligation to obey God's command does not depend on understanding its content. The first man was punished for the very violation of God's command.

Abandonment of Intellectual Apprehension

Maimonides proposes a different approach:

> Years ago a learned man propounded as a challenge to me a curious objection.... This is what the objector said: It is manifest from the clear sense of the biblical text that the primary purpose with regard to man was that he should be, as the other animals are, devoid of intellect, of thought, and of the capacity to distinguish between good and evil. However, when he

2. See the mystical formulation of a similar approach in R. Chayyim Volozhiner's *Nefesh ha-Chayyim*, gate 1, chap. 6.

disobeyed, his disobedience procured him as its necessary consequence the great perfection peculiar to man.... Now it is a thing to be wondered at that man's punishment for his disobedience should consist in his being granted a perfection that he did not possess before, namely, the intellect....

[The answer:] For the intellect that God made overflow unto man and that is the latter's ultimate perfection, was that which Adam had been provided with before he disobeyed. It was because of this that it was said of him that he was created in the image of God and in His likeness. It was likewise on account of it that he was addressed by God and given commandments, as it says: "And the Lord God commanded," and so on (Genesis 2:16). For commandments are not given to beasts and beings devoid of intellect. Through the intellect one distinguishes between truth and falsehood, and that was found in Adam in its perfection and integrity. Fine and bad, on the other hand, belong to the things generally accepted as known, not to those cognized by the intellect. For one does not say: it is fine that heaven is spherical, and it is bad that the earth is flat; rather one says true and false with regard to these assertions.... However, when he disobeyed and inclined toward his desires of the imagination and the pleasures of his corporeal senses, inasmuch as it is said: "That the tree was good for food and that it was a delight to the eyes" (Genesis 3:6), he was punished by being deprived of this intellectual apprehension. He therefore disobeyed the commandment that was imposed upon him on account of his intellect and, becoming endowed with the faculty of apprehending generally accepted things, he became absorbed in judging things to be bad or fine.

(*Guide of the Perplexed* 1, 2)

Maimonides distinguishes here between "intellectual cognitions" and "things generally accepted as known." Before he sinned, man was able to understand everything with his intellect; he conducted himself in accordance with pure and absolute logic. His sin began the moment he inclined toward his desires, seeing the tree as "a delight to the eyes." Then he was deprived of his intellectual cognitions. When man ate from the tree, he was completely transported into the world of things generally accepted as known, to a world of relative social norms. Maimonides understands the words "And you shall be like *elohim*" as meaning "like judges who rule over states." According to Maimonides, as understood by his commentators, the Tree of Knowledge symbolizes the world of pleasure and desire.

Nature Versus Civilization

Abravanel suggests a different understanding:

> The general intent of this great section is to tell us that God created man in His intellectual image.... And He also created everything essential for his existence – food, drink, the fruits of the trees of the garden that He had planted, and the waters of its rivers. This was all made available in the natural world, so that there would be no need for effort, toil, or human activity. Everything that man needed was ready and available to him at all times, so that he would not have to trouble his soul to seek out what his body needs, but rather to perfect his soul for which he had been created. For this reason, God commanded man to content himself with the natural things that he had created for his needs, and not to allow himself to be drawn after luxuries which require work.... All this notwithstanding, the man of his own free will and choice walked in darkness.
>
> (Abravanel, Commentary to Genesis 3)

In Abravanel's view, the sin connected to the Tree of Knowledge lay in the man's submission to his passion for luxuries, which led to the development of civilization. Man is capable of meeting all his needs with what nature provides. It is the pursuit of unnecessary luxuries that brings him to develop civilization and corrupt his culture. Abravanel, as is well known, was greatly repelled by civilization, viewing it as corrupt and destructive. In this respect, he resembles the philosopher Rousseau, who saw man as noble by nature but corrupted by civilization.

Free Will

Nachmanides takes a totally different approach:

> "And the tree of the knowledge of good and evil." The commentators have suggested that its fruit gave rise to sexual passion, and therefore they [Adam and Eve] covered their nakedness after having eaten of it. They [i.e., the commentators] cite a similar expression, the saying of Barzillai the Gileadite: "Can I distinguish between good and evil?" (II Samuel 19:36) – meaning that he no longer had sexual desire. But in my opinion this interpretation is incorrect, for the serpent said: "And you shall be like Elohim, knowing good and evil" [i.e., knowledge of good and evil cannot be understood as a material quality, because the serpent attributes it to God]. And if you say that the serpent lied to her [Eve], surely, "And the Lord said, Behold man has become like one of us knowing good and evil" (Genesis 3:22)....
>
> The correct interpretation seems to me to be that man's original nature was such that he did whatever was proper for him to do naturally, just as the heavens and all their hosts do, faithful workers whose work is truth, and who do not change from their prescribed course, and whose deeds are not driven by love or hatred. But the fruit of this tree gave rise to will and desire, that those who ate it should choose a thing or its very opposite, for good or for evil. This is why it was called the Tree of Knowledge of good and evil, for "knowledge" in our language is used for the will....
>
> Now at that time sexual intercourse between Adam and his wife did not result from passion; rather, at the time of begetting offspring they came together and procreated. Therefore, all their bodily parts were, in their eyes, as the face and hands, and

> they were not ashamed of them. But after having eaten of the fruit of the Tree of Knowledge, he [Adam] acquired the power of choice; he could now do evil or good to himself or to others as he pleased. On the one hand, this is a divine attribute; but it was bad for man in that he acquired a will and desire.
>
> (Nachmanides, Commentary to Genesis 2:9)

Nachmanides' explanation is sensational. He says that eating from the Tree of Knowledge brought man free will. On one hand, free will is an advantage, for it is one of God's traits, as described by the words "And you shall be like God." Practically speaking, however, it is to man's disadvantage, for it leads him to sins of passion and desire.[3] Many differed with Nachmanides on this point, arguing that free will is a great advantage. Here, for example, is what Abravanel says:

> As the Sages have said: "'And behold, it is good' – this refers to the good inclination; 'very [good]' – this refers to the evil inclination." They meant to say that all of man's goodness and perfection stems from his ability to choose between good and evil in accordance with his inclination. Were this not so, man would not be man, and God would not have commanded him: "Of every tree of the garden you may freely eat; but of the Tree of Knowledge of good and evil, you shall not eat of it" (Genesis 2:16–17). For a commandment only applies to one who has choice and will.
>
> (Abravanel)

Another argument may be raised: if man lacked free will before he sinned, then how could he have sinned?

---

3. In his commentary to *Parashat Nitzavim*, Nachmanides goes so far as to say that in the messianic period we will once again be like the first man, stripped of free will.

Maturity

Let us conclude with the words of Rabbi Mordechai Breuer, who follows Nachmanides' approach. He, too, sees in the Tree of Knowledge a mixture of gain and loss, rather than total loss:

> Thus, man passed all at once from childhood to adulthood. The slow development that passes over every individual, little by little, fell upon Adam suddenly and all at once. A moment earlier he had been perfect and innocent, pure as a child – and now he is already an adult. Together with all the good in an adult's world, he acquired also all the bad – the splitting and the rift, the shame and the sin. In contrast to the adults in our world, however, it was he who brought all this evil upon himself.
>
> (*Pirkei Bereishit* I, p. 113)

Gain or Loss

As the discussion this chapter demonstrates, there are two main currents of thought regarding Adam's sin in the Garden of Eden. One views the outcome as advantageous to man; the other sees it as having been to his detriment. The various opinions cited above can be classified in accordance with this division:

Detriment

Ibn Ezra: Sexual desire.

Maimonides: Acquisition of things generally accepted as known rather than those apprehended by the intellect.

Abravanel: Submission to passion for luxuries.

S.R. Hirsch: Surrender to desire (which existed even before the sin).

Benno Jacob: The tree itself had no special properties (the sin consisted of Adam's failure to obey).

Advantage

Nachmanides: Free will. (Nachmanides, however, presents it as a disadvantage for man, even though it is a divine quality.)

Rabbi Mordechai Breuer: Spiritual maturity.

Proofs That Knowledge of Good and Evil Was Detrimental

1. Immediately following the sin, the verse states: "And they knew that they were naked" (Genesis 3:7), implying that there is an immediate connection between the sin and sexual desire. Shame appears (i.e., shame of nakedness and the sense of guilt resulting from the sin), because of which the man and the woman hide from God. Note that this new awareness was so deeply implanted in the man that he failed to realize that by saying "And I was afraid, because I was naked" he was exposing his new awareness, attesting admission of his sin.

2. In II Samuel 19:36, we find a similar formulation, "Can I discern between good and evil," and it is clear from the context that the reference is to physical desire and pleasure.

3. As pointed out by Abravanel, it would seem strange for God to withhold a certain advantageous quality from man and then allow him to attain it only by sinning.

Proofs That Knowledge of Good and Evil Was Advantageous

Twice this characteristic is attributed to God Himself: in the words of the serpent ("And you shall be as God, knowing good and evil" [3:5]), and in the words of God ("The man is become like one of us, knowing good and evil" [3:22]). Below, we shall propose a refutation of this compelling proof.

Suggested Understanding

In conclusion, I wish to suggest an explanation that I find most persuasive. It inclines in the direction set by Rabbi Samson R. Hirsch, but with certain additions and changes. According to this understanding, sexual pleasure existed even before the sin involving the Tree of Knowledge, but there was no sexual impulse, in the sense of a wild, uncontrollable drive. Before he sinned, man ruled over his impulses and inclinations, and allocated to himself practical and emotional opportunities for pleasure – but in the appropriate place, time, and manner. (It is difficult for us to distinguish between pleasure and impulse, but the distinction is certainly possible, and even self-evident at the level of principle.) The impulse is what makes man lose control, bringing shame in its wake. Only after the sin – after the impulse came into being – is Adam ashamed of his nakedness. Adam and Eve allowed the impulse to develop within them when they succumbed to the seductions of the serpent. (This resolves the question of how they were seduced if there was no impulse. We argue that from the very outset there was pleasure, and they willingly chose pleasure over the fulfillment of God's command.)

The serpent refers to God as Elohim rather than by the Tetragrammaton, which appears throughout the entire section. When Adam was commanded, he enjoyed the personal revelation of God. The sin lowered him to the natural level of relating to Elohim, the source of all forces, which has no moral meaning or command. The serpent's words "And you shall be like God" should be understood against the background of the primitive perception of sensuality, which sees God as the pinnacle of power and passion. In other words, we are not dealing here with a true description of God, but with a false description uttered by the serpent (i.e., the evil impulse). The true problem is how to understand the words of God Himself: "The man is become like one of us, knowing good and evil." Unless we are ready to chop the verse into pieces, as was done by Onkelos and other commentators, we must conclude that God is employing irony that comports with man's intentions and poor understanding: He is saying, in effect, man thinks he has now become like one of us. Ibn Ezra alludes to this interpretation, and Abravanel adopts it. This interpretation is problematic, but there is apparently no ready alternative.

The punishment for sin is estrangement. When the impulse

came into being, each person began to see the other as an object for the satisfaction of his own desires and passions, rather than as a partner and mate. This estrangement finds expression first and foremost in death, for prior to his sin, man was not destined to die (thus it was only after the sin that God was concerned that Adam would eat of the Tree of Life): death is man's estrangement from the world (and within man himself, the estrangement of his spiritual side from his material side; it is difficult to ignore God's belittling tone when He said: "For you are dust, and to dust shall you return" [Genesis 3:19]: you have proven that your element of dust has overcome your spiritual side).

There are other levels of alienation: (1) Between man and nature – "Cursed is the ground for your sake; in sorrow shall you eat of it all the days of your life; thorns also and thistles shall it bring forth to you" (ibid., 17–18). (2) Between man and the animal kingdom – "And the Lord God said to the serpent…I will put enmity between you and the woman" (ibid., 14–15). (3) Between man and man, and especially between man and his wife – "And yet your desire shall be to your husband, and he shall rule over you" (ibid., 16). The insertion of desire into the relationship between the man and the woman resulted in a hierarchy and in domination. Their relationship was henceforth based on mutual exploitation. Before the sin, the man called his wife *isha*, as a sign of the partnership and equality she shared with him. After the sin, she is Eve – mother of all living – a functional role (we shall deal with this in a subsequent chapter).

The element of estrangement also finds expression in Adam's hasty placing of the blame for his sin on his wife. When they succumbed to their passions, Adam and Eve entered into a period of alienation and struggle. The challenge of the confrontation with human passions accompanies mankind to this very day.

Guilt and Shame

Guilt, Shame, and the Tree of Knowledge

Guilt and shame are fundamental components of our emotional and spiritual world. Their first appearance is in *Parashat* Genesis, in the wake of Adam's sin involving the Tree of Knowledge:

> And they were both naked, the man and his wife, and they felt no shame.... And the eyes of them both were opened, and they knew that they were naked; and they sewed fig leaves together, and made themselves loincloths. And they heard the voice of the Lord God walking in the garden in the breeze of the day; and the man and his wife hid themselves from the presence of the Lord God among the trees of the garden. And the Lord God called to the man, and said to him, Where are You? And he said, I heard your voice in the garden, and I was afraid, because I was naked, and I hid myself. And He said, Who told you that you were naked; have you eaten of the tree, of which I commanded you that you should not eat?
>
> (Genesis 2:25–3:11)

This passage describes two emotions that man experiences for the very first time. First, there is shame. Following their sin, Adam and his wife are ashamed of their nakedness; according to the plain sense of the text, each felt shame in the presence of the other, even before God appeared to them. In addition to the shame, there is a second emotion: a sense of guilt that has arisen in them as a consequence of the sin. When the man hides from God and God calls to him, he tries to pretend that he was hiding out of shame rather than guilt. God, however, sees right through him: shame is also an emotion that was born out of the man's sin: "Who told you that you were naked?" It is important to note that shame has become such an essential element in Adam's world that he can no longer remember a time when he was free of shame, and he fails to understand that his feeling of shame has exposed him.

The source of the man's feeling of guilt is clear: he feels bad because of his sin. He feels guilty; he feels that he has conducted himself improperly. But what is the source of the shame? Why has the man become ashamed of his nakedness as a result of his sin? The two emotions may be directly related. In the man's eyes his nakedness is connected to his sin. But it may also be that the connection is more indirect; nakedness may not be connected to the specific sin of which the man was guilty, but to the evil inclination, which he has suddenly become aware of. As long as the man had ruled over his desires, he felt no shame in his nakedness. When he lost control, his nakedness began to symbolize his shame, his inability to control himself.

Nachmanides proposes a similar idea:

> Now at that time [i.e., before the sin] sexual intercourse between Adam and his wife did not result from passion; rather, at the time of begetting offspring they came together and procreated. Therefore, all the bodily parts were, in their eyes, as the face and hands, and they were not ashamed of them. But after having eaten of the fruit of the Tree of Knowledge, he acquired the power of choice; he could now do evil or good to himself or to others as he pleased. On the one hand, this is a divine attribute; but it was bad for man in that he acquired a will and desire.
>
> (Commentary to Genesis 2:9)

Nachmanides argues that it was only after he sinned that the man was given free will; along with the capacity to sin came also the feeling of shame. In the preceding chapter, we dealt with the various understandings of the sin of the Tree of Knowledge. No matter how we understand the Tree of Knowledge, we can still adopt Nachmanides' explanation of the origins of the feelings of guilt and shame. Rabbi Samson Raphael Hirsch has a different understanding of the sin and its consequences, but he, too, emphasizes the emergence of shame in the wake of sin:

> As soon as man becomes subjugated to his passions, and fails to strive to elevate his sensuality to the realm of sanctity, but on the contrary, his sensuality lowers his sanctity to its realm – he immediately becomes ashamed of his nakedness.
>
> (Commentary to Genesis 2:25)[1]

Before concluding this section, we shall quote another passage from Rabbi Hirsch, in which he distinguishes between the function of guilt and conscience and the function of the Torah:

> The voice of God that echoes in man – his conscience, whose messenger is shame – only warns man in general to be good and to turn away from evil, but it is from the mouth of God that he is told what is good and what is evil.
>
> (Ibid., Genesis 3:1)

Shame and Guilt: Good or Bad?

In the modern period, different attitudes arose toward the feeling of guilt.[2] One of the prevailing attitudes today is highly critical

---

1. See Radak's picturesque description in his commentary to Genesis 3:7.
2. This chapter is heavily based on Prof. Shalom Rosenberg's article "Matzpun ve-Ashma ba-Hagut ha-Yehudit" in C. Navon (ed.), *Teshuva u-Pesikhologiya*, (Alon Shevut, 5761), pp. 19–47.

of the idea of guilt. The philosopher Friedrich Nietzsche argued that guilt is merely the turning inward of man's aggressive feelings. Society, he claimed, has erected walls of social morality within the individual that rein in his primal instincts: enmity, cruelty, and joy in pursuit and destruction. But these passions do not disappear. They turn inward, instead of outward, and are transformed into a "bad conscience."

> This is the origin of "bad conscience." The man who lacked external enemies and opposition and was forced into an oppressive narrowness and regularity of custom, impatiently tore himself apart, persecuted himself, gnawed away at himself, grew upset, and did himself damage.
>
> (Nietzsche, *On the Genealogy of Morality*, essay 3)

In Nietzsche's system, once human society put restrictions on aggressive behavior, people began to turn their aggressive inclinations inward against themselves. This is human conscience, through which man gnaws away at himself. Note that in this view the human conscience does not flow from man's inner purity, but, on the contrary, from his latent aggressiveness.

Freud, the father of psychoanalysis, developed a similar direction of thought. The feeling of guilt is not inborn in man's personality, but results from social pressures nurtured by the individual in order to allow for the perpetuation of an orderly society. The growing child internalizes the prohibitions taught by his environment, creating within himself his super-ego, that is, his conscience, which torments him because of his evil impulses.[3] The super-ego punishes us not only for the offenses we commit, but even for negative thoughts that stir up pangs of conscience within us. The

3. On this point, Freud's description is very different from that in the book of Genesis, where guilt and shame appear spontaneously without any social pressure whatsoever.

strengthening of the super-ego is "a most precious cultural asset," without which human civilization would not be possible.

If not for the internalization of social norms, according to Freud, society would be a collection of egotistical murderers who would stop at nothing to achieve their desired ends. On the other hand, when the super-ego becomes too strong or demanding, it results in neurosis – extreme emotional tension that expresses itself in distorted behavior.

> In our research into, and therapy of, a neurosis, we are led to make two reproaches against the super-ego of the individual. In the severity of its commands and prohibitions it troubles itself too little about the happiness of the ego, in that it takes insufficient account of the resistances against obeying them – of the instinctual strength of the id [in the first place], and of the difficulties presented by the real external environment [in the second]. Consequently we are very often obliged, for therapeutic purposes, to oppose the super-ego, and we endeavor to lower its demands.
>
> (*Civilization and Its Discontents*, vol. 8)

In other words, Freud recognized the necessity of the super-ego and conscience for the establishment of human society, but felt that man's conscience can be too rigid, and so must often be tempered with the help of psychological treatment.

Admonitions regarding the destructiveness sometimes latent in the feeling of guilt are also found in Jewish thought. Consider, for instance, this extract from an early Chasidic work attributed to the Ba'al Shem Tov:

> The evil inclination sometimes misleads a person, convincing him that he has committed a grave transgression, even though the sin was merely a stringency, or not a sin at all. [The evil inclination] wishes that a person will be filled with sadness, so that in his sadness he will neglect the service of the Creator,

> blessed be He. A person must understand this deception, and say to the evil inclination, "I do not heed the stringency of which you speak, for your intention is that I should neglect His service; you speak lies. Even if it really is a little sinful, it will be more pleasing to my Creator if I do not heed the stringency of which you speak so as to cause me sadness in His service. On the contrary, I shall serve Him with joy, for my intention in [His] service is not for myself, but to do what is pleasing before God, blessed be He. Therefore, even if I do not heed the stringency of which you speak, the Creator will not be angry with me, for the whole reason that I do not heed it is so that I should not neglect His service. For how can I neglect His service for even a moment?" This is a great principle in the service of the Creator, blessed be He, that a person should watch out for sadness to the best of his ability.
>
> (Ethical Will of Rivash)[4]

Rabbi Abraham Isaac Kook wrote in a similar vein:

> The pangs of conscience of spiritually great people who wish to rid themselves of all spiritual dross and filth can sometimes grow excessively in strength, for nothing can stand in the way of man's spirit. This can sometimes lead to a loathing of the world, life, and everything done under the sun.
>
> (*Ayin Ayah*, *Berakhot* 2, p. 326)

As a rule, however, Judaism attaches great value to the feeling of guilt, the conscience. Guilt feelings can at times impair an individual's emotional health, but generally speaking, in normal situations, feelings of guilt are beneficial and necessary. We believe that the feeling of guilt is not an internalization of the prohibitions

---

4. Note that the author of the ethical will of Rivash is not concerned about the emotional crisis that guilt can create, but about its negative impact on the worship of God.

imposed by society, but a fundamental feeling that God gave man, allowing him to feel his sins and make amends. Guilt is not a destructive force, but a beneficial one.

Rabbi Joseph B. Soloveitchik emphasizes this point, citing Aristotle's understanding of the blessing found in pain, the idea that suffering is a warning sign that precedes the degeneration of the body. Many tragedies occur because pains are only discerned when it is too late. Sin is also an illness, and, therefore, it, too, finds expression in suffering. Pangs of conscience are often sharper and more painful than any bodily suffering. But they are also a blessing, for they warn us of the need to treat the disease of sin (*On Repentance*, p. 194).

Judaism, as a moral religion that demands a certain lifestyle in addition to obedience to God's commandments, does not perceive the conscience as a destructive force that ruins the emotional health of an individual. On the contrary, it is our conscience that makes it possible for us to achieve spiritual health and emotional wholeness.

Rabbi Soloveitchik, aware that guilt can be an inhibiting and negative force, distinguishes between two types of guilt feelings. There is guilt that focuses exclusively on the sharp pain over sins committed in the past. Guilt feelings of this type are indeed degenerating and paralyzing. There is, however, a second type of guilt feeling that is healthy and healing:

> If guilt and other feelings of penitence are not torn like a single leaf out of the book of life, and channels of communication are kept open between them and their antithetic emotions (in this case, faith in one's recuperative power and the aptitude for reconstruction), then the same feelings of depression may bring about outbursts of creative energy. Guilt might be the gateway to a greater and richer life.
>
> (*Out of the Whirlwind*, p. 194)

The context of the preceding statement is Rabbi Soloveitchik's view that our emotions must be complex and not absolute. Every experience of joy must contain some measure of sadness, and vice versa. In this context, the feeling of guilt and remorse must not be entirely negative. Guilt must always be accompanied by an optimistic faith in the possibility of renewal and change, by a thin line of the breaking of dawn at the end of the night.

Martin Buber added that the conscience is not an internalization of society's moral norms, but just the opposite.[5] Conscience is the ideal image of man that one sets before one's eyes and toward which one aspires. Not only is the conscience vital for the survival of the moral individual, but it leads him to his essence, his very self. This stands in absolute contradistinction to Freud's approach.

Let us conclude with the impressive words of Prof. Shalom Rosenberg on the spiritual importance of the conscience and guilt feelings. Rosenberg observes that the relativism of the post-modern world has made guilt an even dirtier word than it was in the modern world. If there are no absolute values, and every individual has his own truth, why should anyone ever feel guilty? It is precisely for this reason that we must raise the banner of guilt and conscience and recognize their great importance. Prof. Rosenberg argues that only an Orthodox Jew can be a sinner. A person who rejects every objective standard of good, erasing the gap between "commandment" and "sin," cannot commit sins. "Woe to us, for we have sinned"; but fortunate are we that we are guilty, that we still feel guilt. Let us not give up this spiritual virtue.

> Now we can understand the meaning of the *tashlikh* ceremony, the act of casting away sin. We pray to God: "And You will cast all their sins into the depths of the sea" (Micah 7:19). The sins will disappear, not if we concentrate them in a sewer of evil, but only if we dilute them in a sea of good deeds. If we fill that

5. See Martin Buber, *Penei Adam*, pp. 296–297.

sea, God will dilute our sins in His infinite and absolute sea of loving-kindness.

(Rosenberg, "Matzpun ve-Ashma ba-Hagut ha-Yehudit," in *Teshuva u-Pesikhologiya* [Alon Shevut], 5761, pp. 46–47)

The Woman in Creation

In this chapter we shall not deal with the general question of the status of women; that issue is too broad for a single unit. We shall content ourselves here with a discussion of the woman's place in creation.

The Plain Sense of the Text

Let us start with the plain sense of the scriptural verses. The second chapter of Genesis describes the creation of the woman in an optimistic atmosphere of partnership and friendship.

> And the Lord God said, It is not good that the man should be alone: I will make him a help to match him. And out of the ground the Lord God formed every beast of the field, and every bird of the air; and brought them to the man to see what he would call them: and whatever the man called every living creature, that was its name. And the man gave names to all cattle, and to the birds of the air, and to every beast of the field; but for the man there was not found a help to match him. And the Lord God caused a deep sleep to fall upon the man, and he slept: and he took one of his ribs [alternatively: sides], and closed up the flesh in its place, and of the rib [alternatively:

> side] which the Lord God had taken from the man, he made a woman, and brought her to the man. And the man said, This is now bone of my bones, and flesh of my flesh; she shall be called woman [*isha*], because she was taken out of man (*ish*). That is why a man leaves his father and his mother, and cleaves to his wife; and they become one flesh.
>
> (Genesis 2:18–24)

The story starts with the man's loneliness. "It is not good that man should be alone." He is searching for a "help." This is immediately followed by the account of the creation of the animals and how the man gave them names. What is this doing here?

According to the plain sense of the text, the answer is simple: the man is searching among the animals for a helpmate. He names all the animals, trying to understand their essential nature. But still, "for the man there was not found a help to match him"; the animals do not fill man's need for society.

God then decides that the man's mate will only be found in a creature closely resembling him, one fashioned out of one of his ribs. That is how the woman comes into being. The man calls her "woman" (*isha*) as a symbol of the similarity between them and her source in him (*ish*): "She shall be called woman, because she was taken out of man."

The story ends on an optimistic note: "That is why a man leaves his father and his mother, and cleaves to his wife; and they become one flesh." The woman is part of the man; for this reason a man leaves his parents' house in order to find a woman to whom he can cleave.

Sin, however, brought this idyllic situation to an abrupt end. The sin, as we learned in an earlier chapter, allowed unrestrained desire to enter into the relationship. Uncontrollable desire causes us to relate to others merely as a means for the satisfaction of our own needs. Thus, the man quickly blames his wife: "The woman whom You gave to be with me, she gave me of the tree" (Genesis 3:12).

Following the sin, the relationship between the man and the woman undergoes a change. We all remember the woman's punishment:

> Unto the woman He said, I will greatly multiply the pain of your childbearing; in sorrow you shall bring forth children; and yet your desire (*teshukatekh*) shall be your husband, and he shall rule over you.
>
> (Genesis 3:16)

What is meant by the words "And yet your *teshuka* [usually translated as 'desire'] shall be your husband"? Rabbi Abraham ibn Ezra offers a surprising interpretation:

> *Teshukatekh* – your obedience, meaning that you will do whatever he commands you [to do], for you are under his authority to do what he wants.
>
> (Ibn Ezra, commentary ad loc.)

The term *teshuka* is usually understood as "desire," but Ibn Ezra interprets it here in the sense of "obedience." What brought Ibn Ezra to this interpretation? Perhaps he was prompted by the real-life observation that a woman's desire is not necessarily any greater than a man's; perhaps he failed to understand how desire could be regarded as a curse; or perhaps he was guided by the parallelism with the final clause of the verse: "And he shall rule over you."

The classical commentators as well as modern biblical scholars adduce proof for Ibn Ezra's position from the verse regarding Joseph: "And according to your word shall all my people be ruled (*yishak*)" (Genesis 41:40), where *teshuka* is equivalent to "rule." According to this interpretation, we understand how God's words are a curse; and there is no difficulty from observable human conduct. This is apparently also the way to understand the verse further on regarding Cain, "And to you shall be his *teshuka*, and yet you shall rule over him" (Genesis 4:7), where once again we find a juxtaposition of *teshuka* and "rule."

Rabbenu Bachya ibn Pekuda proposes a different interpretation. The verse does not mean to say that a woman's desire is greater than a man's, but rather that, in contrast to others in a subservient position, such as slaves, she yearns for her husband, and therefore makes no attempt to escape her bondage. In any event, Rabbenu Bachya also understands the verse as related to a man's domination over his wife.

It is important to emphasize that we are dealing here with a curse, and not with the ideal state. Some have tried to use these verses to perpetuate the subservience of women to their husbands. But the verses refer to a *curse* against which we are *commanded* to fight, and thus the message of this passage is the very opposite.

Let me relate a personal anecdote. The wife of a friend of mine was in the delivery room with a woman whose husband had forbidden her to have an epidural so that she would be better able to fulfill the imperative, "in sorrow shall you bring forth children."[1] My friend asked the husband whether he was equally careful to fulfill the command, "in the sweat of your face shall you eat bread." This is totally erroneous: we are dealing here with a curse, not a command. The words "and he shall rule over you" should be understood in the same way. We are being given here the important and surprising message that male domination and oppression of women are a curse, and not at all part of the optimal social order.

Let us continue and see what happens in the aftermath of the sin. Adam names his wife for a second time:

> And the man called his wife's name Eve; because she was the mother of all living.
>
> (Genesis 3:20)

1. In 1591 a midwife named Agnes Simpson was burned at the stake for trying to alleviate the pain of birthing mothers by using various potions, in violation, as it were, of the divine command.

There is an enormous difference between the names given to the woman before and after the sin. This point was noted by Rabbi Isaac Arama, author of *Akeidat Yitzchak*:

> Originally, Adam had called Eve *isha*, emphasizing her parity with man, i.e., *ish*. After the episode with the Tree of Knowledge, he called her Eve, emphasizing the female element within her, and the fact that she was the mother of all subsequent human beings. Between these two names, the two functions of woman are defined. On the one hand, as the *eshet chayil*, "woman of valor," she possesses all the ingredients that can raise her to the status of prophetess; on the other hand, her function is to become a mother. A woman who fails to give birth, just like a man who is sterile, has not forfeited her major function in life, as is proven from Isaiah 56:3–5: "Let not the barren proclaim I am but a dried-out tree." We hold the view that man's major function is the performance of good deeds, something quite independent of procreation. If Jacob had been angry at Rachel for demanding children, or else her life would not be worth living, it was precisely for this reason.
>
> (*Akeidat Yitzchak*, Genesis 9)[2]

Before the sin, the man called his wife Isha, giving expression to her essential nature as well as to her origin. Now he calls her Eve, a name that expresses the benefit she brings him. He does not relate to his wife's essential nature and personality, but only to the fact that she provides him with children, that she is "the mother of all living." He relates to her functionally, attempting to examine the benefit Eve can bring him.

This leads naturally to the next stage:

---

2. Rabbi Arama, however, does not develop the idea that we have presented here about the change effected by the sin. Ralbag explains that the name "Eve" alludes to the fact that in a certain respect the woman belongs to the class of animals, albeit the highest among them. According to him, the name itself emphasizes the female's inferiority.

> And Lamech took to him two wives; the name of the one was Adah, and the name of the other Zillah.
>
> (Genesis 4:19)

As pointed out by Radak, Lamech was the first to take two wives. The taking of two wives reflects a way of looking at a woman not as a partner in marriage, but as a source of benefit. A man who marries two women does not expect to "cleave to his wife and become one flesh," but to derive gain and benefit. Rashi's comment on this verse cites the words of the Sages:

> This was the custom of the generation that lived before the time of the Flood; they had two wives, one for childbearing, the other for frivolous companionship and charm; the latter was given a cup of some drug to drink in order that she might become barren, and was dressed up like a bride and fed with the best food, while her fellow-wife was left without her husband's companionship and ever mourned like a widow.
>
> (Rashi, commentary ad loc.)

At first glance, it would appear that the woman designated for the man's companionship should be happy; in truth, however, they are both wretched. When a woman is set aside for a particular purpose, whether for procreation or for companionship, she is being treated as an object from which benefit may be derived. Dividing the various functions of a wife among several women is the ultimate expression of relating to a woman from the perspective of the functional benefit that may be derived from her. The message of *Parashat Bereishit* is that the ideal situation is harmony and friendship between husband and wife, and that exploitation follows from exaggerated desire and sin.

What the Commentators Say

The positions of the commentators on this issue vary widely. We shall present their views without unnecessary apologetics, and allow the intelligent reader to choose for himself the view that he thinks most closely corresponds to the plain sense of Scripture and his own outlook.

The Image of God

The commentators disagree on the question of whether only the man or also the woman was created in the image of God. The dispute stems from the fact that the biblical verse passes from the singular to the plural: "In the image of God He created him; male and female He created them." This makes it possible to understand creation as relating to both of them, but the image of God only to the man. That is how Abravanel, for example, understood the verse:

> Even though the two of them were of one species, they were not equally in the image of God. This is why the verse states: "In the image of God He created him; male and female He created them." That is, man alone was created in the image of God.... For the primary creation was that of the male, he alone being created in the image of God, as it is stated in the singular: "In the image of God, He created Him." For it is he who would perceive the mysteries of wisdom, and not the female, whose wisdom is limited to the spindle.
>
> (Commentary to Genesis 1:27)

Rabbi Naftali Tzvi Yehuda Berlin, the Netziv, developed this idea further:

> "Male and female He created them." The verse does not come to explain that this species, more so than all the other creatures, has a male and a female. Rather, [it comes] to teach you that they are two beings, as will be explained below. This is because the male of this species is not at all similar in his character to the female of the same species. As the Ecclesiastes says: "One man among a thousand I have found; but a woman among all

> those I have not found" (Ecclesiastes 7:28). That is, a man of virtue resembling his Creator in the image of God is found one in a thousand; which is not the case regarding women.
>
> (*Ha'amek Davar*, Genesis 1:27)

The Netziv wonders why it is that only about man is it stated that his species was created male and female; surely, the same could have been said about every other member of the animal kingdom! He answers that Scripture adopted this formulation in order to indicate that there is a difference in level between the human male and female. Among human beings, only a man can attain the image of God, and so the verse uses the singular in reference to the image of God. The Netziv explains the entire creation story in the same spirit.

Rabbi Abraham ben ha-Maimonides rejected the idea that "the image of God" refers to man alone. He argues that even if we say that God created "the man" (and only "the man") in His image, the verse is referring to the entire human race:

> The term *adam* has more than one meaning. It denotes the first human being, as will be explained, and also the human species, which divides into men and women. The reference in this and the following verses is to the species, for it is stated: "Male and female he created them."
>
> (Commentary to Genesis 1:27)

According to Rabbi Abraham, the verse stating that God created "the man" in His image refers to the entire human race, and not only to males. Rabbi Samson Raphael Hirsch built on this idea. His conclusion, based on what Chapter 1 of Genesis says about the creation of the male and the female, is the very opposite of the Netziv's.

> "Male and female He created them." All living creatures were created male and female, but Scripture mentions this only in connection with the creation of man. Thus, the Torah teaches

> us that the two sexes were created directly by God, and both were created in His image. This is given special emphasis by the transition from the singular to the plural, *oto* ("him") to *otam* ("them"). The one human being was created in God's image, he being both male and female. Only the two sexes together constitute the full man.
>
> (Commentary to Genesis 1:27)

The Netziv argues that the Torah's emphasis on the division between male and female informs us of the gap between them. Rabbi Hirsch argues just the opposite: it teaches us about their equality. The Netziv understands the statement "In the image of God, He created him" as referring to the male alone. Rabbi Hirsch arrives at the very opposite conclusion: only when the two sexes come together do they constitute a whole creature that is in the image of God. Rabbi Hirsch explains the entire passage in this spirit.

The Woman's Creation from the Man's Rib

The fact that the woman was created from the man's rib seems to suggest that the male is superior to the female. That was how Ralbag understood it:

> Woman was created from man because he is the reason for her existence, that is to say, she was created to serve him.... She was created from him so that she would be more obedient to him and perform the services he requires.... This is not the case regarding other living creatures. And for this reason they were created together from one place.
>
> (Commentary to the Torah)

At the end of the passage, Ralbag claims that it is only in the human species that the female is inferior to the male. Therefore, it was only the man who was created alone without his wife, she being created only afterward.[3]

It is interesting that Plato also alluded to a hierarchy among men and women, and he, too, based it on the order of creation:

> At first only males were created, and according to the reasonable explanation, all those of faint heart who lived evil lives would pass into women at their second birth.
>
> (Plato, *Timaeus*)

Rabbi Samson Raphael Hirsch's explanation of the creation of the woman was quite different from Ralbag's. He says that the fact that the woman was created from the man testifies to her superiority.

> The creation of the man was not the same as the creation of the woman. The material of the man's body was taken from the earth, and God took one side of his body, and formed the woman from it.... The man was built out and arranged as a woman.... Thus, Scripture attests to the complete equality of women. Our Sages also ascribe to this all the special characteristics of the woman: her voice, her character and temperament, as well as the earlier spiritual and mental maturity of women.... She was formed out of the body of the man, which already had feeling, sensitivity, and vitality, in contrast to the man, whose body was created out of earth.
>
> (Commentary to Genesis 2:22)

Rabbi Hirsch says that the man was created from the earth,

---

3. A similar interpretation was offered by Ra'avad, *Ba'alei ha-Nefesh*, pp. 14–14. The *Ba'alei ha-Tosafot* (in their commentary to the Torah) suggest that it was owing to the woman's inferiority and subjugation to the man that she was created specifically out of his rib: "There is a question: Why was the woman created out of a rib and not some other organ? So that the woman should be bent down before and subservient to her husband [i.e., kneel and prostrate herself before him]."

whereas the woman was created from the man, and so enjoys higher status.

The narrative in the first chapter of Genesis describes a single joint creation of the man and the woman, in contrast to the second chapter, where the male is created first. Nonetheless, even with respect to the account in the second chapter, the Sages understood the primal creature not as a male, but as both male and female.

> Rabbi Shemuel bar Nachman said: When the Holy One, blessed be He, created the first man, he created him a hermaphrodite. Rabbi Levi said: When man was created, he was created with two body fronts, and He sawed him in two, so that two backs resulted, one back for the male and another for the female. An objection was raised: "And He took one of his ribs" (Genesis 2:21). He answered: The word should be rendered "of his sides," as it is written: "And for the second side of the tabernacle" (Exodus 26:20).[4]
>
> (Leviticus Rabba 14, 1)

This, of course, is not the plain sense of the text, but midrash. It embodies, however, an important message: Essentially, the man was not created before the woman; both were created together. (There is also an additional message, unrelated to our present discussion, concerning the deep connection between man and woman, who can cleave together and form a single flesh.)

The Sin

Certain thinkers and biblical commentators emphasized the woman's guilt and responsibility for the sin involving the Tree

4. Resh Lakish understands that the verse which states that God took one of Adam's *tzela'ot* (Genesis 1:21) is not referring to what we call a *tzela*, i.e., a rib, but to one of Adam's sides. Resh Lakish's interpretation of *tzela* as "side" is indeed the plain sense of the word (though the picture he paints of Adam being created with two faces is certainly not the plain sense of the verse). A similar account appears in Plato's *Symposium*.

of Knowledge.[5] Thus, for example, Rabbenu Bachya ibn Pekuda writes:

> "That God has made man upright" (Ecclesiastes 7:29). In other words, He created [man] entirely rational, that in all his qualities he should only follow [his] intellect. But when the woman emerged from him, having been taken from his ribs, he then sinned and veered from the path of the intellect because of her, for she caused him to sin and think evil of God as a result of the wicked adviser.... For he had never sinned when he was by himself, until the woman came. But once she came, sin came [as well].
>
> (*Kitvei Rabbenu Bachya*, p. 550)

The Torah states that the woman ate of the forbidden fruit first, but it does not say that she seduced the man. It only says that she gave him of the fruit and he ate. It was only Adam who tried to blame his wife, hanging the sin upon her. *Midrash ha-Gadol* depicts the woman as having seduced her husband, but it is precisely her weakness and inferiority that it puts forward in her defense:

> Adam said to the Holy One, blessed be He: "Master of the universe, when I was by myself, I did not sin before You. But when this woman came to me, she led me astray, as it says: 'She gave me of the tree, and I ate.'" The Holy One, blessed be He, said to him: "I gave her to you as a help, yet you are ungrateful, saying: 'She gave it to me.' You should not have listened to

5. Christianity greatly developed the idea of the woman's responsibility for the primeval sin. As Paul said: "I permit no woman to teach or to have authority over men; she is to keep silent. For Adam was formed first, then Eve; and Adam was not deceived, but the woman was deceived and became a transgressor. Yet woman will be saved through bearing children, if she continues in faith and love and holiness, with modesty" (1 Timothy 2:12–15).

> her, for she is subordinate to you, whereas you are not subordinate to her."
>
> (*Midrash ha-Gadol*, Genesis 3:12)

In general, the story of the sin illuminates Eve in a negative light. It is by no means certain, however, that we are dealing with a general model that teaches us about the weakness of all women.

"It Is Not Good That Man Should Be Alone"

Although in general the Netziv follows the interpretation that emphasizes the woman's inferiority, he also suggests an interpretation of a wholly different sort. When the verse says "It is not good that man should be alone," it is not referring to the fact that the male needs the female, for that is the case with all the world's creatures, and why should man be different? What is the novelty in a man needing a woman? What the text really means to say is as follows:

> It is not good that [man] should have a female counterpart like those of the other creatures, who, rather than being a help throughout the course of life, only present themselves at mating time; it is not good that man should be in such a situation.
>
> (*Ha'amek Davar*, Genesis 2:18)

Human coupling is based not only upon sexual union, but also upon partnership and joint living. We might add that even on the purely sexual plane, there is a difference between man and other living creatures. Most other animals have a limited mating season, at which time the males join with their female counterparts. Only man comes together with his wife at all times of the year. This, too, gives expression to the need of man and woman to be together at all times.

Violence

The First Act of Violence

Cain's slaying of his brother Abel was the first act of violence in the history of the world. A British lord once said rather sarcastically that today's youth are no worse than the youth of old, for even when there were only two young men in the world, Cain and Abel, one of them was a criminal.

The story of Cain and Abel is pessimistic as well as tragic. There are only four people in the entire world, all of them members of the same family, and yet a murder is committed. In proportional terms, Cain killed a greater part of the world's population than any other person. Cain sowed the seeds of the evil and violence that would accompany mankind ever after. The Sages described the period of innocence that preceded the murder as follows:

> *Mishna:* Know that capital cases are not like monetary cases. In monetary cases, a person gives money and atones for himself. In capital cases, his blood and the blood of his descendants hang on him until the end of the world. For thus we find regarding Cain, who killed his brother, as it is said: "Your brother's bloods cry out" (Genesis 4:10). It does not say "your brother's blood," but "your brother's bloods" – his blood and the blood of his descendants.

> *Gemara:* Rav Yehuda the son of Rabbi Chiyya said: This teaches that Cain inflicted many bruises and many wounds on his brother Abel, for he did not know from where the soul departs, until he reached the throat.
>
> (*Sanhedrin* 37a–37b)

Rav Yehuda the son of Rabbi Chiyya tells us why the phrase "your brother's bloods" is in the plural. Cain wanted to kill his brother, but did not really know how to go about killing another human being. Thus he inflicted many wounds on Abel, and blood spilled out of all of them. This was the last time that a murderer did not know how to kill his victim.

After Cain, we hear of another killing – the murder committed by Lamech, one of Cain's descendants:

> And Lamech said to his wives, Ada and Zillah, Hear my voice, wives of Lamech, hearken to my speech; for I have slain a man for wounding me, and a young man for my hurt. If Cain shall be avenged sevenfold, truly Lamech seventy and sevenfold.
>
> (Genesis 4:23–24)

The Sages understood that Lamech had killed unintentionally. According to certain modern scholars, however – and this seems to be the plain sense of the text – Lamech is singing in praise of himself for having succeeded in killing his enemies. He proclaims that the revenge he took from his enemies is far greater than the revenge God took from Cain. Murder is no longer a shameful sin, but an accomplishment to take pride in.

The Background to Abel's Murder

Since Cain's murder of Abel was an archetypal event, it is critically important to understand what led up to it. According to the plain sense of the text, Cain killed Abel out of jealousy. Abel was the younger brother, yet it was his offering that God favored. That is why Cain killed Abel. The plain sense of the passage describes a conflict rooted in inequality and the resulting jealousy.

The plain meaning, however, leaves an important question unanswered. The verse states:

> And Cain said to Abel his brother; and it came to pass, when they were in the field, that Cain rose up against Abel his brother, and slew him.
>
> (Genesis 4:8)

What did Cain say to his brother? And why did the Torah leave the sentence dangling? The commentators propose several approaches:

> "And Cain said to Abel." He began an argument, striving and contending with him, to seek a pretext to kill him.
>
> (Rashi, ad loc.)

Rashi teaches us an important principle of human psychology. Sometimes a person hates his fellow, conspires against him, and then looks for a pretext to harm him. According to Rashi, the Torah does not record the precise wording of the conversation because it is unimportant: Cain was merely looking for an excuse to kill Abel.

Rabbi Abraham ibn Ezra suggested a different interpretation:

> "And Cain said." It appears to me that Cain related to Abel a full account of the rebuke with which God had reproached him.
>
> (Ibn Ezra, ad loc.)

Ibn Ezra explains that this verse is a direct continuation of the previous incident: Cain shares his troubles with Abel as a prelude to the murder. Seforno offers a similar explanation:

> "And Cain said to Abel his brother." [He told him] how annoyed he was, and how his countenance fell because of his brother.
>
> (Seforno, ad loc.)

Seforno implies that the words *el Abel achiv* (translated here as "to Abel his brother") do not describe a conversation between Cain and Abel. Rather, Abel was the subject of what Cain said.

Nachmanides goes in a different direction:

> But in my opinion it is connected with the following words of Scripture: "And it came to pass, when they were in the field," meaning that Cain said to Abel, "Let us go forth into the field," and there he secretly killed him.
>
> (Nachmanides, ad loc.)

Nachmanides introduces an additional factor into the picture – premeditation. Cain cold-bloodedly planned the murder in advance.

Rabbi Yosef Bekhor Shor takes this approach to the extreme:

> "And Cain said to Abel his brother." What the Holy One, blessed be He, had told him. He approached him with guile, for he sensed that Abel was guarding himself against him. He said to him: "This is what the Holy One, blessed be He, said to me, and we made peace with each other, and I am no longer upset..." And Abel thought that [Cain] had been appeased, and so he no longer kept his guard up against him.
>
> (Rabbi Yosef Bekhor Shor, ad loc.)

We are not dealing here with a spontaneous reaction of explosive fury, but with cold, calculated planning with malice aforethought. According to secular law, this would be reason to impose a more severe punishment. Halakha does not recognize a formal difference between premeditated and unpremeditated murder, provided that the killer was fully aware of his actions. The Torah raises the level of responsibility that it imposes upon man; as a rule, it does not view a spontaneous outburst of anger as an extenuating circumstance, notwithstanding the fact that the requirement of previous warning means that a person is only liable for punishment if he clear-mindedly assumed responsibility for his action. In any event, Nachmanides' approach clearly magnifies Cain's sin.

An explanation in *Midrash ha-Gadol*, however, implies just the opposite:

> "And Cain talked." This teaches that they argued with each other (*nitamru*).

According to *Midrash ha-Gadol*, Cain and Abel argued and fought with each other. According to this explanation, the murder may have been the spontaneous consequence of a fraternal argument. We shall see below that the Sages enlarged upon this approach. Some even assigned blame to Abel:

> "And Cain said to Abel his brother." This means that he related to him the words of the Holy One, blessed be He, and what he had said to Him. He indicated that he was very angry that God had not shown him the same regard that He had shown Abel. *And Hevel was glad.* "And Cain rose up against Abel his brother, and slew him."
>
> (Da'at Zekenim mi-Ba'alei ha-Tosafot)

There are other interpretations as well. The author of *Ha-Ketav veha-Kabbala*, for example, understands the first half of the verse as the answer to God's question, "Why are you angry?" Cain answers: "Because of Abel my brother." Cassuto suggests, on the basis of Near Eastern parallels, that Cain arranged to meet his brother in the field. Others have proposed that the verse reflects Cain's thoughts, musings, and designs with respect to his brother Abel.

The Background to Human Violence

Thus far, we have dealt with the plain sense of the biblical account. The Sages exploited the obscurity of the passage to broaden the canvas with a midrashic interpretation that treated Cain's slaying of his brother as the archetype of all future acts of murder. Thus, they expanded upon the factors that led to the killing:[1]

> "And Cain spoke unto Abel his brother, etc." What were they quarreling about? They said: "Come, let us divide the world." One took the land, and the other the movables. The one said: "The land you are standing on is mine," and the other responded: "What you are wearing is mine." The one said: "Undress"; the other retorted: "Flee [off my land]." Out of this quarrel, Cain rose up against his brother Abel.
>
> Rabbi Yehoshua of Siknin said in the name of Rabbi Levi: Both took land and both took movables, but about what did they quarrel? The one said: "The Temple will be built in my borders," while the other responded: "It will be built in mine."
>
> ...Yehuda bar Ami said: Their quarrel was about the first Eve. Rabbi Aibu said: The first Eve had returned to dust. About what then was their quarrel? Rabbi Huna said: An additional twin was born together with Abel, and each claimed her. The one claimed: "I will take her, because I am the firstborn"; while the other argued: "I will take her, because she was born with me."
>
> (Genesis Rabba 22:7)

As pointed out by Nechama Leibowitz, the Sages saw the confrontation between Cain and Abel as the model for violence and conflict throughout human history. The Sages proposed various explanations for the confrontation. Another point should be mentioned. As we will see below, the Christians viewed Abel as an archetype of their Messiah. The Sages emphasize that Abel was

1. In the discussion that follows, I have made use of the book *Sippurei Reishit.*

human, and that he was afflicted with the same lusts and desires that plagued Cain.

According to the first opinion cited in the midrash, Cain and Abel argued about property and power. Disputes involving property, money, and power have been at the center of an endless number of conflicts throughout the course of history, both on the interpersonal and the international level. Let us cite the well-known words of the French philosopher Rousseau regarding this point:

> The first man, who, after enclosing a piece of ground, took it into his head to say, "This is mine," and found people simple enough to believe him, was the true founder of civil society. How many crimes, how many wars, how many murders, how many misfortunes and horrors, would that man have saved the human species, who pulling up the stakes or filling up the ditches should have cried to his fellows: "Be sure not to listen to this imposter; you are lost if you forget that the fruits of the earth belong equally to us all, and the earth itself to nobody!"
>
> (*Discourse on the Inequality Among Mankind*, pt. II)

Like the midrash, Rousseau maintains that property and the acquisition thereof are the root of innumerable crimes, wars, and murders. He makes some controversial assumptions, however. First, he claims that the very concept of property is artificial, that there is no property in nature, and that property is a human convention. Second, Rousseau claims that mankind would be better off without property. This argument is quite problematic: If the farmer was not promised the fruits of his field, he would have little incentive to work it. In order to agree with Rousseau, we must assume that man is fundamentally so good that he would be prepared to work with no guarantee of receiving anything in return. Or else, that man could make do with what nature provides, without having to invest special effort to increase nature's yield. Rousseau himself seems to incline toward the second assumption. Karl Marx, on the other hand, inclined toward the first.

He maintained that the abolition of private ownership would resolve the problems of society and morality when combined with continual technological advancement:

> The history of all hitherto existing societies is the history of class struggles. Freeman and slave, patrician and plebeian, lord and serf, guild-master and journeyman, in a word, oppressor and oppressed, stood in constant opposition to one another, carried on an uninterrupted, now hidden, now open fight.... In this sense, the theory of the Communists may be summed up in the single sentence: Abolition of private property.... In proportion as the antagonism between classes within the nation vanishes, the hostility of one nation to another will come to an end.
>
> (Marx, *Communist Manifesto*)

The midrash suggests a second cause (third in the text itself) of conflict, war, and violence: the fight over women – the sexual drive. On the individual level, we are all familiar with personal conflicts based in romantic rivalries. On the international level, it is more difficult to see sex as a cause of conflict, although it is said that the Trojan War began as a struggle over the beautiful Helen of Sparta.

Sigmund Freud heavily underscored sex as a root of conflict and tension. He argued, however, that the aggressive impulse is an independent entity, sex being only one of its outlets.

In addition, Freud vigorously rejected the Communist position that property is the source of all controversy and violence. Communism holds that man is good by nature, but has been corrupted by the institution of private property. If we abolish private property, there will no longer be any reason for ill-will and hostility among men. Freud describes this approach as "an untenable illusion." If we abolish private property, he warns, people will fight over sex.

> If we do away with personal rights over material wealth, there still remains prerogative in the field of sexual relationships, which is bound to become the source of the strongest dislike and the most violent hostility.... If we were to remove this factor, too, by allowing complete freedom of sexual life ..., we cannot, it is true, easily foresee what new paths the development of civilization could take; but one thing we can expect, and that is that this indestructible feature of human nature will follow it there.
>
> (*Civilization and Its Discontents*, 5)

Freud claims that sex is a stronger and more conniving force than property, but that these are all means and expressions of the aggressiveness latent in man.

The third suggestion proposed by the midrash is that Cain and Abel argued about the site of the future Temple: would it be built on Abel's portion or Cain's? This suggestion is very close to the plain meaning of the scriptural text, which implies that Cain was envious because Abel seemed to have been favored by God. But the midrash shows us how easy it is for a religious dispute to turn into an issue of special interests. Jealousy of another person's nearness to God is certainly a religious issue. The argument over the site of the Temple opens the door to economic and territorial interests: Who will have more influence and prestige?

Either way, according to this proposal, religious disagreements can lead to war and violence. This claim is not scorning religion; on the contrary, it recognizes its great importance and significance. It is, however, sending warning that we must not let religious controversy turn into violence. It should be added that most wars are not primarily about religion, but are struggles over power and territory. Some conflicts, however, do revolve around religious issues.

Rabbi Yehuda Halevi offered a similar explanation of the conflict between Cain and Abel:

> The Land [of Israel] was also the first object of jealousy and envy between Cain and Abel, when they desired to know which of them would be Adam's successor, and heir to his essence and intrinsic perfection; to inherit the land, and to stand in connection with the divine influence, while the other would be a nonentity.
>
> (*Kuzari* I, 14)

Elsewhere, Rabbi Yehuda Halevi has the king of the Khazars relating to religious debates and wars:

> There must, no doubt, be a way of acting, pleasing by its very nature, but not through the medium of intentions. If this be not so, why, then, do Christian and Muslim, who divide the inhabited world between them, fight with one another, each of them serving his God with pure intention, living either as monks or hermits, fasting and praying? For all that, they vie with each other in committing murders, believing that this is a most pious work and brings them nearer to God. They fight in the belief that paradise and eternal bliss will be their reward.
>
> (Ibid. I, 2)

The Christian thinker Augustine also saw in Abel's murder the archetype of human violence, especially violence committed against a religious backdrop. He, however, places the emphasis not on disputes between religious people, but on disputes between those who serve God and those who disregard Him, between the "good" and the "wicked":

> Of these two first parents of the human race, then, Cain was the first-born, and he belonged to the city of men; after him was born Abel, who belonged to the city of God.... Thus the founder of the earthly city was a fratricide. Overcome with envy, he slew his own brother, a citizen of the eternal city, and a sojourner on earth.... he was moved by that diabolical, envious

> hatred with which the evil regard the good.... the carnal lusts of two men, good but not yet perfect, contend together, just as the wicked contend with the wicked.
>
> (*The City of God*, bk. xv)

Unfortunately, religious violence is not always between the wicked and the righteous, and often is between two sets of righteous people. For this reason at least, if not for other reasons, every effort should be made to avoid war, even wars fought in the name of religion. There is no better way to conclude this chapter than with the words of Rabbi Naftali Tzvi Yehuda Berlin (Netziv), who went on at great length to warn against violence stemming from religious beliefs:

> The matter that is explained in the Song of *Ha'azinu* in the verse, "He is the Rock, His work is perfect...just and right is He" (Deuteronomy 32:4): The praise "right" comes to justify the rightness of the judgment of the Holy One, blessed be He, regarding the destruction of the Second Temple, which occurred in "a perverse and crooked generation." As we have explained, [the people of that generation] were righteous and pious people who toiled in Torah study, but they did not act uprightly in the ways of the world. Because of the unjustified hatred in their hearts, anyone whom they saw as acting not in accord with their own view of the fear of God was suspected of being a Sadducee or a heretic. This led to bloodshed and all the evils of the world until the Temple was destroyed. The justification of [God's] judgment comes from this, that the Holy One, blessed be He, is right, and does not tolerate righteous people of this sort. For even with regard to the ways of the world they must walk in the right path, and not in perversity, even if they are acting for the sake of heaven. This was a praiseworthy attribute of the patriarchs, who besides being righteous and pious, lovers of God in the best possible way, were also upright, that

is, they related to the nations of the world, even the despicable idol worshippers, with love and concern for their welfare.

(*Ha'amek Davar*, introduction to Genesis)

The Impulse of Man's Heart

In the Torah

Parashat Bereishit ends with God's pessimistic evaluation of man:

> And the Lord saw that the wickedness of man was great in the earth, and that all the impulse of the thoughts of his heart was only evil continually. And the Lord repented that He had made man on the earth, and it grieved Him at His heart.
>
> (Genesis 6:5–6)

We shall not deal here with the theological challenge of how God repented or grieved; didn't He know from the outset how things would develop? Here we shall deal with a different question: man's natural inclination. Is man essentially good, or is he corrupt and egotistical? In this case, the Torah seems to be making a clear and unequivocal assertion. Moreover, God repeats the idea a second time, in a positive context. Following the flood, God concludes that the evil heart of man is good reason to be lenient about punishing him:

> And the Lord said in His heart, I will not again curse the ground any more for man's sake, for the impulse of man's heart

> is evil from his youth; neither will I again smite any more everything living, as I have done.
>
> (Genesis 8:21)

Here is Nachmanides' representative interpretation of the verse:

> "For the impulse of man's heart is evil from his youth." He is trying to defend them, that by their very creation they have an evil nature in their youthful days but not in their old age. And therefore, for these two reasons it would not be right to smite all living things.[1] For from the beginning of youth, it [the evil impulse] is with them.... Alternatively, from youth – that is to say, on account of youth – the evil impulse is in man, for youth causes him to sin.
>
> (Commentary to Genesis 8:21)

Thus, the Torah's view on this topic seems to be quite clear. Man controls his own destiny and personality, as we see in God's words to the dissatisfied Cain – "and you shall rule over it" – but his natural inclination is to do evil rather than good. The gates of interpretation, however, remain open, and there is always room to say that the Torah is here describing only one aspect of man, one period of time, or the like. According to the simplest understanding along these lines, the Torah relates to only one component of man's personality – "the impulse of man's heart," that is to say, the evil inclination. But, in addition, man also has a godly soul, the good inclination.[2]

Rabbi Samson Raphael Hirsch proposed another explanation along these lines to the verse "for the impulse of man's heart is evil from his youth":

1. First, that man is born with an evil inclination; and second, this evil inclination influences him primarily during his youth, and less so in his old age.
2. See, for example, Maimonides, *Guide of the Perplexed* III, 22.

> Now, to the best of our knowledge, the commentators have erred in their interpretation of the continuation of the verse "for the impulse of man's heart is evil from his youth."...The words "for the impulse, etc.," are in parentheses: If the impulse of the heart of man will be evil again, and even in his youth, and the only way of saving it would be the destruction of the generation, nevertheless I will not curse them again, as I did before.... Youths are neither righteous nor evil. Woe unto him who thinks that the average child is evil! Anybody familiar with children will say: No, it is not true. Youth is not corrupt, and the impulse of man's heart is not evil from his youth. It is not in his youth that man will aspire to evil. In normal times one finds a much greater number of adults than of youths whose hearts and minds are directed to evil.
>
> (Commentary to Genesis 8:21)

Rabbi Hirsch reads the verse not as making an assertion but as setting a condition: Even if the heart of man will be evil from his youth, even then I shall not destroy mankind. Under normal circumstances, says Rabbi Hirsch, the heart of youth is not evil. And, indeed, we should remember that in Scripture itself we find verses which bear a message that is the very opposite of the message of our verses. Thus, for example, the famous verse in Ecclesiastes:

> God has made man upright, but they have sought out many inventions.
>
> (Ecclesiastes 7:29)[3]

The question of man's fundamental nature has long been the subject of dispute among Jewish sages and gentile thinkers. It is one of the most important and decisive issues in our spiritual world.

3. Many, however, understand this verse as pertaining specifically to the first man.

The Jewish Sages

Rabbi Abraham Isaac Kook believed that man is fundamentally good and beneficent. As the spirit of God lies deep within him, he is essentially good, not bad. Rabbi Kook saw this as an educational and moral guideline:

> An upright man must believe in his life, that is to say, he must believe in his own life and feelings that follow a straight path from the foundation of his soul, that they are good and upright and that they lead him along the straight path.... A Jew is obligated to believe that the soul of God is found within him, that his entire essence is one letter of the Torah.
>
> (*Orot ha-Torah*, chap. 11)

This position has become widespread and popular in our day. It is based upon Rabbi Kook's mystical outlook, according to which even evil, when viewed in a larger context, is part of the world's general tendency toward goodness and holiness:

> After the divine light has shined upon the entire universe, after everything that exists has been repaired, it will become clear that everything is absolutely good. When we look at certain aspects of the world we encounter exceedingly evil sights, but this is only because we do not see all of God's great work from beginning to end.
>
> (*Olat Ra'aya*, 1, p. 210)

In contrast, some of the major exponents of the Musar movement presented a very pessimistic view of man. To illustrate this point, we advance here the words of Rabbi Yitzchak Blazer:

> Because man was formed from dust of the ground, his heart inclines to material desires, to eat, drink, and be merry, to covet fortune and riches, to love honor and power, to don

> haughtiness and pride to swell his heart, to delight in carnal pleasures, in every lowly trait and every despicable desire.
>
> And with this, the impulse of his heart is only evil continually, namely the evil inclination of his spiritual element.[4]...
>
> Unlike these are the ways of fear, the fear of heaven and the fear of His punishment, blessed be His name; for this fear is not in man's nature.
>
> (*Sha'arei Or*, in *Or Yisrael* 6b–7a)

According to Rabbi Yitzchak Blazer, man's nature contains two evil inclinations: first, his carnal desires, and second, the Satan who seeks devices to cause man to stumble and commit evil sins.[5] In contrast, man's fear of heaven is not natural or inborn.

Rabbi Joseph B. Soloveitchik's position is more complex. He maintains (as did Rabbi S.R. Hirsch) that man is neither fundamentally good nor fundamentally bad. Man, he says, has great potential and is called upon to exploit it positively. As opposed to Rabbi Kook, who speaks of the need to *uncover* the good in man, Rabbi Soloveitchik speaks of the need to *create* the good in man. We are not dealing here with a given, but with a mission:

> Indeed, Judaism has sanctified man, teaching that he contains within him a divine spark; Judaism has never accepted the position that man is in a state of sin by his very nature. On the contrary, we have taught that the challenge standing before man and the possibilities open to him are boundless. In the eyes of Judaism, man is *in potentia* a good creature, a developing creature. He often finds himself, however, in the grips of an overwhelming and irresistible force that drags him downward....
>
> In short, Scripture trusts man, but also suspects and has its doubts about him.
>
> (*Divrei Hagut ve-Ha'arakha*, pp. 252–253)

---

4. The force that seeks ways to make man stumble in sin.
5. This distinction is found in R. Yisrael Salanter's *Iggeret Mussar*.

Rabbi Soloveitchik illustrates this by recounting a family tradition. His grandfather, Rav Chayyim, was known for his great acts of loving-kindness. Rabbi Soloveitchik tells us, however, that this was not one of Rav Chayyim's inborn qualities, but one that he developed on his own. By nature, he was not good at all.

> [Rav Chayyim's] warm and magnanimous heart was shaped and formed by the force of internal will. My father, of blessed memory, told me that Rav Chayyim had once told him: "Moses, do not think that I am good. By nature, I am bad. Man must seize loving-kindness by force. Man must break himself. I worked rigorously until I eradicated the trait of cruelty from within me."
>
> (*Yemei Zikkaron*, p. 79)

The position that raises doubts about man's innate goodness is supported not only by the scriptural verses cited above, but, even more, by the very existence of Halakha. As a detailed system of laws and guidelines, the Halakha appears to rest on the assumption that man by his very nature will not necessarily do what is good, and therefore must be forced to do so by a detailed system of commandments and laws. If man were fundamentally good, it would be unnecessary to force him to do what is good. The heavy emphasis that Judaism puts on Halakha gives expression to a certain skepticism about man's innate nature.[6]

I often offer the following example to illustrate the Halakha's at-

6. (1) It might be argued that all the Torah does is preserve man's fundamentally good nature. If so, we must say that at the very least man has a natural inclination to moral erosion. (2) It should be noted that the compulsory nature of existing Halakha is generally not accompanied by external force, but relies on man's willing desire to obey it. In any event, then, it reflects a certain degree of trust. Nevertheless, the very formulation of moral instructions as binding commandments leads from an educational perspective to a feeling of obligation that does not depend exclusively on man's good will and sensitive conscience.

titude on this matter. The *Shulchan Arukh*, the most accepted and influential halakhic code in the Jewish world, opens with a stormy demand:

> One should strengthen oneself like a lion to get up in the morning for the service of the Creator. One should rise early enough to usher in the dawn.
>
> (*Orach Chayyim* 1:1)

Rema's gloss, however, immediately adds:

> One should at any rate not get up too late to pray the morning prayer service at the time that the community pray it.

Rema lowers the *Shulchan Arukh*'s excitement and intensity to the plane of reality. We don't all get up in the morning filled with enthusiasm and vigor; one can say with reasonable certainty that most people get up in the morning more like cats than like lions. It is fitting, therefore, to establish clear and unequivocal guidelines that do not depend upon the good will and enthusiasm of the individual. Rema's dry and prosaic attitude is a bit disappointing after the poetic tempest of the *Shulchan Arukh*, but it is more meaningful to most people who get up in the morning for prayer.

Thus we see the way of Halakha, the divine command: meticulous concern with well-defined and finely detailed laws, with all their branches and particulars, and unconcealed skepticism about religious feeling that is not firmly fixed in absolute definitions and measurements. Rabbi Soloveitchik once said that if Halakha had a *mitzva* to prepare a "holiday-tree," many chapters in the *Shulchan Arukh* would be devoted to a clarification of its precise form, the number of branches, who is bound by the obligation and who is exempt, where the presents should be hung, if at all, and other precisely formulated particulars. Halakha does not rely on man's good will and emotional identification. Thousands of years of history have proven time and again how justified is its skepticism. This attitude assumes a certain understanding of human nature.

Non-Jewish Thinkers

One of the most important philosophical controversies in the modern era focuses upon human nature: Is man by his nature good, or is he fundamentally evil?

Two important Western traditions see man's basic nature as dubious at best. The first tradition is Christianity, which holds that in the wake of the "primal sin," every human is born, literally or figuratively, a sinner. One of the outstanding representatives of this tradition is Augustine, one of the church fathers of the fourth century of the common era. In a famous passage of his *Confessions*, Augustine notes that even infants are sinners: they eat voraciously, they show no respect to those who are older and wiser, and they are indignant when others do not do what they demand. He concludes the passage as follows:

> The infant's innocence lies in the weakness of his body and not in the infant mind. I have myself observed a baby to be jealous, though it could not speak; it was livid as it watched another infant at the breast.... But is this innocence?
>
> (*Confessions*, chap. VII)

Augustine maintains that man is born an evil sinner; his inclination to sin is present even in newborn infants. This is a position that goes far beyond the realistic skepticism of Halakha. Augustine's view of human nature is exceeding pessimistic.

The second tradition that casts doubt upon man's natural righteousness is the English philosophical tradition from the eighteenth century on. The English philosophers were skeptical about man's nature. Thus, for example, the philosopher and economist Adam Smith saw man as fundamentally egotistical, not overly concerned about the suffering of others. He wondered what would happen if the Chinese empire were suddenly swallowed up by an earthquake. How would a typical European, who has no personal connections to the inhabitants of China, react to such a calamity? Smith answers: He would certainly express sorrow about the tragic occurrence and about the precariousness of human life. But what next?

> And when all this fine philosophy was over, when all these humane sentiments had been once fairly expressed, he would pursue his business or his pleasure, take his repose or his diversion, with the same ease and tranquility, as if no such accident had happened. The most frivolous disaster which could befall himself would occasion a more real disturbance. If he was to lose his little finger tomorrow, he would not sleep tonight; but, provided he never saw them, he will snore with the most profound security over the ruin of a hundred millions of his brethren.
>
> (*The Theory of Moral Sentiments*, pt. III, chap. 1, par. 46)

The English philosopher Thomas Hobbes reasoned that human society was established because people wished and needed to protect themselves from the aggression that lies concealed in human nature. People are prepared to live in communities and forfeit the freedom of solitary life, in order to "get themselves out from that miserable condition of war." Only collective social compulsion can prevent outbreaks of violence and struggle; it does so by punishing those who violate the social order. Only social coercion can provide the individual with security.

> For the laws of nature, as justice, equity, modesty, mercy, and, in sum, doing to others as we would be done to, of themselves, without the terror of some power to cause them to be observed, are contrary to our natural passions, that carry us to partiality, pride, revenge, and the like.
>
> (*Leviathan*, pt. II, chap. 17)

Hobbes assumes that human nature would lead to a miserable

existence marked by war and hatred, were it not for the fact that social institutions have been established to punish criminals and compel the proper way of life.

To these two traditions, the Christian and the English, was added a third tradition in the twentieth century: the psychoanalytic approach. Sigmund Freud uncovered – or claimed to have uncovered – man's truly loathsome essence. In Freud's eyes the two basic drives that move man are Eros, sexual love, and Thanatos, aggression. Society's institutions and internal inhibitions are the only things that prevent us from behaving like wild beasts. Man is not "a gentle creature who wants to be loved," and is capable at most of defending himself against those who attack him. According to Freud, aggression is one of the basic human impulses. For man, the other is not only a potential friend and partner, but also the object of exploitation, dominion, humiliation, and even torture and killing (*Civilization and Its Discontents*, chap. 5).

Freudian psychoanalysis maintains that the powerful drives of lust and aggression, hidden by the mask of our personality, are what truly pull the strings of our conduct. *Homo homini lupus* ("Man is a wolf to man"), affirms Freud. Therefore we must not let sentiment lead us into error about man's problematic nature.

The Renaissance and the Enlightenment, however, also saw the birth of a different tradition in the West. This tradition skipped pass Christianity and reconnected with the classical period, Greek and Roman philosophy, arguing that man is by nature good and praiseworthy. The French philosopher Montesquieu rejected the position taken by Hobbes.

> Hobbes inquires, "For what reason go men armed, and have locks and keys to fasten their doors, if they be not naturally in a state of war?" But is it not obvious that he attributes to mankind before the establishment of society what can happen but in consequence of this establishment, which furnishes them with motives for hostile attacks and self-defense?
>
> (*The Spirit of the Laws*, bk. 1, chap. 2)

Montesquieu argued, in contrast to Hobbes, that evil conduct is not a given of human nature, but a result of perverted social institutions. Jean-Jacques Rousseau developed this idea, arguing, exactly in opposition to Hobbes, that natural man is better and nobler than modern man, and that it is only the institutions of society that have corrupted him:

> Let us lay it down as an incontestable maxim that the first movements of nature are always right. There is no original perversity in the human heart. There is not a single vice about which one cannot say how and whence it came.
>
> (*Emile*, bk. II, par. 267)[7]

Rousseau taught that compassion is a feeling that was more developed in primitive man. According to him, Hobbes missed this point. A philosopher's sleep is disturbed by the idea of human suffering; but were one real person to be murdered outside his window, he would shut his ears and convince himself on logical grounds that he should not intervene. In contrast, primitive man dedicates his entire being to the feeling of compassion and identification.

> It is the populace that flocks together at riots and street-brawls, while the wise man prudently makes off. It is the mob and the market-women, who part the combatants, and hinder gentle-folks from cutting one another's throats.
>
> (*Dissertation on the Origin and Foundation of the Inequality of Mankind*, pt. 1)

It is important to note that two separate issues have become intermingled here. All agree that the situation today is not good. Therefore, the higher we elevate the worthiness of natural man,

---

7. See also *Emile*, bk. I, par. 10: "Everything is good as it leaves the hands of the author of things, everything degenerates in the hands of man."

the more we are forced to blame the institutions of society. Conversely, the more we question man's basic nature, the more we will see society's institutions as a necessary constraint, without which we could not live at all. This point was emphasized by Antoin Nicolas Condorcet in the eighteenth century:

> Is there any vicious habit, any practice contrary to good faith, any crime, whose origin and first cause cannot be traced back to the legislation, the institutions, the prejudices of the country wherein this habit, this practice, this crime can be observed?
>
> (*Sketch for a Historical Picture of the Progress of the Human Mind*, chap. 10)

In order to illustrate the uniqueness of Condorcet's position, let us bring in contrast the words of Alexander Hamilton, one of the authors of the *Federalist Papers*, a collection of essays intended to explain the American Constitution:

> Why has government been instituted at all? Because the passions of men will not conform to the dictates of reason and justice, without constraint.
>
> (*Federalist*, 15)

Punishment

"By Man Shall His Blood Be Shed"

In *Parashat Noach*, following the disembarkation of Noah and his family from the ark, God defines the rigid moral principles that were to accompany mankind from that time on. One of these fundamental principles in particular stands out:

> Whoso sheds man's blood by man shall his blood be shed; for in the image of God made He man.
>
> (Genesis 9:6)

What is the meaning of the rationale, "for in the image of God made He man"? Rabbi David Kimchi (Radak) understands it as follows:

> "For in the image of God made He man" – for he is more venerable than all the lowly creatures, to the extent that God created him in His image, with the intelligence that He implanted within him. Therefore, the rest of creation should fear him, and also one person his fellow, so that he not destroy his body and image. For if he kills him, he has destroyed the work of God, the most venerable among the lowly creatures. God had fashioned him in His image, and this one destroyed him, thus acting against God to nullify His work....
>
> God also commanded that a man's blood be shed when he

> sins, as He [later] commands in the Torah of Moshe Rabbenu with respect to those deserving the death penalty according to their sin, each sinner according to what he deserves. For [the sinner] corrupted his image first when he transgressed God's commandment.
>
> (Radak, Genesis 9:6)

Note that Radak proffers two explanations of "for in the image of God made He them." The first explanation relates to the victim: the murderer deserves to be punished because the victim was fashioned in the image of God. The second explanation relates to the murderer: he deserves to be punished because by committing murder he corrupted the image of God within himself. One may add that it is precisely the godly image in the murderer that justifies his punishment, for it is on account of that image that he bears responsibility for his acts.

Rabbi Yosef Bekhor Shor and, following him, Chizkuni, understand the matter differently:

> "For in the image of Elohim made He them." In the image that he should be a judge (*elohim*), and not that people should scorn and kill him, as it is written: "You shall not revile the judges (*elohim*), nor curse the ruler of your people" (Exodus 22:27). For if they scorn the great ones, who will judge between them, and to whom shall they listen? Every man will do what is right in his own eyes, and the world will be destroyed in the absence of judgment and justice."
>
> (Rabbi Yosef Bekhor Shor, Genesis 9:6)

What Rabbi Yosef Bekhor Shor is saying is not entirely clear: do the words "in the image of Elohim" refer to the victim, to whom the murderer should have related respectfully as a fellow human being, or to the judge? The plain sense seems to follow the second possibility (this is Nechama Leibowitz's understanding as well): man was created in the image of God, and therefore it is his duty to execute justice and judgment.

We have already seen that according to Radak special justification is necessary for imposing punishment upon man: "God also commanded that a man's blood be shed when he sins, as He [later] commands in the Torah of Moshe Rabbenu.... For [the sinner] corrupted his image first when he transgressed God's commandment." That is the issue we shall deal with in this chapter: the justification for punishment meted out by man. Bear in mind that we shall not be dealing here with the punishments inflicted upon man by God, but only with those imposed by man upon his fellow.

Recompense and Justice

Punishment is founded, first and foremost, on the principle of recompense. By right, a person who commits a sin must be punished, the primary reason being the very fact that he has sinned and therefore deserves to be punished. This is the idea implied by the Torah's formulation of the punishment administered to a person guilty of inflicting bodily injury:

> And if a man maim his neighbor; as he has done, so shall it be done to him; breach for breach, eye for eye, tooth for tooth; as he has maimed a man, so shall it be done to him. And he that kills a beast, he shall restore it; and he that kills a man, he shall be put to death.
>
> (Leviticus 24:19–21)

In actual practice, it is only in the case of murder that this law has been carried out in its literal sense; in other cases, the Oral Law has softened the punishment. It seems, however, that the Torah chose the formulation "as he has done, so shall it be done to him" in order to teach us that from the perspective of pure justice, this would have been the appropriate way to punish a person who maims his neighbor. Here we consider the principle of just recompense in and of itself. Punishment based on the principle of "measure for measure" is, indeed, the clearest manifestation of punishment based upon justice and recompense.

This spirit also underlies the following verses:

> You shall take no ransom for him that is fled to the city of his refuge, that he should come back to dwell in the land, until the death of the priest. So you shall not pollute the land in which you are; for blood pollutes the land, and the land cannot be atoned of the blood that is shed therein, but by the blood of him that shed it. And you shall not defile the land which you shall inhabit, in which I dwell: for I the Lord dwell among the children of Israel.
>
> (Numbers 35:31–34)

Mention is made here of the idea of atonement, to which we shall devote a separate discussion below. The passage, however, speaks of the "land's atonement" and is apparently referring to the realization of justice on the land. In any event, the moral passion expressed here shows that we are not dealing with deterrence.

We saw earlier that Radak also embraces this idea: "God also commanded that a man's blood be shed when he sins, as He [later] commands in the Torah of Moshe Rabbenu with respect to those deserving the death penalty according to their sin, each sinner according to what he deserves. For [the sinner] corrupted his image first when he transgressed God's commandment." According to Radak, punishment is the fitting and just recompense for the destruction of the divine image in man.

Among the non-Jewish thinkers, Plato has Protagoras reject the idea of punishment for the sake of recompense and justice:

> No one punishes the evil-doer under the notion, or for the reason, that he has done wrong, only the unreasonable fury of a beast acts in that manner. But he who desires to inflict rational

> punishment does not retaliate for a past wrong which cannot be undone; he has regard to the future, and is desirous that the man who is punished, and he who sees him punished, may be deterred from doing wrong again.
>
> (Plato, *Protagoras*)

On the other hand, the philosopher Immanuel Kant vigorously advocates punishment for the purpose of executing justice. The only valid purpose of punishment is just recompense for the criminal. If we punish for the purpose of deterrence, we act unjustly toward the offender. We must never use a person as a means for achieving other goals, important as they may be. Who has authorized us to punish one person in order to bring benefit to other people?[8] The only legitimate justification for punishment is just recompense of the criminal himself. This line of thought leads Kant to the fascinating conclusion:

> Even if a civil society resolved to dissolve itself with the consent of all its members – as might be supposed in the case of a people inhabiting an island resolving to separate and scatter themselves throughout the whole world – the last murderer lying in the prison ought to be executed before the resolution was carried out. This ought to be done in order that everyone may realize the desert of his deeds, and that blood-guiltiness may not remain upon the people.
>
> (*The Science of Right*, pt. II, 49, E, 1)

Our generation is marked by a moral relativism that questions the right of one person to judge another. According to this approach, the justification for punishment must lie in deterrence, prevention, or some other purpose, as we shall discuss below. The psychologizing of human behavior has given an additional push in this direction. It diminishes the criminal's guilt by arguing that

8. See C.S. Lewis, *The Problem of Pain* (Glasgow, 1981), pp. 81–82.

man lacks free will, and his behavior is dictated by psychological factors beyond his control. It is important, therefore, to emphasize that the Torah acknowledges that punishment may be imposed merely for the purpose of fitting recompense. The Torah's approach is not relativistic; it recognizes that a given deed may be judged in absolute terms as good or evil.

Deterrence

There are four categories of people about whom the Torah states: "So that they shall hear, and fear." That is to say, the punishment imposed upon these four types of offenders is primarily for the sake of deterrence. They are: one who incites others to worship idols, a rebellious son, a rebellious elder, and false, conspiring witnesses. In these cases, the factors of deterrence and prevention seem to have special significance. We cite here the law pertaining to the inciter as an example:

> If your brother, the son of your mother, or your son, or your daughter, or the wife of your bosom, or your friend, who is as your own soul, entice you secretly, saying, Let us go and serve other gods, which you have not known, you, nor your fathers, of the gods of the peoples who are round about you, either near to you, or far off from you, from the one end of the earth even to the other end of the earth; you shall not consent to him, nor hearken to him; nor shall your eye pity him, nor shall you spare, nor shall you conceal him. But you shall surely kill him; your hand shall be first upon him to put him to death, and afterward the hand of all the people. And you shall stone him with stones, that he die; because he has sought to draw you away from the Lord your God, who brought you out of the land of Egypt, from the house of bondage. And all Israel shall hear, and fear, and shall do no more any such wickedness as this is among you.
>
> (Deuteronomy 13:7–12)

Here is how Maimonides summarized the laws applying to the inciter in light of the rationale "and all Israel shall hear, and fear":

> The laws applying in the case of a person suspected of incitement to idolatry are not the same as those applying in other capital cases. Witnesses may be concealed in order to apprehend him, and he does not require a warning, as do other capital offenders. If a court exonerated him, and someone came forward claiming that he has something to say that would incriminate him, the case is returned to court. If he was found guilty, and someone came forward claiming that he has something to say in his defense, the case is not returned to court. We do not suggest arguments in defense of the inciter. He is tried by a court that includes an old man, a eunuch, and one who has no children, so that he be shown no mercy. For cruelty to those who lead the people astray after vanity is mercy for the world.
>
> (*Hilkhot Sanhedrin* 1:5)

The special need for deterrence leads to heightened stringency with respect to the inciter. Truth be told, however, Maimonides views deterrence as the general purpose of punishment and its fundamental reason, not just in the four categories we mentioned, but in all cases:

> If a criminal is not punished, injurious acts will not be removed in any way and nobody intent upon transgression will be deterred.
>
> (*Guide of the Perplexed* II, 35)

This also follows from the four factors that Maimonides lists as affecting the severity of punishment: the severity of the transgression, its frequency, its appeal to possible perpetrators, and the difficulty of executing it (*Guide* II, 41). At the very least, the last three factors are explicitly connected to deterrence.

The way we comprehend the need for a mechanism of punishment affects the severity of the punishment. This effect may lead either to stringency or to leniency. If we understand that the reason for punishment is deterrence, we may sometimes rule leniently regarding a grave offense because it is relatively rare; similarly, we may rule stringently regarding a light offense on account of its frequency. The emphasis upon deterrence also results in punishment that attaches greater significance to the practical result of the transgression and less importance to the offender's intentions.

Rabbenu Sa'adya Gaon also stresses the significance of deterrence as a central component of punishment:

> Man was ordered to be put to death by means of four different forms of execution. I realized that all this was for his benefit, and that it was not contrary to reason. For it is in accordance with the verdict of reason that, just as the individual recognizes that the cutting off of one of the members of his body, which has been rendered useless by poison or disease, is a corrective necessary for the preservation of the rest of his body, so the human species must recognize that the slaying of one of its members who has become corrupted and is causing trouble on earth is a corrective necessary for preserving the rest of the species. As Scripture says: "And those that remain shall hear, and fear."
>
> (*Book of Beliefs and Opinions* IV, 2)

Rabbi Ya'ir Bachrach, the author of *Chavvot Ya'ir*, also maintains that the primary objective of the Torah's punishments is deterrence. He argues further that the guilty party must be punished for the benefit of society as a whole, even if the sinner himself may suffer spiritual damage as a result. In other words, deterrence takes precedence over rehabilitation. Rabbi Bachrach discusses the case of a person who had violated the prohibition against drinking gentile wine, and the community was now debating whether to punish him. The local rabbi advised against punishing the sinner, so as not to reject him altogether, lest he ultimately commit more severe transgressions. Rabbi Bachrach disagrees:

> The rabbinic authority incorrectly objected to the community's conduct, and I am afraid that he may have sinned. On the contrary, it would be fitting for him to don zealotry for the God of hosts, and excommunicate and punish [the sinner], until he comes to do penance and sin no more. Were we to be concerned about this, God forbid, evil people would continue to act as they pleased.... The Sanhedrin was never concerned about this while the Temple stood, lest because of this concern the number of sinners would grow. Regarding such a case, the Sages said: "They too cause the number of murderers in Israel to grow"...for we should be concerned about the benefit to the community, even when it is detrimental to the individual.... We should also conduct ourselves in this manner, acting in accordance with the law and the rules of our Torah. We should not be concerned about the deterioration of the corrupt person who has sinned, even in the case of one individual against another. All the more so when there is concern about the corruption of others. The punishment administered to the wicked is directed primarily at [the prevention of such corruption], as the Torah has written in several instances: "And the others will hear, and fear."...How very much must we be concerned about the corruption of the generation.
>
> (*Chavvot Ya'ir*, no. 141)

Rabbi Bachrach argues that the primary objective of the Torah's punishments is deterrence, based on a concern for the welfare of the community. Concern about the further corruption of the criminal pales in the presence of this consideration.

Rabbi Abraham Isaac Kook also believes that the chief purpose of punishment is deterrence. Rabbi Kook bases his argument upon a moral assertion. As opposed to Kant, who said that punishment for the purpose of deterrence is immoral, Rabbi Kook holds that punishment for the purpose of deterrence has greater moral value than punishment administered as recompense. His point of departure is the law stating that a slave-owner who kills his slave is, in certain circumstances, exempt from the death penalty:

> Many ask: Why does a slave lose his right to life by virtue of his being his master's chattel, so that the law applying to a slave differs from the law applying to a free man? In my opinion, this law, too, rests on the pillars of true compassion for the human species. For it is clearly the law of our holy Torah that we do not administer justice in order to take revenge even in the case of the most heinous sinner, but only to fill in the breach so that the evil will spread no further. If so, in a matter that has another fence, it is unnecessary to be stringent regarding the fence of punishment, for nothing will remain of it aside from the benefit of lowly revenge. Therefore, regarding a person who strikes his neighbor, were the matter not controlled by way of the death penalty, sinners wishing to kill their neighbors because of a certain benefit that may accrue to them as a result of their deaths would multiply. But as for a person killing his own slave, who is his money and property – it is human nature to care for one's property.... Therefore the Torah states that if the slave continues a day or two, his owner shall not be put to death. For in such a case punishment would constitute revenge, not something leading to the perfection of the world. And this would not be right according to the law of He who is merciful over all his works, including sinners. And [the Torah] offers the rationale that there is no need for a fence, for [the slave] is his money and he will have compassion. Very rarely, therefore, will a person strike his own possession with composure, losing money thereby, to the point that there is no reason for concern that the evil will spread further.
>
> ("Ta'amei ha-Mitzvot," *Nitzanei Eretz* 12, pp. 12–13)

Rav Kook explains that the whole purpose of punishment is deterrence, and not revenge. Therefore, in a case where there is no concern that the transgression will become widespread, there is no need to impose punishment. The case of a slave-owner who kills his own slave is exceptional, and there is no concern that it would become widespread, for the slave is the property of the slave-owner. Hence there is no logical reason to punish him.[9]

Among non-Jewish thinkers, the philosopher David Hume emphasized the significance of punishment as a deterrent, even at the cost of justice:

> When any man, even in political society, renders himself by his crimes, obnoxious to the public, he is punished by the laws in his goods and person; that is, the ordinary rules of justice are, with regard to him, suspended for a moment, and it becomes equitable to inflict on him, for the benefit of society, what otherwise he could not suffer without wrong or injury.
> (*Enquiry Concerning the Principles of Morals*, sec. III, pt. I)

Twofold System

In his *Derashot*, Rabbenu Nissim of Gerondi (Ran) states that in Jewish law, punishment has two objectives: the execution of justice and deterrence. Thus, there is a twofold system of punishment; on one level it worries about doing justice, and on another level it is concerned with deterrence:

> For the king that we set over us will complete that [political] correction. But the objective of the judges and the Sanhedrin was to judge the people with true justice, just in itself. This will cause godliness to cling to us, whether public matters become perfectly ordered therewith, or not. For this reason, some of the laws of the gentile nations may be closer to the perfect political

9. Rabbi Kook expressed a similar idea in one of his letters. See *Iggerot ha-Ra'aya* I, letter 89.

> order than some of the laws of the Torah. We, however, lack nothing, for whatever is missing from the perfect order, the king would complete.
>
> (*Derashot ha-Ran*, no. 11)

Ran claims that punishment has two main objectives: the execution of justice and deterrence. He says that the Jewish people are supposed to be governed by two parallel judicial systems, the one whose goal is the execution of justice, and the other whose purpose is deterrence. The courts judge according to Halakha, which always gives expression to absolute justice – the punishment the convicted party truly deserves. Often, however, the deterrent factor would totally disappear if we were to judge solely on the recompense the offender truly deserves according to strict justice. That is why there is a second judicial system – the monarchy. The monarchy's goal is to eradicate sin and evil, even if from time to time an injustice is committed against specific individuals.

Prevention

One of the exceptional punishments about which the Torah says, "And all Israel shall hear, and fear," is the punishment administered to the rebellious son:

> If a man have a stubborn and rebellious son who will not obey the voice of his father, or the voice of his mother, and that, when they have chastened him, will not hearken to them, then shall his father and his mother lay hold of him, and bring him out to the elders of the city, and to the gate of his place; and they shall say to the elders of his city, This our son is stubborn and rebellious, he will not obey our voice; he is a glutton, and a drunkard. And all the men of his city shall stone him with stones, that he die. So shall you put evil away from among you; and all Israel shall hear, and fear.
>
> (Deuteronomy 21:18–21)

The Sages explain that we are not dealing here with a punishment aimed at deterrence, but with a punishment whose goal is prevention, that is, preventing the offender from causing additional offense in the future:

> *Mishna:* A stubborn and rebellious son is tried on account of his ultimate destiny: Let him die innocent and let him not die guilty.
>
> *Gemara:* It has been taught: Rabbi Yose the Galilean said: Did the Torah decree that the rebellious son shall be brought before a court and stoned merely because he ate a *tartemar* of meat and drank a *log* of Italian wine? But the Torah foresaw his ultimate destiny. For at the end, after dissipating his father's wealth, he would [still] seek to satisfy his accustomed [gluttonous] wants, but being unable to do so, he would go forth at the crossroads and rob. Therefore the Torah said, "Let him die while yet innocent, and let him not die guilty." For the death of the wicked benefits themselves and the world; [and the death] of the righteous injures themselves and the world.
>
> (*Sanhedrin* 71a–71b)

At first glance it might seem that our concern here is with the spiritual welfare of the rebellious son, that he should die innocent and not guilty. The baraita, however, teaches that his death is "beneficial to him and beneficial to the world." That is to say, we are also concerned with the welfare of the community, that it should be spared confrontation with a confirmed criminal.

Maimonides offers another example of punishment whose goal is prevention when he explains that the law regarding a *moser* ("informer") is similar to and parallels the law regarding a *rodef* ("pursuer"):

> One is permitted to kill a *moser* in all places, even in our times when we do not judge capital cases. And one is permitted to

> kill him even before he informs, once he says "I plan to denounce so-and-so."…We warn him and say to him, "Do not denounce." If he dares to say, "No, I plan to denounce him," there is a *mitzva* to kill him, and whoever goes ahead and kills him gains merit. It seems to me that if the *moser* did as he had planned and denounced, it is forbidden to kill him.... It happened throughout the ages in the cities of the West that they executed *moserim* who were known to denounce money belonging to a Jew.
>
> (*Hilkhot Chovel u-Mazik* 8:10–11)

According to Maimonides, one is only permitted to take counteraction against a *moser* before he makes his denunciation, in order to prevent it. We are clearly dealing here with a punishment whose objective is prevention.[10]

In modern society, quite apart from capital punishment, incarceration has a preventative effect. The removal of the offender from society for an extended period renders him unable to cause additional harm.

Rehabilitation and Improvement

Many biblical sources treat punishment as a rehabilitative process that may help to refine the offender's personality. This principle appears repeatedly in the book of Proverbs:

> He that spares the rod hates his son; but he that loves him chastises him early.
>
> (Proverbs 13:24)

> When the scorner is punished, the simple man is made wise.
>
> (Proverbs 21:11)

10. Regarding the law of *rodef*, this is quite evident, for according to the simplest understanding, killing a *rodef* is not a punishment, but an act of self-defense: "if someone is coming to kill you, go first and kill him."

> You shall beat him with the rod, and shall deliver his soul from She'ol.
>
> (Proverbs 23:14)

The Sages of the Midrash emphasize this point:

> "He that spares the rod hates his son; but he that loves him chastens him early" (Proverbs 13:24).... Anyone who refrains from punishing his son causes him to fall into evil ways and will come to hate him. Thus we find regarding Ishmael, who behaved rebelliously against his father Abraham, but he did not punish him, and thus he fell into evil ways, so that he hated him and cast him forth empty-handed from his house.... What happened to him in the end? After he sent him away, he sat at the crossroads, and robbed and molested passers-by, as it says: "And he shall be a wild ass of a man; his hand shall be against every man" (Genesis 16:12). Another example: "Now Isaac loved Esau" (ibid. 25:28). Hence, he fell into evil ways, because he did not punish him.... Similarly, because David did not rebuke or punish his son Absalom, he fell into evils ways, seeking to kill his father, sleeping with his concubines, and becoming the cause of his wandering barefooted and crying, and of the killing of many thousands and tens of thousands of Israelites, as well as endless other troubles.... David treated Adonijah in a similar fashion, neither rebuking nor punishing him, and therefore he fell into evil ways....
>
> But a father who punishes his son causes the son to love him more and to honor him.
>
> (Exodus Rabba 1:1)

These sources relate only to educational punishment within the family, and not to criminal punishment meted out by the court; but the principle can be used to explain certain criminal punishments as well. For example, a similar explanation has been offered in our generation regarding the punishment of a thief who is sold into slavery when he does not have the means to make restitution. Living in the house of his master, who is bound to care for his needs and watch over him, will contribute to the thief's social and moral rehabilitation.

Atonement

In a religious framework, punishment has one additional objective: atonement.[11] Although atonement is somewhat similar to recompense and justice, its objective is not to repay the sinner in kind, but to wipe out his sin and make him repent before God so that he will not suffer divine punishment. This aim finds striking expression in the punishment administered to the inadvertent killer. The talmudic discussion in *Makkot* (2a–2b) implies that atonement is for the sinner's benefit. For this reason, a serious offender is sometimes denied the punishment of exile so that he will not be able to atone.

11. It may be argued, however, that atonement is not the primary reason for punishment, but only a secondary result.

The Tower of Babel

The Story of the Tower of Babel

One of the most intriguing episodes in the book of Genesis is the story of the tower of Babel. The scriptural account is interesting because it is not exactly clear what is happening. Let us examine the relevant passage:

> And the whole earth was one language, and of one speech. And it came to pass, as they journeyed from the east, that they found a plain in the land of Shinar; and they dwelt there. And they said to one another, Come, let us make bricks, and burn them thoroughly. And they had brick for stone, and slime had they for mortar. And they said, Come, let us build us a city and a tower, whose top may reach to heaven; and let us make us a name, lest we be scattered abroad upon the face of the whole earth. And the Lord came down to see the city and the tower, which the children of men were building. And the Lord said, Behold, the people is one, and they have all one language, and this they begin to do; and now nothing will be withheld from them, which they have schemed to do. Come, let us go down, and there confound their language, that they may not understand one another's speech. So the Lord scattered them abroad from there upon the face of all the earth; and they ceased to build the city. Therefore is the name of it called Babel; because the Lord did there confound the language of all the earth. And

> from thence did the Lord scatter them abroad upon the face of all the earth.
>
> (Genesis 11:1–9)

A critical element in the affair is totally obscure. What was the sin or the error of the people of Babel? Why did God punish them? What did they do wrong?

The words of the Sages on this question are well known:

> "And of one speech": They spoke against two who were unique [lit., "one"], namely, against Abraham who was one (Ezekiel 33:24) and against "The Lord our God, the Lord is one" (Deuteronomy 6:4). They said: "This Abraham is a barren mule and cannot produce offspring." And against "The Lord our God, the Lord is one," they said: "He has no right to choose the upper worlds for Himself and give us the lower world. But come, let us build a tower, place an idol at its top, set a sword in its hand, which will thus appear to wage war against Him."
>
> Another explanation: "And one speech" – united in possessions, what belongs to the one belongs to the other....
>
> Because the generation of the deluge was immersed in robbery, as it is written: "They remove the landmarks, they violently take away flocks and feed them" (Job 24:2), therefore not a remnant of them was left. But these [i.e., the generation of the dispersion] loved one another, as it is written: "And the whole earth was of one language," therefore a remnant of them was left....
>
> Another explanation: "And of one speech (*achadim*)" – they spoke sharp words (*chadim*), saying: "Once in one thousand six hundred and fifty-six years the heaven totters;[1] therefore let us go and make supports for it, one in the north, one

1. The reference is to the precedent of the flood.

> in the south, one in the west, while this spot will be its eastern support."
>
> (Genesis Rabba 38:6)

The Sages propose several explanations, all of which share the same basic approach. The first suggestion sees the tower of Babel as an ordinary act of idolatry, committed by the community as a whole and in public. The generation of the dispersion rebelled against God, and their rebellion reached its climax in the tower of Babel.[2] The second suggestion emphasizes the unity of the generation: "What belongs to the one belongs to the other." All property was jointly owned, a sort of proto-communism. In the continuation, the midrash emphasizes the generation's unity, which stood them in good stead even after they sinned. The midrash closes with another idea: The generation of the dispersion wished to prevent another flood, and therefore tried to erect supports for the heavens. They related to the flood not as a miracle, but as a law of nature (similar to the attempts to explain the splitting of the Red Sea as the result of a natural occurrence). It was in this that they sinned, and also in their revolt against God and their thinking that they could prevent His plan from being actualized.

In order to find a scriptural basis for this or any other explanation, we must examine the generation's objective in building a city and a tower: "Lest we be scattered abroad upon the face of the whole earth." Rashi explains:

> "Lest we be scattered abroad": That He shall not be able by bringing some plague upon us, to scatter us from here.

According to Rashi, the tower-builders' objective was to confront

2. According to this explanation, the scorn for Abraham demonstrated by the members of the generation of the dispersion might have related to the fact that Abraham was the great fighter against idolatry, and his mockers thought that his legacy was about to disappear.

God. But what is the meaning of "and let us make us a name"? Seforno's commentary may prove helpful on this point:

> "Let us make us a name": Idolatry.

The *Da'at Mikra* commentary understands the words "and let us make us a name (*shem*)" as relating not to the builders' objective, but to their means: the word *shem* in this context does not mean "name," but "wall."

Modern biblical scholars suggest that the people of Babel had two objectives – to make a name for themselves and to prevent their dispersion. In line with this thinking, they propose that the biblical narrative combines two different stories. Some talk about the story of "the city" and the story of "the tower." Rabbi Mordecai Breuer speaks about the story of "the whole earth" and the story of "the plain."

Seforno adds an explanation of how the scattering of mankind might prevent or at least minimize idolatry:

> The opposite of this will happen when there are divisions between the nations regarding their strange gods, for each one of them believes that there is a "god of gods" with whom all other gods agree, and through him their governance and the governance of all existence reaches perfection.

Seforno explains that when there are many false gods, those who believe in them are forced to concede that there must be one true God above all the others. Dispersion and division lead to a recognition of the relativism of human spiritual achievements. When there are a variety of beliefs, people are more likely to question their own achievements and opinions, recognizing thereby that there exists a supreme God whom they do not know.

Rabbi Nissim Girondi (Ran) proposes a slightly different interpretation of this idea. He moves the discussion from the spiritual plane to the political arena: division into separate nations is necessary in order to allow men of spirit to survive the persecution of power-hungry rulers.

> There is no doubt that for the righteous of those generations the division into nations and governments was good and beneficial. For when they were oppressed by a nation living in one country, they would wander to another country where they would be able to worship God as they pleased. As has happened to us in our exile today, for when persecution is renewed in the land of Ishmael, the survivors flee to another country, and from there [back] to Ishmael. This ensures us partial subsistence in times of trouble and slavery....
>
> Although there was no immediate evil [in the building of the tower of Babel], the gathering was bad for them and bad for the world.... For there is no doubt that all those generations were trying to exalt their idols and cause the name of the Holy One, blessed be He, to be forgotten. But they did not succeed because of the division into governments and lands, because those who worshipped God had a [place of] refuge.
>
> (*Derashot ha-Ran* 1)

Translating the Ran's point into modern terms, we might say that he is alluding to the problematic nature of totalitarian regimes, which cannot tolerate nonconformists. Only a plurality of different regimes can guarantee the survival of those who are hated by their own governments. Ran's solution is not utopian, for he does not talk about the establishment of an ideal regime; it is realistic, in that it limits the authority of any one particular government.

Thus far, following the approach first proffered by the Sages, we have seen the tower of Babel as embodying the sin of idolatry. This understanding suggests why the Torah emphasizes the etymology of the name Babel, deriving it from the word *balal*, "confound." Prof. Yehuda Elitzur states that this etymology was intended to mock the Babylonians, who connected the name of their city to the name *bab-ili*, "gate of god," an expression obviously connected to idolatry. The Torah is saying: not the gate of god, but the gate of confusion.

Other commentators propose different approaches, although they usually develop motifs already found in the Sages. For example, Rav Yehuda Kil, author of the *Da'at Mikra* commentary, proposes the following:

> Unless we construct a walled and strongly fortified city, our enemies may come upon us, bring us to submission, and scatter us abroad upon the face of the whole earth.... With this argument, the builders exposed their true feelings, that they no longer rely upon God, who saved their forefathers from the flood. They prefer to put their trust in their own power and might.
>
> (*Da'at Mikra*)

According to Rabbi Kil, the primary sin was not idolatry in the ordinary sense, but rather the fact that they trusted in their own might, and not in God. The generation of the dispersion sinned through their pride and haughtiness.

Others emphasize the social dimension of their sin:

> "Let us make a name for ourselves." An idol which will be situated in the tower. The fame of its height, and the huge size of the city, will spread among the whole human race in such a manner that this deity will be considered the "deity of deities" among mankind, and all will seek it out. The intention was that he who rules over the city will rule over the entire human race, for the city contains that which all seek out.
>
> (Seforno)

Seforno is proposing an intermediate position. We are dealing here not merely with idolatry, moreover, but with a desire to gain control over other people. We can learn something from this about how dictators and demagogues exploit ideology in order to gain power.

The social problem in and of itself is emphasized in the following midrash:

> There were no stones with which to build the city and the tower. What did they do? They made bricks and fired them like a potter, until they built it seven miles high.... If a person fell and died, their hearts would not go out to him, but if a brick fell, they would sit, and weep, and say: When will another one go up in its place? Abraham ben Terah passed by and saw them building the city and the tower, and he cursed them in the name of God.
>
> (*Pirkei de-Rabbi Eliezer* 24)

This midrash emphasizes the strained social relations among the tower builders themselves. Their obsession with the gigantic project made them forget their own humanity. The midrash is reminiscent of what Stalin said when asked why he put so many people to death: "You can't chop wood without making chips fly."[3] The midrash cited earlier related to the generation of the dispersion as an example of a unified mankind. This midrash teaches that unity among the majority is sometimes achieved at the expense of the minority. There are times when it is precisely unity built around a common ideology that leads to the most inhuman behavior.

Rashbam gives expression to yet another approach:

> Because the Holy One, blessed be He, had commanded them, "Be fruitful and multiply, and fill the earth," and they chose for themselves a place in which to settle, saying, "Lest we be scattered" – therefore, He scattered them abroad from there through His decree.

3. Or in the formulation attributed to Napoleon: "You can't make an omelet without breaking the eggs."

Radak offers a similar explanation:

> They were indeed the descendants of Adam, who walked after the stubbornness of their own hearts, rejecting the deed of God. For He wanted the earth to be settled from east to west, and they thought to settle only one place in the world, thinking that they would overrule God's will.

According to this interpretation, the primary objective of the generation of the dispersion was to establish a military and cultural center that would concentrate all of mankind in one place. They sinned in that they rejected the mission assigned them by God: "Be fruitful and multiply, and fill the earth" (Genesis 1:28; 9:1). The problem here is not necessarily pride and arrogance, but the practical one of upsetting God's plan for the development of the world.

This explanation is supported by the fact that the Torah makes no mention of any sin; it merely recounts the dry facts. Nor is the punishment very severe; it is merely an attempt to neutralize the builders' activities.

All of these explanations focus on one point: the potential danger resulting from the development of civilization and unification of society. The generation of the dispersion made technological advances: they succeeded in producing bricks and constructing a magnificent tower. Unity and technological advances, however, give rise to many dangers. They are liable to lead to unity in worshipping false gods, because they make people forget the limitations of human achievement, as suggested by Seforno, or because a totalitarian regime offers no refuge for nonconformists, as argued by Ran. They are liable to give rise to pride and a false sense of power. They are also liable to lead to social injustice and to oppression of certain segments of the populace for the sake of grandiose projects.

Professor Shalom Rosenberg depicts communism as manifested in the twentieth century as a modern-day expression of the generation of the dispersion. The Communists, too, imagined that they could build a tower that would prevent the sky from caving in – economic and social crises. The Sages long ago suggested that the builders of the tower advocated communal ownership: "What belonged to the one belonged to the other." The Communists' presumption in the economic and social realm was combined with the mocking, primitive atheism that characterized the Soviet Union. (The accident at the atomic reactor at Chernobyl demonstrate the failure of the ridiculous presumption of building a "tower whose top may reach the heaven.") In the end, communism deteriorated into hatred and contempt for other human beings, just as the Sages spoke about the tower-builders who wept over a lost brick but not over a fellow worker who died. The Communists worried about their five-year plans, about the welfare of society and its classes; but they showed no concern whatsoever for the individual.

> The generation of the dispersion gave expression to an ideal that had beautiful elements. The Sages compared the generation of the flood "who were immersed in theft" to the generation of the dispersion "who loved one another," or at least proclaimed their love for each other. The vision of the modern generation of the dispersion presented a difficult challenge to religious belief. The collapse of the modern generation of dispersion that is unfolding before our eyes teaches us about its true nature from the very beginning.
>
> (Rosenberg, *Be'ikvot ha-Kuzari*, p. 16)

The generation of the dispersion may be seen as symbolizing not only communism, but, in general, the dangers posed by the development of human civilization and scientific progress. We shall therefore examine various positions regarding civilization in general.

Civilization

Are civilization and human progress good or bad? Abravanel, in light of his experience in the service of the royal courts of Portugal, Spain, and Naples, condemned civilization as negative and unnecessary:

> The overall intention of this great section[4] is to inform us that God created man in His intellectual image.... And He also created everything essential for his existence – food, drink, the fruits of the trees of the garden that He had planted, and the waters of its rivers. This was all made available in the natural world, so that there should be no need for effort, toil, or human activity. Everything that man needed was ready and available to him at all times, so that he would not have to trouble his soul to seek out what his body needs, but rather could perfect his soul for which he had been created. For this reason, God commanded man to content himself with the natural things He had created for his needs, and not to allow himself to be drawn after luxuries which require work.... All this notwithstanding, the man, of his own free will and choice, walked in darkness.
>
> (Abravanel, Commentary to Genesis 3)

Abravanel offered a similar explanation for the sin of the generation of the dispersion:

> And likewise the sin of the generation of the dispersion was similar to the sin of Adam, Cain, and his sons. Even though they had an abundance of the natural things necessary for their existence coming from God in heaven, and even though they were free from all work and toil, and available to engage themselves in the perfection of their souls, they were not satisfied with what their Creator had prepared for them with His

4. Regarding the sin committed by Adam.

> expansive natural gifts. They wished to send out their hands and set their minds on finding the crafts necessary to build a city (which includes all the crafts), with a tower in its center, in order to join together there, and become political creatures, instead of being men of the field. They thought that their special objective was to establish a polity and develop cooperation and society, and that this is the highest human goal. And this despite all that would follow from it – appointments, offices, imaginary honors, lust for amassing wealth, robbery, theft and bloodshed, all of which did not exist when they were out in the field.
>
> (Abravanel, Commentary to Genesis 11:1)

Abravanel claims that nature is superior to the artificiality of civilization. Nature suffices to provide for all of man's needs. Civilization leads only to unnecessary luxuries, and with them worries and distraction from the fear and service of God. This is what made Abel superior to Cain.[5] Abravanel sees the pinnacle of human existence in the life of the hunter-gatherer, the most primitive form of human existence. Similar ideas echo in the approach of Jean-Jacques Rousseau, which we discussed in a previous chapter. Rousseau also held that natural man is superior to civilized man:

> If I consider him, in a word, such as he must have issued from the hands of nature; I see an animal less strong than some, and less active than others, but, upon the whole, the most advantageously organized of any; I see him satisfying the calls of hunger under the first oak, and those of thirst at the first rivulet; I see him laying himself down to sleep at the foot of the same

---

5. Similar explanations were proposed by Rabbis S.R. Hirsch and Hillel Zeitlin. See Rabbi Elchanan Samet, *Iyyunim be-Farshat ha-Shavu'a*, Genesis, pp. 6–17; and Y. Rosenson, "La-Fetach Chatat Rovetz," *Megadim* 3 (5747).

> tree that afforded him his meal; and behold, this done, all his wants are completely supplied.
>
> (*On the Inequality Among Mankind*, pt. 1)

Abravanel and Rousseau maintain that man can survive perfectly well without civilization, and that technological and social progress has been detrimental to him. They describe the natural life as romantic and perfect. But anyone whose yearnings for the natural life are aroused by Abravanel and Rousseau should try to imagine life without a roof over his head to protect him from the elements, without running water for a shower, without antibiotics. We are aware today of the limitations of civilization in such matters as ecology. Man's technological development is liable to be catastrophic. But Abravanel and Rousseau put forth a much more radical argument: civilization corrupts man's very essence.

How different are the famous words of Rabbi Joseph B. Soloveitchik on this issue. Rabbi Soloveitchik praises modern man for his ability to build hospitals and develop new therapeutic techniques to save the lives of countless numbers of sick people; for bridging continents with modern means of transportation and conquering nature for the betterment of human society. He sees all these activities in a positive light:

> In doing all this, Adam the first is trying to carry out the mandate entrusted to him by his Maker, who, at dawn of the sixth mysterious day of creation, addressed Himself to man and summoned him to "fill the earth and subdue it."
>
> (*The Lonely Man of Faith*, pp. 11–16)

Rabbi Soloveitchik does not see civilization as a curse, but as a blessing; not as a sin, but as a mission and destiny. The lesson to be learned from this disagreement is, perhaps, that one must try to exploit the benefits of civilization but at the same time recognize its deficiencies and strive to avoid them so as not to repeat the mistakes of those who built the tower of Babel.

The Road to Faith

In this chapter we shall deal with the road to faith. Finding one's road to faith is not a one-time event. Faith is an ongoing mission with which we must struggle every day. When we buy a car, we sometimes think that all we have to do now is start the engine in the morning and drive off. We soon discover that the car requires upkeep: tune-ups, oil changes, payments, attention.... In the same way, faith is not something we acquire in one shot and then put away in our briefcase.

It is true, however, that it is easier to clarify the road to faith when we consider a path that is altogether fresh and new, and not the path we have already trodden many times. We shall therefore begin our discussion with the road to faith taken by the first Jew – Abraham our father. His trailblazing foray has much to teach us about our own ongoing journeys.

Faith: Natural or Acquired?

We first meet Abraham at the end of *Parashat Noach*. The first time that God addresses him is at the beginning of *Parashat Lekh Lekha*, when he is already an old man:

> Now the Lord said to Abram, Get you out of your country, and

> from your kindred, and from your father's house, to the land that I will show you. And I will make of you a great nation, and I will bless you, and make your name great; and you shall be a blessing. And I will bless them that bless you, and curse him that curses you; and in you shall all the families of the earth be blessed. So Abram departed, as the Lord had spoken to him; and Lot went with him: And Abram was seventy-five years old when he departed out of Haran.
>
> (Genesis 12:1–4)

It as if we have been brought in to see a play that is already in its third act. What did Abraham do before he reached the age of seventy-five? Why did God choose to reveal Himself to Abraham of all people? Nachmanides raises both of these questions:

> This section of Scripture does not clarify the entire story. Why did the Holy One, blessed be He, say to Abraham: "Leave your country, and I will bestow unprecedented good upon you," without first explaining that Abraham served God or that he was a perfectly righteous man? Or else it should have stated as a reason for his leaving the country that the very journey to another land would be regarded as an act of drawing near to God.
>
> (Commentary to Genesis 12:2)[1]

The Torah may have chosen not to write about Abraham's earlier deeds precisely because it wished to leave room for the imagination. Perhaps it was because the Torah does not want us to think that there is only one path to God, that it forces us to think about the many ways through which Abraham may have come to recognize Him.

---

1. In his answer to this question, Nachmanides mentions the approach taken by the Sages that Abraham fought against idol worship throughout the years that he lived in Ur of the Chaldees.

Although the Sages dealt with the question of how Abraham found God, we shall begin with Maimonides and Ra'avad, who followed in the Sages' footsteps with respect to this issue:

> After [Abraham] was weaned, while still an infant, his mind began to reflect. By day and night he was thinking and wondering: "How is it possible that this [celestial] sphere[2] should continuously be guiding the world and have no one to guide it and cause it to turn round; for it cannot be that it turns round of itself." He had no teacher, no one to instruct him in anything. He was immersed, in Ur of the Chaldees, among silly idolaters. His father and mother and the entire population worshipped idols, and he worshipped with them. But his mind was busily working and reflecting till he had attained the way of truth, apprehended the correct line of thought, and knew that there is one God, that He guides the celestial spheres and created everything.... Abraham was forty years old when he recognized his Creator.
>
> Having attained this knowledge, he began to refute the inhabitants of Ur Kasdim, arguing with them and telling them, "The course you are following is not the truth." He broke the images and commenced to instruct the people that it was not right to serve anyone but the God of the Universe.... When he prevailed over them with his arguments, the king sought to slay him. He was miraculously saved, and emigrated to Haran. He then began to proclaim to the whole world with great power and to instruct the people that the entire universe had but one Creator and that Him it was right to worship. He went from city to city and from kingdom to kingdom, calling and gathering together the inhabitants till he arrived in the land of Canaan.
>
> (Maimonides, *Hilkhot Avoda Zara* 1:3)

2. The reference is to the sphere in which the stars are set, according to the scientific knowledge of Maimonides' day.

> "Abraham was forty years old when he recognized his Creator." [Rabbi] Abraham [ben David] said: There is an aggada [that states that] he was three years old. As it says: "Because (*eikev*) you have obeyed My voice" (Genesis 22:18) – the numerical value of *eikev*.[3]
>
> (Ra'avad, *Hassagot* on Maimonides, ad loc.)

Maimonides and Ra'avad disagree about whether Abraham recognized his Creator at the age of forty or at three. There are rabbinic sources in support of each position (*Nedarim* 32a, *Pesikta Rabbati* 21:81). This disparity indicates that we are dealing with two very different paths to faith. Maimonides' Abraham followed a very difficult road. He searched and investigated, examined and scrutinized, until finally he arrived at the true faith. Abraham worked hard to acquire faith. In contrast, Ra'avad's Abraham attained faith when he was only three years old, which is just about the earliest age at which a child can even begin to conceive of the world. The disagreement between them is a disagreement about the nature of faith: Is faith implanted in man from the day he is born, or does it require hard work and continuous effort in order to be revealed?

Another midrash follows the same general direction taken by Ra'avad, emphasizing the naturalness of Abraham's faith:

> "But his delight is in the law of the Lord.... And in His law does he meditate day and night" (Psalms 1:2). Rabbi Shimon bar Yochai said: His [Abraham's] father did not teach him, nor did he have a teacher; whence then did he learn the Torah? The fact is, however, that the Holy One, blessed be He, made his kidneys serve like two teachers for him, and these welled forth and taught him wisdom.
>
> (Genesis Rabba 61:1)

---

3. *Eikev* (*ayin* [70], *kof* [100], *bet* [2]) years – 172 years; that is to say, for 172 of his 175 years Abraham obediently obeyed the voice of God. Thus, we see that it took him only three years to arrive at the true faith.

This midrash emphasizes the naturalness of Abraham's faith. Abraham had no need for teachers or rabbis; his kidneys, heart, and feelings were his teachers. We sometimes encounter a caricature of this position among ordinary people. During my army service, fellow soldiers who were not *shomrey mitzvot* often said to me: "I don't need a rabbi. I believe on my own." Unfortunately, we are not all Abraham, and therefore we need rabbis and teachers. According to this approach, however, rabbis and teachers merely help us to uncover the faith that is already within us.

It is important to emphasize that two concepts of Abraham's faith, as expounded by Maimonides and Ra'avad, are not necessarily mutually contradictory. A certain layer of faith may be natural, while another may have to be acquired from outside. It may also be that some people have a simpler and more natural faith than others.

In *The Varieties of Religious Experience*, the psychologist and philosopher William James describes a great many people whose faith was simple and natural. One of them, the Christian author and preacher Dr. Edward Everett Hale, wrote:

> Any man has an advantage, not to be estimated, who is born, as I was, into a family where the religion is simple and rational; who is trained in the theory of such a religion, so that he never knows, for an hour, what these religious or irreligious struggles are. I always knew God loved me, and I was always grateful to him for the world he placed me in. I always liked to tell him so, and was always glad to receive his suggestions to me.
>
> (*Varieties of Religious Experience*, lecture IV)

In contrast, the philosopher Søren Kierkegaard emphasizes the complexity of faith and the great effort and devotion it requires:

> Today nobody will stop with faith; they all go further.... In those old days it was different. For then faith was a task for a whole lifetime, not a skill thought to be acquired in either

> days or weeks. When the old campaigner approached the end, had fought the good fight, and kept his faith, his heart was still young enough not to have forgotten the fear and trembling that disciplined his youth and which, although the grown man mastered it, no man altogether outgrows.
>
> (*Fear and Trembling*, p. 42)

According to Kierkegaard, faith is a continuous mission, and cannot be easily acquired or maintained. He speaks of faith as a struggle rather than a natural asset.

The *Chafetz Chayyim* says that even if Abraham acquired faith through a difficult struggle, that is not necessarily the appropriate path for us to day:

> Even if the Sages told us that Abraham our father investigated with his mind, came up with novel ideas, and discovered that the world has a master.... This was only because he was the first, and did not receive the principles of Judaism from his forefathers. But we are the descendents of our forefathers, who received the Torah at Mount Sinai; why should we spend time on such investigation and start again from the very beginning?
>
> (*Chafetz Chayyim* on the Torah, pp. 24–25)

By Way of the Intellect or Experience?

Maimonides raises another important point. Even if we agree that one must work and search hard in order to come to faith, we must begin by answering the question of where one begins the search. As Maimonides sees it, one comes to faith through the intellect, for the road to faith is an intellectual quest:

> For it is not logical that man's major purpose is to eat or to drink or to engage in copulation or to build a house or to be a king, because these are all passing occurrences and do not add to his essence. Moreover, he shares all these activities with other types of living creatures.... For man, before he acquires

knowledge, is no better than an animal, for he is not different from other types of animals except in his reason. He is a rational living being. The word "rational" means the attainment of rational concepts. The greatest of these rational concepts is the understanding of the Oneness of the Creator, blessed and praised be He, and all that pertains to that divine matter.

(Introduction to the Commentary on the Mishna)

One only loves God with the knowledge with which one knows Him. According to the knowledge will be the love. If the former be little or much, so will the latter be little or much. A person ought therefore to devote himself to the understanding and comprehension of those sciences and studies which will inform him concerning his Master, as far as it lies in human faculties to understand and comprehend.

(*Hilkhot Teshuva* 10:6)

This God, honored and revered, it is our duty to love and fear....

And what is the way that will lead to the love of Him and the fear of Him? When a person contemplates His great and wondrous works and creatures and from them obtains a glimpse of His wisdom, which is incomparable and infinite, he will straightaway love Him, praise Him, glorify Him, and long with an exceeding longing to know His great Name; even as David said, "My soul thirsts for God, for the living God" (Psalms 42:3). And when then he ponders these matters, he will recoil affrighted, and realize that he is a small creature, lowly and obscure, endowed with slight and slender intelligence, standing in the presence of Him who is perfect in knowledge.

(*Hilkhot Yesodei ha-Torah* 2:1–2)

Maimonides maintains that the path to God is through scientific-philosophical speculation about nature and the wisdom it embodies. Intellectual speculation brings us not only to recognize the existence of God, but also to love and fear Him.

There are, however, other ways to reach God. The philosopher Immanuel Kant thought that he had succeeded in demonstrating that there is no rational proof for the existence of God. It would appear, then, that an approach that presents the recognition of God as dependent upon the rational intellect collapses. If so, how is it possible to know God? Must a person who does not find faith naturally implanted in his heart give up in despair? Rabbi Joseph B. Soloveitchik thinks not. According to him, the philosophical denial that it is impossible to demonstrate the existence of God through logical argument was actually beneficial to the religious world. Instead of continuing a barren search for intellectual proofs, religion focused on human encounters with God that are not mediated by the mind:

> This view came to uproot, but ended up planting; it came to deny, but ended up believing. It denied man's ability to draw indirect conclusions through proofs.... But instead of eradicating all these proofs from its book, it accepted and reaffirmed them as non-mediated experiences that are not based on logic, but rather are expressed through sudden revelation and illumination.
>
> (*Uvikashtem mi-Sham*, pp. 127–128)

Rabbi Soloveitchik argues that Kant freed us from the need to tie our faith to our limited and restricted intellects. Our encounter with God is direct and experiential. We encounter God through existential experiences: the experience of enjoying nature, the experience of moral strength, of aesthetic pleasure – we may encounter God in any or all of these. The encounter is experiential, not intellectual. Imagine someone who must prove the existence of his mother through his intellect. The attempt would only limit and strangle his family relationships. We experience God's existence with full inner certainty, and there is no need to restrict it with the formulas of mathematics and logic.

Furthermore, and this is an important point, those who do not experience God directly can often experience God's presence by a process of elimination. Most people cannot really imagine a world empty of God, a world that is cold and cruel, arbitrary and haphazard.

Through Nature or Through History?

As we have seen, man's encounter with God can take place through nature; and this encounter can take place by using intellectual analysis, or as experiential meeting. There is, however, another arena in which to meet God – history. Rabbi Yehuda Halevi considered this point at length:

> I believe in the God of Abraham, Isaac, and Jacob, who led the children of Israel out of Egypt with signs and miracles; who fed them in the desert and gave them the land, after having made them traverse the sea and the Jordan in a miraculous way; who sent Moses with His law, and subsequently thousands of prophets, who confirmed His law by promises to the observant, and threats to the disobedient.
>
> (*Kuzari* I, 11)

Rabbi Yehuda Halevi emphasizes man's encounter with God through history, as opposed to Maimonides, who stresses his encounter with God through nature.[4]

Revelation

Thus far we have seen several approaches to Abraham's path to

4. Note that this does not answer the question of whether Rabbi Yehuda Halevi holds that man encounters God through his intellect; for the search for the God of history may also be carried out with the assistance of reason. Halevi's position on the matter is more complex than generally acknowledged.

faith. We raised several fundamental questions. First, is faith natural and simple or acquired through extended spiritual effort? Second, is the spiritual quest better aided by the tools of logic or by the instrumentality of experience? And third, in what realm is God to be sought: will we encounter Him in nature or in history?

We find yet another important approach to the issue in the words of the Sages. This approach, which is connected to the third question, is reflected in the following well-known midrash:

> Said Rabbi Yitzchak: This may be compared to a man who was traveling from place to place when he saw a building in flames. "Is it possible that the building lacks a person to look after it?" he wondered. The owner of the building looked out and said, "I am the owner of the building." Similarly, because Abraham our father said, "Is it conceivable that the world is without a guide?" the Holy One, blessed be He, looked out and said to him, "I am the guide, the sovereign of the universe."
>
> (Genesis Rabba 39, 1)

This is a very interesting midrash. First of all, Rabbi Yitzchak describes a person who sees "a house burning" or "a house shining." It is not clear whether the fact that the house is burning and gives off light strengthens his faith that it has an owner, or whether it plants uncertainty within him, because the house may be ownerless and of concern to no one. According to this approach, which has been accepted by certain modern scholars, Abraham is described here as a man of doubt. The lesson of the midrash, then, is that it is possible to be a great believer even while harboring doubts and uncertainties.

Whatever the case, the man fails to resolve his uncertainties on his own: "The owner of the house looked out at him." According to this midrash, man is unable to climb up to God on his own. God must come down to him.

This is the way the midrash was understood by Rabbi Chasdai Crescas:

> The Sages said in the Midrash: "This may be compared to a man who was traveling from place to place when he saw a building in flames. 'Is it possible that the building lacks a person to look after it?' he wondered.... The Holy One, blessed be He, looked out and said to him: 'I am the guide, the sovereign of the universe.'" This means that while he was inclined to the truth, he did not remove himself from all uncertainty until God bestowed His light upon him, that is, prophecy.
>
> (*Or ha-Shem*, 1, 3, chap. 6)

This is the road to faith taken by the king of the Khazars in Rabbi Yehuda Halevi's *Kuzari*:

> To the king of the Khazars came a dream, and it appeared as if an angel addressed him, saying: "Your way of thinking is indeed pleasing to the Creator, but not your way of acting." Yet he was so zealous in the performance of the Khazar religion that he devoted himself with a perfect heart to the service of the temple and sacrifices. Notwithstanding this devotion, the angel came again at night and repeated: "Your way of thinking is pleasing to God, but not your way of acting." This caused him to ponder over the different beliefs and religions, and finally become a convert to Judaism together with many other Khazars.
>
> (*Kuzari*, 1, introduction)

Rabbi Yehuda Halevi describes the Khazar king's journey to Judaism as starting with divine revelation. The principle of revelation is central to Judaism. Revelation means that God descends from heaven to earth. On the historical plane, God revealed Himself to us at Mount Sinai. Rabbi Soloveitchik emphasizes, however, that the consciousness of revelation continued even after the direct revelation ceased, as it were. Judaism preserves the Mount Sinai experience, and through it, every generation is able to taste of the experience of divine revelation. Even today God continues to shine His face upon us.

On the other hand, it is important to pay attention to the fact that the owner of the house only revealed himself after Abraham had already pondered the significance of the burning house. This is also what happened to the king of the Khazars: The angel appeared to him in his dreams when he was already devoted to the Khazar religion. Faith makes two demands upon us: to search for God and to answer His call. Samuel David Luzzatto (Shadal) took this idea a step further, arguing that without the necessary spiritual preparation, one will gain nothing from divine revelation:

> Were God to reveal Himself to an individual or to a nation in order to inform them of His unity, it would of necessity serve no purpose. For if someone is accustomed to polytheism, then even were God to reveal Himself to him and tell him that there is only one God, he would not be obligated to incline his heart toward Him and accept monotheism. For a doubt will always remain in his heart, perhaps this god said this for his own glory, so that he will not serve any other god, but tomorrow "another" god might appear to him and tell him that there is no other god but he, or that he, too, is a god like the first one. Therefore, when all the nations were accustomed to polytheism, it would have been impossible for God to reveal Himself to them.... And therefore after Abraham our father arose and through his understanding recognized that there is only one God, the Holy One, blessed be He, immediately appeared to him, and drew him near His service.
>
> (Commentary to Exodus 20:3)

According to Shadal, one can only interpret divine revelation properly if one is spiritually prepared for it.

Inborn Essence and Selection

The Choice of Abraham and His Descendants

This chapter differs slightly from the other chapters in the book. In this chapter we shall focus more on scriptural analysis than on a conceptual issue. I shall present what I believe to be the correct understanding of the scriptural texts under analysis. The theoretical backgroud of this chapter was discussed in chapter 7.

Religious Torah students generally accept Rabbi Yehuda Halevi's position regarding the book of Genesis. He sees the events described in the book as an account of the evolving stages of divine influence. Here is how he describes the transitional stages between Abraham and the sons of Jacob:

> The essence of Abraham passed over to Isaac, to the exclusion of the other sons, who were all removed from the land, the special inheritance of Isaac. The prerogative of Isaac descended on Jacob, while Esau was sent from the land which belonged to Jacob. The sons of the latter were all worthy of the divine influence, as well as of the country distinguished by the divine spirit. This is the first instance of the divine influence descending on a number of people, whereas it had previously only been vouchsafed to isolated individuals.
>
> (*Kuzari* 1, 95)

Rabbi Yehuda Halevi argues that the descendants of Noah and Abraham who were chosen were those who carried the divine essence – the innate genetic ability to attain prophecy. Those who did not carry the essence were pushed aside. Many find support for this position in the opening words of *Parashat Lekh Lekha*, which offer no justification for God's selection of Abraham, and say nothing about his earlier life. This proves, they assert, that Abraham was not chosen on account of his good deeds, but because of his inborn essence.

As we saw in the preceding chapter, however, Nachmanides held that it was precisely this point that troubled the Sages:

> Now this section of Scripture is not sufficiently clarified. Why did the Holy One, blessed be He, tell Abraham to leave his country, and [promise that] He would act favorably toward him in an unprecedented manner, without first stating that Abraham served God or that he was a righteous and perfect man? Or it should offer as a reason for his leaving the country that the very journey to another land was an act seeking the nearness of God....
>
> However, the reason [for God's promising Abraham this reward] is that the people of Ur Kasdim did him much evil because of his belief in the Holy One, blessed be He. He ran away from them to go on to the land of Canaan, staying for a while in Haran. God then told him to leave these places as well and do as he had originally intended, namely, that his worship of God and his call to the people to [serve] God should be performed in the chosen land. There He would make his name great, and these nations would bless themselves by him.
>
> (Commentary to Genesis 12:2)

Nachmanides, following the Sages, emphasizes that Abraham was chosen on account of his deeds. Even according to its plain sense, Scripture emphasizes the deeds by virtue of which Abraham was chosen:

> Because Abraham obeyed My voice, and kept My charge, My commandments, My statutes, and My laws.
>
> (Genesis 26:5)

> For I know him, that he will command his children and his household after him, and they shall keep the way of the Lord, to do justice and judgment.
>
> (Genesis 18:19)

> And in your seed shall all the nations of the earth be blessed; because you have obeyed My voice.
>
> (Genesis 22:18)

Following Nachmanides' approach, we shall present in this chapter a reading of the book of Genesis that differs from that of Rabbi Yehuda Halevi. According to my understanding, God's selection of those whom He loves does not follow from any natural quality latent in them. Nor does His rejection of the others result from their lack of that quality. The chosen ones were selected on account of the deeds they chose to do, and the rejected were pushed aside on account of the acts that they selected. Both were judged on their ways and their decisions, and not on the basis of metaphysical qualities concealed within them from the moment of birth.

Our discussion here will focus on the selection of the descendants of Abraham, the line that established God's nation. In my opinion, however, this principle is also true with respect to the earlier generations.[5] Selection follows not from any natural essence, but from willful decisions, from the way of life a person adopts for himself. Throughout the book of Genesis, the natural firstborns are pushed aside – Cain, Ishmael, Esau, Reuven, Manasseh – by

---

5. The Torah indicates that Cain was rejected and Abel selected because Abel brought a more appropriate offering: "And Abel also brought from *the firstlings* of his flock and of *the fat parts thereof*" (Genesis 4:4). And therefore: "And the Lord had respect to Abel and to his offering" (ibid.). As we have seen, this is true of Abraham as well.

their younger, more deserving brothers. This is the lesson of the book of Genesis: A person's fate is not fixed by the natural qualities with which he enters the world. It is the actions he chooses to do or not do that determine how his life will play itself out. God chooses the person who demonstrates his readiness to serve Him, rather than the one who cannot control his natural qualities.

As was stated above, this distinction appears to be true with respect to every generation. But my main argument in this chapter is that after Abraham was chosen to establish God's nation (12:1–3), the selection of his heirs rested on the very specific principle that the ones to be pushed aside were those who set themselves apart from their family. We are no longer talking about rejection stemming from inappropriate behavior in general. After Abraham was commanded about his chosen destiny, his descendants were only released from the actualization of that destiny if, with their very own hands, they cut themselves off from Abraham's family and from the realization of his vision.

Lot

When God speaks to Abraham for the first time, He informs him, "I will make of you a great nation" (Genesis 12:2). Later, after Abraham has already arrived in the land of Israel, God goes into greater detail: "To your seed will I give this land" (verse 7). It stands to reason that at this stage Lot was still included in the promise. The general term "your seed" might well have included Lot, Abraham's blood relative, who accompanied him on all his travels.[6] This also follows from what Nachmanides says in his commentary to Deuteronomy. Nachmanides notes that the descendants of Lot were given their inheritance along the eastern bank of the Jordan, in an area that had been promised to Abraham

6. It is characteristic of Scripture to waive precision when describing family relationships. Thus, for example, the sons of Jacob refer to Dinah as "our daughter" (Genesis 34:17). See also Genesis 31:23 and Rashi, ad loc.

in the *berit bein ha-betarim,* and that Israel had been commanded not to capture it. Nachmanides writes:

> Scripture states only "Because I have given it unto the children of Lot for a possession" (v. 19), in order to say that even though it was part of Abraham's inheritance, the Holy One, blessed be He, gave it to the children of Lot for Abraham's sake.
>
> (Commentary to Deuteronomy 2:10)

It follows from Nachmanides' comment that even after his rejection, which we shall discuss below, Lot still received a portion of Abraham's estate. All the more so was he entitled to a portion before he was pushed aside, and before Isaac was born.[7]

It later becomes clear to Abraham that Lot will not be his heir. This is the implication of the announcement made to Abraham concerning his seed, which is emphatically repeated "after Lot was separated from him" (13:14). Indeed, we later discover that Abraham believes that his servant Eliezer will inherit him, and not Lot (15:2–3; as long as Lot was in the picture, he clearly enjoyed priority over Eliezer). In the *berit bein ha-betarim* Abraham is explicitly told: "Out of your own bowels shall be your heir" (15:4). This formulation clarifies that the promise he had received relates to a real son, rather than the likes of Lot or Eliezer.

What happened in the interim? Why did Abraham first think that Lot would inherit him, and only later find that Lot would not be his heir? If from the outset Lot had never been destined to inherit Abraham, why was this not made clear to Abraham? My argument is that Lot was in fact meant to be Abraham's heir, or at least to be included among Abraham's primary heirs alongside his future son. Lot, however, chose to pull himself away from the family of Abraham. Chapter 13 of Genesis describes the quarrel between the shepherds of Abraham and the shepherds of Lot, in the aftermath of which Abraham and Lot parted ways, Lot turning

7. See Rabbi Yoel Bin-Nun's article in *Megadim* 17, p. 37.

to the cities of the plain. It is at this point that Lot set himself apart from the future of the family of Abraham.

In order to clarify the significance of Lot's step, we must understand the geographical context. It is generally accepted today that the cities of the plain were situated on the eastern bank of the Jordan.[8] Y. Grossman noted that everyone who was rejected in the book of Genesis headed east: Adam ("And He placed the *keruvim* at the east of the garden of Eden, and the bright blade of a revolving sword"; Genesis 3:24), Cain ("And dwelt in the land of Nod, to the east of Eden"; 3:16), the sons of Keturah ("He sent them away…eastward, to the east country"; 25:6), Esau (who lives in "Seir, the country of Edom"; 32:4), and we shall see below that the same applies to Ishmael.

It must be emphasized, however, that Lot is not cast away eastward; Lot chooses of his own accord to travel eastward, and thus leave the boundaries of the tiny land of Israel! Abraham understands that he must separate from Lot, and makes the following offer:

> Is not the whole land before you? separate yourself, I pray you. If you will take the left hand, then I will go to the right. Or if you depart to the right hand, then I will go the left.
>
> (Genesis 13:9)

As translated by Onkelos, Abraham suggests to Lot that he move "to the right (*yamina*)" – south (compare "on the south side southward (*teimana*)" [Exodus 26:18]), or "to the left (*semola*)" – north (compare "which is on the left hand (*misemol*) of Damascus" [Exodus 14:15]). The land of Israel, as we all know, is long and narrow. Abraham wants Lot to remain within the boundaries of the

8. See *Atlas Da'at Mikra*, p. 72, and *Encyclopedia Mikra'it*, vol. 7, s.v. *tzo'ar*, pp. 690–695. Even Rabbi Y. Bin-Nun, who disagrees with the accepted identification of the cities of the plain, locates them on the east bank of the Jordan. See his article in *Shomrom u-Binyamin* 1 (Jerusalem, 1991).

western Israel, and therefore suggests to him that he move southward or northward. In these directions Lot can distance himself from Abraham, while still staying within the borders of Israel.[9]

Lot, however, opts for a possibility that Abraham did not even propose, and may even have feared. He turns eastward, and crosses the borders of the heart of the land of Israel. As if this were not enough, Lot chooses to live among the evil men of Sodom (13:12). Thus, Lot chooses to separate himself from the family of Abraham and to abandon his vision and destiny.

This, indeed, is what happens. God accepts Lot's decision. Lot is pushed to the sidelines; he is set aside from the inheritance of Abraham in western Israel, and he receives his portion on the east bank of the Jordan, next to Esau. As we know, the *berit bein ha-betarim* only defined the northern and southern boundaries of Israel: "From the river of Mitzrayim to the great river, the river of Perat" (Genesis 15:18). The eastern border of Israel was not defined, perhaps because the east bank of the Jordan enjoys an intermediate status: it became the inheritance of the descendants of Lot and Esau, descendants of Abraham who separated themselves from the family and their destiny.[10] When Lot de-

9. Hermann Gunkel offers the very opposite explanation. He argues that the dialogue between Abraham and Lot is given precisely because Lot's decision to go eastward fully realized Abraham's proposal to Lot to choose between going east or west. His understanding, however, is very problematic, because the Hebrew expression "right or left" in a geographical context always means "south or north." For when one faces eastward (*kedem*), the south is on one's right. A clear example is found in Job 23:8–9: "Behold, I go *forward* (*kedem*), but he is not there; and *backward* (*achor*), but I cannot perceive him: on the *left* hand (*semol*), where he works, but I cannot behold him: he hides himself on the *right* hand (*yamin*), that I cannot see him." Also II *Chronicles* 3:17: "And he set up the pillars before the temple, one on the *right* hand (*yamin*) and the other on the *left* (*semol*)." There are many other examples.

10. See Deuteronomy 2:1–19. As we know, Moses was also not pleased with the request of the tribes of Reuben and Gad to take their portion on the east bank of the Jordan. "And why do you dishearten the children of Israel from going over into the land which the Lord had given them?" (Numbers 32:7). His words imply that the east bank of the Jordan is not included in "the land which the

cides to leave western Israel, he is deciding to leave the family of Abraham. The anxious Abraham is then informed that he will be given other seed that will carry out his mission (Genesis 13:14). It is at this point that Lot seals his fate to be pushed away from the family of Abraham.

Ishmael

Abraham receives the news of the upcoming birth of Isaac (Genesis 17:16) after having been commanded about the covenant of circumcision. At this time, Ishmael is already thirteen years old (Genesis 16:16, 17:1). Abraham is skeptical about the possibility of Sarah's giving birth. Immediately after, Abraham asks: "Oh, that Ishmael might live before You" (Genesis 17:18). Until now Abraham saw no need for such a request, apparently because he thought that he would have no more sons, and that Ishmael would be his heir. Only now is he told: "But my covenant will I establish with Isaac" (Genesis 17:21), and so he begins to worry about what will happen to Ishmael. At first glance this seems to undermine our central argument, for the Torah tells us nothing about Ishmael's earlier deeds, and so it is difficult to say that he had separated himself from the family with his own two hands.

In order to clarify this point, let us reexamine the account of Ishmael's birth. The Torah tells us of Sarah's initiative to give her maidservant to Abraham:

> Behold, now, the Lord has restrained me from bearing children; I pray you, go in to my maid; it may be that I may obtain children by her.
>
> (Genesis 16:2)

Sarah plans to "adopt" Hagar's son and recognize him as her son and legal heir. Rachel will one day do the same thing when she

---

Lord had given them." Regarding the special status of the east bank, see Rabbi Y. Bin-Nun's article in *Megadim* 17, and the bibliography found there.

gives her maidservant Bilhah to Jacob in order to obtain a child through her. And when a child is born, Rachel declares: "God has judged me, and has also heard my voice, *and has given me a son*" (Genesis 30:6); it is also Rachel who gives the baby a name. Even after Rachel has children of her own, her maidservant's children remain part of the family and are eligible to receive a portion of Jacob's inheritance. This was also Sarah's plan. But something goes wrong, and Sarah finally announces: "For the son of this maidservant shall not inherit with my son" (Genesis 21:10).

What happened in the interim? Why did Sarah change her mind about recognizing Ishmael as an heir? Scripture relates what happened:

> And he went in to Hagar, and she conceived. And when she saw that she had conceived, her mistress was despised in her eyes. And Sarai said to Abram, My wrong be upon you; I have given my maid into your bosom; and when she saw that she had conceived, I was despised in her eyes; the Lord judge between me and you.
>
> (Genesis 16:4–5)

Abraham accepts Sarah's complaint and hands Hagar over to her. Sarah deals harshly with her, and Hagar runs away. Here is the parting from Abraham's family; Ishmael is not the one who leaves – it is his mother, Hagar. The harsh treatment brought about by her attitude toward Sarah led her, in the end, to run away from Abraham's house. The angel who tells her to return proves that her running away was not what God had wanted. Hagar should have remained in Abraham's house so that her son would become his heir. By running away, Hagar sealed her son's fate to be severed from Abraham's family.

The angel who reveals himself to Hagar tells her to return, but he intimates that her son Ishmael will not be Abraham's heir. Many read the expression "His hand will be against every man, and every man's hand against him" (Genesis 16:12) as a hint that the descendants of Ishmael would be nomads, without a permanent place of residence. This also accounts for the fact that Scripture never mentions "the land of Ishmael," paralleling the lands of other tribes and nations.[11] It has also been suggested[12] that the expression "and he shall dwell in the presence (*al penei*) of all his brethren" means that he will live east of his brothers, for *al penei* often means "east of," as in "upon the mount of Olives, which is before (*al penei*) Jerusalem on the east" (Zechariah 14:4), and "in the wilderness which is before (*al penai*) Moab, toward the sunrising" (Numbers 21:11). Even during Hagar's pregnancy, Ishmael was pushed out of the land of Israel, and as has been stated, some understand that he was pushed eastward, toward the lands of Lot and Esau.[13]

While Ishmael did not leave the family of Abraham of his own accord, his mother Hagar did. Just as the children of Lot were pushed aside on account of their father's deeds, so, too, Hagar's son was pushed aside on account of his mother's deeds. She provoked Sarah, and it is reasonable to assume that she even tried to take over her position in the household. This led to a quarrel, which ultimately resulted in Hagar's running away from Abraham's house. While the direct responsibility for Hagar's running away falls upon Sarah, who dealt harshly with her (Nachmanides emphasizes that this was a sin), it is Hagar who was responsible for starting the whole process, and it was she who in the end chose flight over confrontation.[14]

---

11. So suggested Y. Kil in *Da'at Mikra*, ad loc.; so, too, Y.M. Emanueli, *Sefer* Genesis, p. 244, in the name of M. Ben Yashar.

12. *Da'at Mikra*, ad loc.

13. Y. Grossman, in his article in *Megadim* 29, argues that Ishmael himself moved south to the wilderness of Paran (Genesis 21:21). Scripture, however, testifies about the descendants of Ishmael: "And they dwelt from Havilah to Shur, that is before Egypt, as you go toward Asshur; and he dwelt in the presence of all his brethren" (Genesis 25:18). In other words, the descendants of Ishmael dwelt in the entire expanse east of the land of Israel, and passed through all of it in their wanderings.

14. It should be noted that even if Ishmael's rejection does not fit the model

I am not suggesting that the punishment for Hagar's wrongdoing consisted of her son's being pushed away from Abraham's legacy. My argument focuses on the human rather than on the theological level: With her own two hands, Hagar uprooted herself from the family of Abraham. Lot could have committed graver sins and still remained Abraham's heir; Hagar could have committed graver sins and still remained the mother of his heir. But they chose to sever themselves, with their very own hands, from their family, and so, too, from their destiny. God merely gave His seal of approval to their decisions.

Esau

Many explanations have been offered for the transfer of the birthright from Esau to Jacob. There are three main elements in the process of this transfer: (1) Rebecca's prophecy "And the elder shall serve the younger" (Genesis 25:23); (2) the sale of the birthright (Genesis 25:29–34); and (3) Isaac's blessing (Genesis chap. 27). In the end, Jacob receives Abraham's blessing from Isaac. For our purposes, this is the most significant element in the story in that it determines the continuation of the house of Abraham (Genesis 28:4). Which of the three stages was the most important in the determination of the heir of Abraham's blessing? Or perhaps, none of them are relevant? How does the process of selecting the heir of the house of Abraham fit in with our general argument that those who were rejected from continuing the legacy of Abraham pushed themselves aside with their own very hands?

Let us begin with an examination of the three main elements mentioned above. First, let us study Rebecca's prophecy, "And the

---

presented here, this would not surprise us. For Ishmael was the son of a maidservant, and it could be argued that he was never accepted into the family, as is the case with the sons of Keturah. God's words in chap. 17, however, imply that Ishmael has an intermediate status, and that in any event he is Abraham's seed. The reason seems to be that Sarah had promised to recognize him as Abraham's legal heir. It was Hagar who separated herself from the family when she ran away, separating her son Ishmael along with her.

elder shall serve the younger" (Genesis 25:23). This prophecy does not seem to mark the point at which it was determined that Jacob would continue the Abrahamic line and not Esau. I say this for two main reasons.

1) First, as was noted by Radak,[15] the wording of the prophecy is unclear, so that it can be interpreted one way or the other. It is not clear who is the subject and who the object ("The elder shall serve the younger" or "the elder – the younger shall serve him"). (Compare Job 14:19: *Avanim shachaku mayim*, "The stones – the waters wear them.")

2) The prophecy does not relate in any way to the blessing of Abraham and the continuation of his line, but rather to the aggressive reciprocal relationship between the two brothers. Abraham's blessing does not mention material domination, and similarly the prophecy of Rebecca makes no mention of the blessing regarding seed and the land.

It seems reasonable to suggest that the central factor in the determination of the heir to Abraham's blessing is Esau's sale of the birthright. The meaning of the birthright here might be the continuation of the house of Isaac and being granted the blessing of Abraham. The firstborn is not necessarily the sole heir, but it may be argued that he was supposed to lead the realization of Abraham's vision and head the family.[16] Esau treated the birthright lightly and sold it for a bowl of lentils, thus demonstrating in the crudest way his contempt for the legacy of Abraham and his derision of the noble mission of Abraham's descendants. In accordance with our general argument, here, too, Esau removed himself from the family; God merely gave His consent to the re-

15. And in his wake, Cassuto (*Sefer* Genesis *u-Mivneihu*, p. 195).
16. The Sages (Genesis Rabba 63, 13) emphasize the spiritual significance of the birthright. Rashi, Seforno, Chizkuni, and Abravanel followed them. See in this context, G. Brin, *Sugyot be-Mikra u-be-Megilot*, pp. 60–62, and notes, ad loc.

moval. It is in this vein that the Rabbis wrote that after the sale "the Holy One, blessed be He, agreed…and established the birthright for Jacob" (Genesis Rabba 63:13). The plain implication is that before the sale, the birthright – including its spiritual components – did not belong to Jacob. The Sages make this point, too, but more explicitly:

> Esau was worthy to bring forth kings, and Jacob was worthy to bring forth priests.... Leah and Zilpah were fit for Esau, and Rachel and Bilhah were fit for Jacob. All these gifts were taken from him. He sold his birthright to Jacob, and immediately it was said about him: "Behold, I will make you small among the nations; you are greatly despised" (Obadiah 1:2).
>
> (*Midrash Zuta Shir ha-Shirim* 1[15])

We see from this midrash that Esau was fit to continue the Abrahamic line alongside Jacob, but was pushed aside on account of his sale of the birthright. Some have asked how this strange commercial transaction could have determined whom God would choose as heir to Abraham's legacy. As we understand the matter, the determining factor was not the legal validity of the sale, but the fact that through the sale Esau demonstrated his severance from the spiritual mission of the house of Abraham. Esau sees no value in the perpetuation of Abraham's legacy: "Thus Esau despised the birthright" (Genesis 25:34).

Upon further examination, however, it appears that this proposal should be rejected, although there are no absolutes on this question. It seems that the birthright is relevant only to the material dimensions of the relationship between the brothers. The description of the relationships between the sons of Jacob implies that the birthright has no relevance regarding spiritual leadership or the determination of a sole heir; it merely determines priority in matters of inheritance. Scripture states (1 Chronicles 5:1–2) that the birthright among the sons of Jacob passed to Joseph. As we know, Joseph's birthright expressed itself in the fact that he received a double portion of the inheritance – Manasseh and Ephraim, and in his national leadership alongside the tribe of Judah. Thus the Chronicles passage does not prove the Sages' understanding, that the birthright had a primary spiritual significance at this stage in the history of the patriarchs.

The third element to be considered is the blessing of Isaac. This element is the easiest to reject, because Isaac's blessing does not deal at all with the establishment of an heir to the house of Abraham. This is so for various reasons.

1) The midrash understands that Jacob sinned when he deceived his father and took the blessing; in fact, he was punished for this.[17] Moreover the words of Isaac already carry a veiled criticism of Jacob's act: "Your brother has come *with cunning*" (Genesis 27:35). It seems unlikely that Abraham's heir was chosen *by virtue* of such a sin.

2) Furthermore, can a father's blessing dictate to God which of two brothers to choose? Malbim raised this argument (Genesis 27:1). Among modern biblical scholars, it was taken up primarily by Cassuto, who vigorously insisted that according to the Torah, a blessing is merely a prayer, devoid of any magical power.[18] The biblical characters may have attached power and influence to blessings, but this did not influence God. The bottom line is that in determining an heir for the house of Abraham, one who would establish the people of Israel, God reserves for Himself the last word.

3) Moreover, as is often pointed out, Isaac's blessing deals exclusively with material things. It does not mention the land and the

17. See the sources collected by Nechama Leibowitz, *New Studies in* Genesis, pp. 264–269.
18. *Sefer* Genesis *u-Mivneihu*, pp. 196–197; *Encyclopedia Mikra'it*, vol. 2, s.v. *berakha*, p. 357.

seed, which is "Abraham's blessing." It is only later that Abraham's blessing is given to Jacob (Genesis 28:4), after Isaac learns that Esau had sold his birthright (Genesis 27:36), and after Rebecca reminds him about Esau's Hittite wives (Genesis 27:46). Only then does Jacob receive the blessing promising him that he will continue the line of Abraham – he and not his brother:

> And may God Almighty bless you, and make you fruitful, and multiply you, that you may be a multitude of people; and give you the blessing of Abraham, to you, and to your seed with you, that you may inherit the land in which you are a sojourner, and which God gave to Abraham.
>
> (Genesis 28:3–4)

It stands to reason that if Esau had not cut himself off from the house of Abraham, the two sons of Isaac would have received Abraham's blessing and continued his work together.

Thus we see that the three elements mentioned above constitute a single continuum that describes the balance of material powers between the two brothers, but does not determine who will continue the Abrahamic line. But if this is so, then why was Jacob chosen to continue the legacy of Abraham? Is this an arbitrary divine decree?

At this point it is necessary to discuss a certain act of Esau's that was no less important than the ones already discussed.

> And he took to wife Judith the daughter of Beeri the Hittite, and Bashemath the daughter of Elon the Hittite; and they were a grief of mind to Isaac and to Rebecca.
>
> (Genesis 26:34–35)

This step testifies to a conscious break from the house of Abraham and his legacy. Esau was surely aware of Abraham's determination not to marry off his son Isaac to one of the daughters of the land (Genesis 24:3). Intermingling with the local Canaanites severs Esau from the heritage of the house of Abraham. Nechama Leibowitz's discussion of Esau's marriages argues that it was because he married the Canaanite women that Esau was denied the blessing of Abraham (*Iyyunim Chadashim be-Sefer* Genesis, p. 195).

The passing of Abraham's blessing from Esau to Jacob is closely associated with the mention of the Hittite women whom Esau married, and to the command directed at Jacob not to marry such a woman:

> And Rebecca said to Isaac, I am weary of my life because of the daughters of Heth; if Jacob take a wife of the daughters of Heth, such as these, of the daughters of the land, what good shall my life be to me? And Isaac called Jacob, and blessed him, and charged him, and said to him, You shall not take a wife of the daughters of Canaan. Arise, go to Padan Aram to the house of Bethuel your mother's father, and take you a wife from there of the daughters of Laban, your mother's brother. And may God Almighty bless you, and make you fruitful, and multiply you, that you may be a multitude of people; and give you the blessing of Abraham, to you and your seed with you; that you may inherit the land in which you are a sojourner, and which God gave to Abraham.
>
> (Genesis 27:46–28:4)

Esau himself recognizes – too late – that the blessing of Abraham has been withheld from him because of his taking strange wives:

> And Esau saw that Isaac had blessed Jacob, and sent him away to Padan Aram to take him a wife from there; and that as he blessed him he gave him a charge, saying, You shall not take a wife of the daughters of Canaan.
>
> (Genesis 28:6)

The root *b-r-kh* ("bless") which appears twice in the verse is clearly connected here to the prohibition against marrying Canaanite women.

Earlier, we proposed that it was Esau himself who cut himself off from his family when he despised the birthright and sold it for a bowl of lentils. It seems, however, that the birthright is not connected to the legacy of Abraham and the perpetuation of his house. According to this understanding, the emphasis should be placed on Esau's second act – his marrying the Hittite women. As stated above, Abraham was most careful not to mix with the people of the land, and to find a wife for his son from among his own family. Esau did not marry a woman from Abraham's house; he chooses his wives from among the people of the land. This is a clear act of cutting himself off from the house of Abraham.[19]

The Sons of Jacob

Based on what has been said so far, it is now necessary to deal with another difficulty. Why were all the sons of Jacob, despite the great sin of selling Joseph, chosen to continue the legacy of the house of Abraham?

The idea I am advancing here explains why the sin did not disqualify them from continued membership in the family or from taking part in establishing the nation of Israel. Ordinary sins do not influence the choice of Abraham's heirs. Only the initiation of a severance from the family can have this effect. Once Abraham

---

19. (1) The connection between Esau's marriage to the daughters of Heth and his rejection from the Abrahamic house was emphasized by Nechama Leibowitz, *New Studies in* Genesis, p. 278; E. Shochet, "Magamot Politiyot be-Sippurei he-*Pirkei Avot*," *Tarbitz* 29, 3 (1955), p. 253; and Rabbi M. Breuer, *Pirkei Bereishit* I, p. 506.
(2) Esau himself chose to leave the land of Canaan (Genesis 36:6–8), and his departure is described in terms that parallel the description of Lot's departure from the land. Esau, however, leaves the land only *after* it becomes clear that he has not received the blessing of Abraham.

and his seed have been chosen, by virtue of his deeds and his beliefs, his sons continue his mission unless they explicitly waive it. The sin of selling Joseph was certainly very grave, but it did not constitute an initiated severance of the brothers from the family and its heritage.

Nevertheless, we are left with an acute problem. The plain sense of the text implies that the sons of Jacob married Canaanite women, for no mention is made of a trip to Haran to find suitable matches, similar to the journeys of Abraham's servant and Jacob. This question is subject to a tannaitic dispute: According to Rabbi Yehuda, the twelve sons were each born with a twin sister, and they later took the sisters as their wives. According to Rabbi Nechemya, they married Canaanite women.[20] Nachmanides suggests a third alternative: The twelve sons of Jacob married strange women, but not from Canaan. They married Egyptian, Ammonite, and Moabite women (Nachmanides, Genesis 38:2). At the very least, however, it is explicitly stated about Simeon, according to the plain sense of the text, that he married a Canaanite woman (Genesis 46:10).[21]

If we reject the assertion that at least some of the sons of Jacob married Canaanite women, there is no problem. If, however, we accept it, we are faced with a very serious difficulty: Earlier we argued that it was precisely because of this sin that Esau was rejected from participating in the perpetuation of the house of Abraham and from receiving the blessing of Abraham. Why then were the sons of Jacob not similarly pushed aside?

20. See *Yalkut Shimoni*, Genesis 143, and Rashi on Genesis 37:35.

21. This also seems to be true with respect to the first wife of Judah (Genesis 38:2), although this depends on the various interpretations given to the passage. 1 Chronicles 2:3 states explicitly that she, too, was a Canaanite woman: "Three were born to him of the daughter of Shuah the Canaanite woman." In any event, the emphasis with respect to one of the sons of Simeon may imply that the rest of his children and the children of his brothers were not of Canaanite descent. At the very least, however, the problem still remains with respect to Simeon himself.

We are forced to conclude that following the selection of Jacob and the rejection of Esau, we enter a new stage in the history of the house of Abraham. After Abraham was chosen, only those descendants who scornfully abandoned his legacy and blessing were pushed aside. Following the selection of Jacob, however, we see a fuller application of the principle "Even if he sinned, he is still part of Israel" (*Sanhedrin* 44a). Jacob's sons continued the house of Abraham regardless of their actions, even if those actions involved a waiver of their mission as heirs of Abraham. The same applies today; according to Jewish law, a Jewish apostate remains a Jew. The sons of Jacob were no longer a band of individuals who carried the vision of Abraham. They were a nation. From that point on, they no longer had the power to relinquish their eternal destiny.[22]

This does not contradict the basic approach that I have proposed. My main argument is that when one party is chosen and another rejected, the rejection does not stem from inborn metaphysical qualities, but from a personal decision by the rejected party. At no point was it said that there must be such a rejection. God does not arbitrarily discriminate between one person and the next, but He may at times choose not to discriminate, even when discrimination would be justified. Jacob was chosen to be the direct father of the nation. That is why Jacob's descendants have no way to escape the eternal destiny cast upon them. Here the destiny begins to be realized; we are no longer dealing with an individual whose heart begins to form a vision of the future, but with an entire family, the kernel of the Jewish people.

22. The Maharal, in dealing with this problem, noted the essential difference resulting from the transition from individuals to a nation, but in a different direction. The Maharal explains (*Gur Arye*, Genesis 38:2) that since we are dealing with a nation and not individuals, marrying Canaanite women is no longer severely prohibited, because now they can become assimilated into the Jewish people.

The Land of Israel

Homeland or Mission?

The first time in the Torah that the land of Israel is connected to the people of Israel is in God's command to Abraham:

> Go you out of your country, and from your homeland, and from your father's house, to the land that I will show you.
>
> (Genesis 12:1)

The land of Israel is not presented here as Israel's homeland. On the contrary, it is the land on behalf of which one leaves his house and homeland. The land of Israel is presented as the antithesis of a homeland, Abraham's place of exile, a place whose name is not even mentioned. The land of Israel is not the natural homeland of the Jewish people, but rather the land that God is giving them so that they can serve Him there.

The Torah emphasizes the fact that the land of Israel is not our natural homeland. There is a twofold danger in seeing the land of Israel as the Jewish people's natural homeland: viewing it as an absolute value, and viewing it as an absolute fact. The *ma'apilim* mentioned in *Parashat Shelach* (Numbers 14:40–45) exemplify those who see the land of Israel as an absolute value. After having been informed of their punishment for their part in the sin of the spies, the people wish to correct their mistake and enter the land of Israel. Moses warns them: "Go not up, for the Lord is not among you; so that you may not be smitten before your enemies!" (Numbers 14:42). But the *ma'apilim* ignore the warning; they fail to understand that the value of living in the land of Israel is conditional upon the will of God, and that when God commands not to go to Israel, going to Israel is a sin. The *ma'apilim* erred in their understanding of the true lesson of the sin of the spies, mistakenly concluding that the land of Israel is above and beyond all other values. In the end, the *ma'apilim* were routed: "Then the Amalekites came down, and the Canaanites who dwelt in that hill, and smote them and discomfited them, as far as Hormah" (Numbers 4:45). This is what happened to those who transformed the land into an absolute value.

There are others who turn the settlement of the land of Israel-into an absolute fact, as if the holiness of the land guarantees that its inhabitants will never be driven out into exile. To counteract this idea, the people of Israel are warned over and over again:

> You shall therefore keep My statutes and My judgments, and shall not commit any of these abominations…*that the land vomit not you out also*, when you defile it.
>
> (Leviticus 18:26–28)

The prophet Ezekiel also comes out against this perception of our continued existence in Israel as a sealed promise:

> Son of man, they that inhabit those waste places of the land of Israel speak, saying, Abraham was one man, and yet he inherited the land; but we are many; the land is given us for inheritance. Therefore say to them, Thus says the Lord God; You eat with the blood, and lift up your eyes toward your idols, and shed blood; and shall you possess the land? You stand upon your sword, you carry out disgusting deeds, and you defile every man his neighbor's wife; and shall you possess the land?
>
> (Ezekiel 33:24–26)

The land of Israel is a *dirat arai* – temporary dwelling place; our continued living there depends at all times upon the will of God, who rewards us for our good deeds. We hope and pray that we will live in the land of Israel forever; but it depends on our behavior.

Not only does our very existence in Israel depend upon God, but also the quality of that existence. The book of Deuteronomy compares the land of Egypt to the land of Israel:

> For the land, into which you go to possess it, is not as the land of Egypt, from whence you came out, where you sowed your seed, and watered it with your foot, like a garden of vegetables. But the land into which you go to possess it, is a land of hills and valleys, and drinks water of the rain of heaven; a land which the Lord your God cares for; the eyes of the Lord your God are always upon it, from the beginning of the year to the end of the year.
>
> (Deuteronomy 11:10–12)

The commentators explain the significance of this passage. In the Land of Israel, adequate watering of the fields is not guaranteed; it depends upon the rainfall. As a result, those who live in Israel depend at all times, openly and explicitly, upon the grace of God. Once again, the same principle is emphasized: Even from an agricultural perspective, the Land of Israel is a *dirat arai*, its living conditions being dependent upon the will of God. These verses are meant to counter the natural inclination to see our settlement in Israel as self-evident, an inclination that in certain circumstances may receive theological support, relying on the sanctity of the land and the eternal connection between it and the people. Over and over again, the Torah stresses unequivocally that our settlement in Israel is neither absolute nor unconditional; the Land of Israel is for us a *dirat arai*.

Rashi's opening words to his commentary on the Torah are often cited in this context:

> Rabbi Yitzchak said: The Torah should have commenced with "This month shall be unto you the first of the months" (Exodus 12:1), which is the first commandment given to Israel. What is the reason, then, that it commences with [the account of] creation? Because of "He declared to His people the strength of His works, in order that He might give them the heritage of the nations" (Psalms 111:6). For should the peoples of the world say to Israel, "You are robbers, because you took by force the lands of the seven nations [of Canaan]," Israel may reply to them, "All the earth belongs to the Holy One, blessed be He; He created it and gave it to whom it seemed proper in His eyes. When He willed He gave it to them, and when He willed He took it from them and gave it to us."
>
> (Rashi, Genesis 1:1)

Rashi is not asserting that God *arbitrarily* willed that the land of Israel should *always* belong to the Jewish people. It is God's will that the land pass over to Israel because of "the sin of the Emorites," because the land vomits out its inhabitants, as is mentioned many times in Scripture. Therefore, Israel, too, if they are not heedful of the Torah, will be spewed forth from the land (in any event, the Land of Israel will not be handed over to another nation). We can prove it from the linguistic context. The midrashic statement that God gave the land "to whom it seemed proper in His eyes" is rooted in the book of Jeremiah:

> I have made the earth, the man and the beast that are upon the ground, by My great power and by My outstretched arm, and have given it to whom it seemed proper in My eyes. And now have I given all these lands to the hand of Nebuchadnezzar, the king of Babel, My servant; and the beasts of the field have I given him also to serve him.
>
> (Jeremiah 27:5–6)

Here the same expression – "and I have given it to whom it seemed proper in My eyes" – is used with respect to Nebuchadnezzar; and later in the chapter Zedekiah is warned that he, too, must submit to the king of Babel! In other words, the formulation used by Rashi emphasizes how tenuous is our presence in the Land of Israel, and how in need it is of constant reinforcement. Israel is not our natural homeland, but rather our mission and destiny. This point is explicitly stated by Nachmanides in his explication of the midrash cited by Rashi:

> Rabbi Yitzchak then explained the reason for it. The Torah began with "In the beginning God created" and related the whole story of the creation until the fashioning of man, how He granted him dominion over the works of His hands, and how He set all things under his feet; and how the Garden of Eden, which is the most select place created in this world, was made the place of his habitation until his sin caused him to be expelled therefrom; and how the people of the generation of the flood were completely banished from the world because of their sin, and the sole righteous one among them [i.e., Noah], together with his sons, was saved; and how the sin of their descendants caused them to be scattered to various places and dispersed to different countries....
>
> If so, it is fitting that when a people continues to sin it should lose its place and another people should come to inherit its land, for this was the rule of God in the world from the beginning. And all the more so regarding that which is related in Scripture, namely that Canaan was cursed and sold as a servant forever. It would therefore not be right that he inherit the most select of places of the civilized world. Rather, the servants of God – the seed of his beloved one, Abraham – should inherit it.... He banished those who rebelled against Him, and settled therein those who served Him so that they know that by serving Him they will inherit it, *but if they sin*

> *against Him, the land will spew them out, just as it spewed out the nation before them.*
>
> (Commentary to Genesis 1:1)

According to Nachmanides, Rabbi Yitzchak means to say that the primary message of the creation saga is that man is judged according to his actions, and that an individual or nation that sins before God is cast out of the land. This message is directed at the Land of Israel even when its inhabitants are Jews.

The same notion finds expression in the Torah portion that is read when the first-fruits are offered:

> And it shall be, when you come into the land which the Lord your God gives you for an inheritance, and possess it and dwell therein; that you shall take of the first of all the fruit of the earth, which you shall bring of your land that the Lord your God gives you, and shall put it in a basket, and shall go to the place which the Lord your God shall choose to place His name there. And you shall go to the priest that shall be in those days, and say to him, I profess this day to the Lord your God, that I am come to the country which the Lord swore to our fathers to give us. And the priest shall take the basket out of your hand, and set it down before the altar of the Lord your God. And you shall speak and say before the Lord your God, An Aramean nomad was my father, and he went down to Egypt, and sojourned there with a few, and became there a nation, great, mighty, and populous.... And the Lord brought us out of Egypt.... And He brought us to this place, and gave us this land, a land flowing with milk and honey.
>
> (Deuteronomy 26:1–9)

What nation opens the description of its historical connection to its homeland with the assertion that the nation's founding father was a nomad, a foreigner, a stranger? Yet that is the essence of the passage recited when bringing first-fruits: a declaration that we are strangers in the land, and therefore what we bring to God belongs to Him, and not to us. Ibn Ezra and Rashbam raised several possibilities regarding the identity of the "Aramean nomad," but both agreed on the conceptual meaning, which emphasizes that dwelling in Israel is dependent on God:

> The likely explanation is that the Aramean is Jacob, as if it said: When my father was in Aram, he was lost, that is, poor and without money.... For I did not inherit the land from my father, he being poor when he came to Aram, and he was also a sojourner in Egypt, and he was also of small numbers, and later he returned with a great people. And You, O Lord, took us out of bondage, and gave us this goodly land.
>
> (Ibn Ezra, Deuteronomy 26:5)

> Abraham was the Aramean, lost and exiled from the land of Aram.... that is to say, our forefathers came to this land from a foreign country, and the Holy One, blessed be He, gave it to us.
>
> (Rashbam, Deuteronomy 26:5)

The same perception is also the basis of the laws pertaining to the Sabbatical and Jubilee years, as well as the laws of tithes: The land belongs not to us, but to God:

> The land shall not be sold forever; for the land is Mine; for you are strangers and sojourners with Me.
>
> (Leviticus 25:23)

Let us conclude this discussion with the piercing words of the Shelah, Rabbi Yeshaya Horowitz:

> One who lives in the land of Israel must always keep in mind the name Canaan, which denotes servitude and submission (*hakhna'a*).... On the contrary, in the land which God cares

> for, one must be more of a servant and more submissive. As King David, may he rest in peace, says: "I am a stranger in the land." That is to say: I make myself more of a stranger in the holy land.... The rule that emerges: Those who live in the land [of Israel] must live in submission, like strangers; they must not see themselves as living in a strong dwelling place.
>
> (*Shenei Luchot ha-Brit* II, 11)

Divine Contraction

There is another fundamental idea regarding the land of Israel that finds expression in Scripture. Even though God is sovereign Lord of the entire universe, Israel is His unique and outstanding portion. This idea is reiterated many times throughout Scripture. Thus, for example, the tribes that settled in western Israel said to the tribes that settled on the eastern side of the Jordan:

> However, if the land of your possession be unclean, then pass over to the land of the possession of the Lord, where the Lord's tabernacle dwells, and take possession among us; but rebel not against the Lord, nor rebel against us, in building an altar for yourselves besides the altar of the Lord our God.
>
> (Joshua 22:19)

King David expressed the same idea:

> For they have driven me out this day from being joined to the inheritance of the Lord [i.e., the land of Israel], saying, Go, serve other gods.
>
> (I Samuel 26:19)

Modern scholars see this as a remnant of ancient idolatry, which restricted the realm of each god to the borders of a particular country. Ezekiel Kaufmann dismissed their arguments:

> Monotheism teaches that there is but one God in the world,

> creator and master of the entire universe, and therefore, of necessity, "universal" in the cosmic sense. However, monotheism is not bound in any essential way to the idea that the one God reveals Himself to all people in equal measure, or that He extends His grace to all of them in the same way....
>
> God rules over all the lands, He acts in Sodom, in Shinar, in Egypt, in Nineveh, in Tarsus, and in all places. But His cultic sanctity He gathered into one land, the place where He is to be worshipped.
>
> (Kaufmann, *Toledot ha-Emuna ha-Yisre'elit*, pp. 613–616)

Rabbi Chasdai Crescas argues that God reveals Himself everywhere in equal measure, so we are not dealing here with a decision on God's part to reveal His Presence in one particular country. But because of the unique qualities of Israel, its inhabitants are specially prepared to reveal and give expression to God's providence:

> As for whether there is more providence in one place than in another, many verses in the Torah indicate that there is a great difference between places.... What must be explained is the reason for this difference in providence between places, if God relates to all of them in the same way. This is not difficult to explain. Even if God relates to all places in the same manner, if those over whom He extends His providence do not relate in the same manner, there will perforce be a difference in the providence.... this explains why in different places there will be a difference in the preparations necessary for true service, such as abstinence and seclusion. This is for heavenly and terrestrial reasons, as alluded to by the Sages, that Israel is unique to the point that they knew by tradition that prophecy rests only in Israel.
>
> (*Or ha-Shem*, *ma'amar* II, 2, chap. 6)

The Uniqueness of the Land of Israel

What is the uniqueness of the Land of Israel, and why was it chosen over all other countries? Many Jewish thinkers did not treat this question at all. Others, however, have suggested a variety of answers.

During certain periods, rational explanations prevailed, referring to the climatic or other such advantages of the land of Israel. Thus, for example, the author of the *Keli Yakar* writes:

> And similarly, the Holy Land is home to peaceful harmony because of its combination of opposites and because it is midway between cold and heat, it being the center of the world and having the middle climate and elevation among the seven climates and elevations, as the verse states: "Beautiful in elevation, the joy of the whole earth" (Psalms 48:3). The mixing of cold and heat corresponds to the quality of peaceful harmony.
>
> (*Ollelot Ephraim* 1, p. 67)

Jewish scholars of the early modern period adopted this position with some modifications:

> So, too, the land of Israel, called Canaan from time immemorial, is distinguished in its merits and qualities over all other lands.... Physical features that distinguish it from all the neighboring countries affect not only its yield and produce, but also the traits of the people living therein.... The winds that blow from the mountains and the ocean blend the air, and therefore the climate of Israel is good, bringing good health to the body.
>
> (Graetz, *Sefer Divrei Yemei Yisra'el*, 1, p. 9)

The English Christian scholar and traveler Henry Baker Tristram felt that the variety of climates and terrains found in Israel had made it a universal focal point:

> This land, which was chosen as the place where God revealed Himself to man and the cradle of the faith that was to spread

> across the entire world, has two impressive qualities: First, there is nothing romantic in its terrain – nothing to shock the imagination or reinforce superstition; and second, the amazing variety of climate, terrain, and yield.... It would have been impossible to find a more fitting place to provide parables for the book...to teach the truth to the peoples of the entire world, from the tropics to the polar regions.
>
> (H.B. Tristram, *The Land of Israel: A Journal of Travels*)

A famous midrash emphasizes not the geographical characteristics of Israel, but its culture:

> When Abraham was traveling through Aram Naharayyim and Aram Nachor, he saw its inhabitants eating and drinking and reveling. "May my portion not be in this country!" he exclaimed. But when he reached the promontory of Zoar and saw them engaged in weeding and hoeing in the proper seasons, he exclaimed: "Would that my portion might be in this country!" Said the Holy One, blessed be He, to him: "Unto your seed have I given this land" (Genesis 15:18).
>
> (Genesis Rabba 39:8)

This midrash does not seem to recognize any unique qualities of Israel other than the culture that developed there. One might argue, however, that the unique qualities of the Land of Israel led to its cultural development in this direction.

Those with a mystical bent have adopted an entirely different approach. Thus, for example, writes Rabbi Solomon Alkabetz:

> Just as some countries yield more agricultural produce than others, and some countries produce more silver, gold, and precious stones than others, so, too, all types of perfection flow from this country. Therefore, it is called "the city of justice," because justice grows there, as do other types of perfection. The sanctity of the land is not like that of other lands; it also has a

> divine element.... Those who reside in its pure air will day and night be surrounded by holy things.
>
> (*Brit ha-Levi*, *Teshuva*, Third principle, 41)

Rabbi Yehuda Halevi was one of the founding fathers of this approach. Halevi understood that the uniquely miraculous qualities of the land of Israel prepare it for the influence of divine revelation:

> You will have no difficulty in perceiving that one country may have higher qualifications than others. There are places in which particular plants, metals, or animals are found.... Priority belongs, in the first instance, to the people which, as stated before, constitute the essence and kernel [of the nations]. In the second instance, it would belong to the country, on account of the religious acts connected with it, which I would compare to the cultivation of the vineyard. No other place would share the distinction of the divine influence, just as no other mountain might be able to produce good wine.
>
> (*Kuzari* 1, 10–12)

A direct continuation of Halevi's approach may be found in the famous statement of Rabbi Abraham Isaac Kook:

> The land of Israel is not a superficial element, a possession external to [the essence] of the nation, merely a means to the goal of [establishing] a comprehensive union and fortifying its material, or even its spiritual, existence. The land of Israel is an essential element connected by way of a living bond to the nation, attached through its inner qualities to its essence.
>
> (*Orot*)

Rabbi Halevi and Rabbi Kook emphasize two points: (1) the mystical uniqueness of *Land of Israel*, and (2) the harmony it enjoys with the inner qualities of the people of Israel.

On the mystical plane, many formulations of the uniqueness of the Israel have been proposed: Only Israel is watched over by God Himself and not by His angels; Israel is closely connected to the gates of heaven; and so on. This feeling was shared by some nonobservant Jews, like the socialist pioneer A.D. Gordon:

> It seems that here [i.e., in the land of Israel], the entire essence of the divine profusion that flows from all the worlds into the soul of man, and especially into the soul of the Jew, is altogether dissimilar, entirely different from [that found] in the lands of the Diaspora. In the language of the soul – and only in the language of the soul – I would say that the essence of the infinite, the essence of truth, sanctity, beauty, might, the essence of all the spheres, is acquired here by the soul in a different manner, in a different way, and absorbed in different combinations.
>
> (Gordon, *Mivchar Ketavim*, p. 203)

Prof. Yehuda Elitzur developed an entirely different approach, raising an interesting idea connected to the issues discussed at the beginning of this chapter. Elitzur held that the verses in Deuteronomy that emphasize the constant dependency of the land of Israel on the will of God with respect to rain are an example of a more general principle: Israel is the land of providence, one that God seeks out at all times. From a political perspective as well, Israel is situated between world empires, and the fate of its inhabitants is always dependent upon God. In the land of Israel the feeling of dependency grows stronger.

> Why were you brought to this land? Because here you are dependent upon divine providence. This is Scripture's definition, stated in the lofty and poetic style that characterizes it. Had we asked an old-time Jew for his definition, his answer would have been: This is a land where one can only survive on miracles.
>
> (Elitzur, *Yisra'el ve-ha-Mikra*, pp. 276–277)

Prof. Elitzur's view is quite profound: The land of Israel was chosen from among all countries precisely because, from all perspectives, continued existence in that country is at all times dependent upon the grace of God. Climactically, politically, economically – it is the feeling of insecurity and utter dependence that sets the land of Israel apart. Those who live in Israel are in greater need of heaven's mercy than the inhabitants of any other country.

Reasons for the Commandments

The first *mitzva* given to the Jewish people was the *mitzva* of circumcision, given to the patriarch Abraham in *Parashat Lekh Lekha.* In this chapter we shall deal with the reasons for the *mitzvot* in general, and afterwards with the reasons for the *mitzva* of circumcision in particular.

Do the *Mitzvot* Have Reasons?

We begin with the question of whether the *mitzvot* do in fact have reasons. What exactly are we asking? In order to properly understand the problem, let us turn to a famous passage from Plato's *Euthyphro.*

> *Socrates:* Consider this question: Is what is pious loved by the gods because it is pious, or is it pious because it is loved?
> *Euthyphro:* I don't understand what you mean, Socrates.
> *Socrates:* Well, I will try to explain more clearly....
> *Socrates:* And what do you say of piety, Euthyphro: Is not piety, according to your definition, loved by all the gods?
> *Euthyphro:* Yes.
> *Socrates:* Just because it is pious, or for some other reason?

> *Euthyphro:* No, because it is pious.
> *Socrates:* So it is loved because it is pious, not pious because it is loved?

Plato is raising a fundamental question: Does a religious worldview leave room for morality and good as independent standards? Plato formulates the problem as follows: Does God desire good because it is good, or is something good because God desires it? In other words, do good and evil exist independently of God, and God chooses that which is good; Or perhaps there is no such thing as independent good, and the term "good" merely represents that which God has arbitrarily chosen?[1]

According to the second possibility, there is no inherent difference between the morning prayer service and murder. Neither act is good or evil in and of itself. The sole difference between them is that God chose the one and not the other, but He could just as well have chosen in the opposite manner.

This question leads directly to the issue of whether the *mitzvot* have reasons. If good and evil exist independently of God, then the *mitzvot* may have reasons. But if good and evil have no independent existence, God's commandments are arbitrary, having no rhyme or reason. According to this understanding, "piety is piety" solely because "it is loved by the gods."

The question raised by Plato has no simple answer from a religious perspective. On the one hand, it is difficult to say that good exists independently of God's will, for that would seem to mean that God is subordinate to something outside Himself. On the other hand, it is no less difficult to assert that good and evil do not exist, and that God charges us with arbitrary commands.

Both approaches find expression in Christianity and Islam. In Judaism, however, the first approach, which recognizes an objective good, enjoys striking dominance, and it is difficult to find

1. According to the extreme versions of this position, God is subordinate neither to logic nor to the "truth," and His actions are absolutely arbitrary.

arguments in favor of the second approach.[2] This may, perhaps, be due to the fact that the book of Genesis early on presents us with an unequivocal stand on this issue in the dialogue between Abraham and God regarding Sodom (18:20–32), which we shall discuss more fully later in this book.

One cardinal point stands out in Abraham's aforementioned exchange with God: Abraham assumes that God acts according to moral criteria, and furthermore, that God's moral criteria are understandable to man. The argument might have been made that absolute standards of good and evil do in fact exist, but are incomprehensible to man. Abraham, however, does not accept this. He approaches God with a moral claim: "Shall not the Judge of all the earth do right?" And God does not reject Abraham's contention, He accepts it. This incident is the primary source for the Jewish position that assumes the existence of an absolute moral good not determined arbitrarily by God.

An alternative position may be proposed, one that denies the existence of reasons for the *mitzvot.* While the commandments as a whole may have a reason, it does not necessarily follow that there is a specific rationale for each and every *mitzva.* There are two possible reasons for the existence of the system of *mitzvot*: (1)

---

2. See, however, the words of the Admor of Piasetzno: "Now the nations of the world, even the best of them, think that truth exists independently, and that God commanded the truth because in and of itself it is true.... This is in contrast with Israel, who say: You are the God of truth; He, may He be blessed, is truth, and there is no truth outside Him. All the truth in the world is [true] only because so God commanded and willed. Since He, may He be blessed, is truth, therefore this, too, is truth. One is forbidden to steal because the God of truth so commanded. Because of the command of the true God, this is true as well. But when God commands the opposite – that property declared by a court to be ownerless is ownerless – then that becomes the truth, that this person's property is ownerless. And when God commanded our father, Abraham, to bind up his son Isaac [as an offering], then it was the truth to bind him. Had He not said to him afterwards, Do nothing to him, it would have been the truth to slaughter him" (*Eish Kodesh*, p. 68). The Admor of Piasetzno's position cannot be detached from his experiences during the Holocaust; at that time, any attempt to explain God's ways seemed groundless.

the subjugation of man and deepening of his submission to God; (2) the intensification of man's sense of connection to God in all areas of life, and anchoring it in specific actions. God does not act arbitrarily, and these two reasons explain why He instituted the system of *mitzvot*. Major significance, however, may not be attached to the specific content of each and every *mitzva*, but only to the system as a whole. God could just as well have ordered us to don *tefillin* on our feet, because the most important thing is the fact that we are fulfilling God's will.[3] This position was proposed by the author of the *Yefe To'ar* commentary to the Midrash:

> If you see *mitzvot* which seem not to have a rationale, such as slaughtering an animal at the throat and not at the neck, know that the words of God are pure, and come to purify man, and test whether he will obey Him or not, and to provide reward for those who observe His word, so that it will provide protection to all who trust in it. For even the *mitzvot* that lack a reason have a reason. For the Holy One, blessed be He, commanded them in order that man should cleave to Him and always remember that it is God who orders and commands them to perform [the *mitzvot*].
>
> (*Yefe To'ar*, Genesis Rabba 44, 1)

3. A general reason of this sort clearly exists, but the simple understanding is that it is in addition to the specific rationale of the *mitzva*. C.S. Lewis proposed such an idea in *The Problem of Pain* (Glasgow, 1981), pp. 88–89. See also Ramchal: "He fulfills thereby His desire in two ways, the one following from the other. That is to say, he fulfills His desire in that He had commanded him to perform this act and he does so, and second, through this act he perfects himself [through the acquisition] of one of the levels of perfection which results from this *mitzva*" (*Derekh ha-Shem* I, chap. 4, 7). And similarly R. Joseph Albo: "About this [the Sages] said: 'Greater is he who acts having been commanded than one who acts not having been commanded.' For one who acts having been commanded accomplishes two thing when he performs the *mitzva* properly: first, he does what is truly good and just; and second, he intends to do the will of his Father in heaven. But he who acts without having been commanded does so only because it is just, but for no other reason" (*Book of Principles* II, chap. 28).

The scope of the *mitzvot* to which he is referring is unclear.[4] In any event, according to the classic Jewish position, individual *mitzvot* do have specific reasons. A clear example of the Jewish attitude may be found in what Maimonides says about the reasons for the *mitzvot*:

> There is a group of human beings who consider it a grievous thing that causes should be given for any law; what would please them most is that the intellect would not find a meaning for the commandments and prohibitions. What compels them to feel thus is a sickness that they find in their souls, a sickness to which they are unable to give utterance and of which they cannot furnish a satisfactory account. For they think that if those laws were useful in this existence and had been given to us for this or that reason, it would be as if they derived from the reflection and the understanding of some intelligent being. If, however, there is a thing for which the intellect could not find any meaning at all and that does not lead to something useful, it undoubtedly derives from God; for the reflection of man would not lead to such a thing. It is as if, according to these people of weak intellect, man were more perfect than his Maker; for man speaks and acts in a manner that leads to some intended end; whereas the deity does not act thus, but commands us to do things that are not useful to us and forbids us to do things that are not harmful to us. But He is far exalted above this; the contrary is the case.... [o]n the basis of its dictum: "For our good always, that He might preserve us alive, as it is this day" (Deuteronomy 6:24). And it says: "Which shall hear all these statutes (*chukkim*) and say: Surely this great community is a wise and understanding people" (Deuteronomy 4:6). Thus

4. Maimonides himself brings the issue of slaughtering at the throat or at the back of the neck as an example of a particular *mitzva* that has no rationale, as opposed to the *mitzva* of slaughter itself, which has a rationale. The *Yefe To'ar* implies otherwise, for he does not distinguish between the *mitzva* itself and its particulars.

> it states explicitly that even all the statutes (*chukkim*) will show to all the nations that they have been given with wisdom and understanding. Now if there is a thing for which no reason is known and that does not either procure something useful or ward off something harmful, why should one say of one who believes in it or practices it that he is wise and understanding and of great worth? And why should the religious communities think it a wonder? Rather things are indubitably as we have mentioned: every one of these six hundred and thirteen commandments exists either with a view to communicating a correct opinion, or to putting an end to an unhealthy opinion, or to communicating a rule of justice, or to warding off an injustice, or to endowing men with a noble moral quality, or to warning them against an evil moral quality.
>
> (*Guide of the Perplexed* II, 31)

Rabbenu Sa'adya Gaon delineated two classes of *mitzvot*: those required by reason (*sikhliyot*) and those practiced solely due to revelation (*shim'iyot*). The second category consists of "things neither the approval nor the disapproval of which is decreed by reason, on account of their own character, but in regard to which our Lord has imposed upon us a profusion of commandments and prohibitions in order thereby to increase our reward and happiness." But "nevertheless, one cannot help noting, upon deeper reflection, that they have some partial uses as well as a certain slight justification from the point of view of reason" (*Book of Doctrines and Beliefs* II, 1). Maimonides, however, disagreed, emphasizing that even *chukkim* ("statutes") demonstrate wisdom and understanding.

Earlier, we mentioned the possibility that a reason may exist for the *mitzvot* as a whole, but not for each particular *mitzva*. Maimonides adopts an intermediate position. A specific reason exists for every *mitzva*, but not necessarily for every particular of any given *mitzva*:

> But no cause will ever be found for the fact that one particular

> sacrifice consists in a lamb and another in a ram and that the number of the victims should be one particular number. Accordingly, in my opinion, all those who occupy themselves with finding causes for something of these particulars are stricken with a prolonged madness.
>
> (*Guide of the Perplexed* II, 26)

According to Maimonides, there are no reasons for the particulars of the *mitzvot*. If this is so, why then, according to Maimonides, are the particulars at all necessary? If there is no reason, why must we offer a lamb rather than a ram, and why didn't God simply command us to sacrifice an animal? Maimonides answers: "In order to refine mankind through them."

It is here that the arguments and principles raised earlier enter into the picture: establishing an awareness of submission to God and anchoring the general ideas in specific actions, thus ensuring that they become deeply implanted in man's consciousness. The particulars of a *mitzva* are necessary in order to intensify the *mitzva*'s effect upon our lives, particularly with respect to the assimilation of the awareness of obligation and submission. For this purpose, it is of no consequence whether, in and of themselves, the particulars are arbitrary.

The approach taken by the Kabbalists is the exact opposite of this. They maintain that each and every particular of every *mitzva* has mystical and metaphysical meaning. Maharal strongly objected to Maimonides' stance on this issue:

> And there is certainly no justification for this explanation, for it is about the entire Torah that the verse states: "And what nation is there so great, that has statutes and judgments so righteous, as all this Torah?" (Deuteronomy 4:8); and it says: "Keep them therefore and do them; for this is your wisdom and your understanding in the sight of the nations, who shall hear all these statutes [and say, Surely this great nation is a wise and understanding people]" (ibid., v. 6). Surely, then, every matter

> in the Torah, general rule as well as particular, are all words of wisdom. And it is not as he [Maimonides] thought, that the particulars have no reason whatsoever, for that would not be a Torah of wisdom.
>
> (*Tiferet Yisra'el*, chap. 7)

In great measure, we are dealing here with a disagreement between rationalists and those who recognize the limitations of reason. The more we rely on the intellect as a tool for understanding the reasons for the *mitzvot*, the more we are inclined to give up on reasons for their particulars, for it is indeed difficult to find logical rationales for them.[5]

Is It Desirable to Seek the Reasons for the *Mitzvot*?

The prevalent position in Judaism is that *mitzvot* do in fact have reasons. But now another question arises: Should we search out the reasons? We know that seeking out the reasons for the *mitzvot* was quite acceptable to the sages of Israel, starting with the great Sages, through the *Rishonim*, and down to the most recent *Acharonim*. Maimonides explicitly encourages believers to ponder the reasons for the *mitzvot*:

> It is fitting for man to meditate upon the laws of the holy Torah and to comprehend their full meaning to the extent of his ability. Nevertheless, a law for which he finds no reason and understands no cause should not be trivial in his eyes.
>
> (*Hilkhot Me'ila* 8:8)

We shall return later to this statement and consider it in its entirety. What interests us now is the assertion that it is fitting to

5. Compare also to Rabbi Yehuda Halevi's *Kuzari* 1, 99. The main point of the *Kuzari* lies in the recognition of the limits of logic, and so it is not surprising that Rabbi Yehuda Halevi claims that there are reasons for the particulars of the *mitzvot*.

occupy oneself in the reasons for the *mitzvot*. Why is so much importance attached to searching for the reasons of the *mitzvot*? We can suggest two answers: (1) Occupation with the reasons for the *mitzvot* can stir up religious enthusiasm and spiritual motivation. This refers primarily to motivation and enthusiasm to observe the *mitzvot* whose rationales are being uncovered, but also to excitement with respect to the worship of God in general. The better we understand the light and wisdom embodied in the *mitzvot*, the more our excitement and joy in the Torah and the worship of God will grow.[6] (2) The study of the reasons for the *mitzvot* can teach us important conceptual principles. Occupying ourselves with the reasons for the *mitzvot* can lead us to an understanding of God's will and of the basic values to which He is directing us.[7]

We have seen that Maimonides encourages students to search out the reasons for the commandments. Rabbi Yehuda Halevi takes a more nuanced approach. His description of the reasons for the *mitzvot* relating to the Temple concludes with the following:

> I do not, by any means, assert that the purpose of the service is the order expounded by me. On the contrary, it entails something more secret and elevated. And I say that it is God's Torah. He who innocently accepts it without scrutiny or argument is better off than he who investigates and analyzes. He, however, who steps down from the highest level to scrutiny, does well

6. Rabbi Chayyim Volozhiner writes in a similar vein: "He who God, blessed be His name, allowed him to comprehend the esoteric aspects of our holy Torah.... [i]t is only for the purpose that each person, in accordance with his intellect and understanding, should contemplate how far-reaching are the particulars of his actions, words, and thoughts, and all his affairs in the upper and lower worlds. And he should be amazed and stirred by this to act and fulfill every *mitzva*, and every aspect of his service of the Creator, blessed be His name, should be done with the utmost precision, with great fear and dread and love, and with holiness and purity of heart" (*Nefesh ha-Chayyim*, *sha'ar* 1, chap. 22).

7. For a summary of the advantages of studying the reasons for the *mitzvot* according to Maimonides, see I. Twersky, *Halakha ve-Hagut* 1 (Tel Aviv, 5755), pp. 31–33.

> to seek the reasons for these matters that are founded upon divine wisdom, instead of abandoning them to evil opinions and doubts which lead man to perdition.
>
> (*Kuzari* I, 26)

Maimonides finds religious value in the search for the reasons of the *mitzvot* because they can clarify the moral and spiritual foundations of the worship of God and enhance one's religious commitment and enthusiasm. Rabbi Yehuda Halevi does not accept this approach. He says that studying the reasons for the *mitzvot* is only necessary as a prophylactic cure for heresy. Those whose faith is unblemished have no need to investigate the reasons for the *mitzvot*. That is only necessary for the weak in faith, who must be reminded why the *mitzvot* have value and meaning. Rabbi Yehuda Halevi says further that we are incapable of uncovering the true reason for any *mitzva*. We can, at most, speak of different layers of reasons, only the outermost of which we manage to understand.

It is not clear whether these two arguments are connected. Perhaps Rabbi Yehuda Halevi feels that there is no value in searching for the reasons of the *mitzvot* primarily because we will not succeed in fully understanding their rationales.

The fear that we may misunderstand the reasons for God's commandments is a significant concern. If we hope to infer spiritual and ideological principles from the *mitzvot*, then a mistake can be of great significance. And if we think that there is little chance of hitting upon God's true reasons, then perhaps the entire effort is superfluous and devoid of meaning. Even if, in the end, we decide to try to understand the reasons for the *mitzvot*, we must certainly exercise extreme caution. This care should express itself in the method we use to derive the reason from the commandment, as well as in our awareness that any rationale we come up with is merely a conjecture.

The Sages raise an altogether different concern about whether it is advisable to inquire into the reasons for the commandments.

> Why were the rationales of the Torah not revealed? For surely regarding two passages where reasons were given, the greatest man in the world stumbled. It is written: "Neither shall he multiply wives to himself, [that his heart not turn away]" (Deuteronomy 17:17). Solomon said: I will take many [wives], but not turn away. And it is written: "For it came to pass, when Solomon was old, that his wives turned away his heart" (1 Kings 11:4). And it is written: "But he shall not multiply horses to himself, [nor cause the people to return to Egypt]" (Deuteronomy 17:16). Solomon said: I will take many [horses], but not cause [the people] to return. And it is written: "And a chariot went out of Egypt" (1 Kings 10:29).
>
> (*Sanhedrin* 21a)

The Sages point here to the danger that our commitment to a *mitzva* may be undermined if we learn its rationale. A person who knows the rationale for a *mitzvah* may regard it as the reason for his commitment to observe the *mitzva*. This leads to the practical concern that he will be lenient regarding the *mitzva* or change it in accordance with his understanding. We see what happened to Solomon, when he thought that the reason for the *mitzva* did not apply. He became the classic proof for the extent to which the reason for the *mitzva* is still valid.

This is not only a practical concern but a spiritual one, too. Even if a person does not actually change the way he observes a particular *mitzva*, his sense that he is fulfilling the *mitzva* not because of a commitment to God, but because he recognizes its value and benefit, entails a great spiritual flaw. The Tur alludes to this concern:

> As for the prohibition against shaving the corners of one's

> beard, Maimonides said about this as well that it is forbidden by Scripture because the idolaters acted in this manner. This, however, is not explicit, and we need not look for a reason for the *mitzvot*. For they are like royal decrees, even if we do not know their reasons.
>
> (Tur, *Yore De'a* 181)

When a person delves into the reasons for the *mitzvot*, there is grave concern that he will observe the *mitzvot* only because he identifies with them and feels at ease performing them. It is difficult to think of one who does this as serving God. The Chatam Sofer clearly identified this concern (after having also explained at length the practical concern about halakhic rulings based on false reasons):

> For we observe God's statutes and teachings as statutes without reasons, the Torah being the decree of the King, may His name be blessed. Even if a person observes the entire Torah and all the commandments as he is required, if in his heart he does so for some particular reason, it is not received by God with favor.
>
> (*Derashot ha-Chatam Sofer* 1, p. 19b)

We are required to observe the *mitzvot*, not because we identify with them, but because God has commanded us to do so.

How can these two concerns be overcome? The Sages differentiate two types of *mitzvot*:

> Our Rabbis taught: "You shall keep my judgments" (Leviticus 18:4) – matters that had they not been written should have been written: idolatry, illicit sexual relations, murder, theft, and blasphemy; "and you shall keep my statutes (*chukkim*)" – matters that Satan argues against [and the nations of the world argue against], such as eating pig, wearing garments made of a mixture of wool and linen, *halitza*, a leper's purification, and

> the sent-away goat. You might say these are meaningless acts. Therefore the verse states: "I am the Lord": I am the Lord who enacted them, you have no right to criticize them.
>
> (*Yoma* 67b)

Part of the Torah – the "statutes" (*chukkim*) – is very hard and, perhaps, impossible to explain. As we shall see, the *Rishonim* taught that this does not mean that the statutes are devoid of reason, but only that the reasons for them are beyond our understanding. The Sages have said (*Yoma* 14a) that even King Solomon, the wisest of all men, declared about the *mitzva* of the red heifer: "I said I will be wise; but it was far from me" (Ecclesiastes 7:23). The statutes have great educational value; they diminish the concern that learning the rationales of the *mitzvot* will create a connection between the reason for the *mitzva* and one's commitment to observe it. Rav Yehuda Amital was once asked at a seminar for *ba'alei teshuva* which *mitzvot* a newly observant person should observe first, if he feels that he is incapable of accepting all the *mitzvot* at once. Rav Amital answered (following Rashi's comment on the *mitzvot* commanded to Israel at Mara; Exodus 15:25) that the newly observant person should choose one *mitzva* pertaining to the relationship between man and his fellow, such as honoring one's parents, one *mitzva* pertaining to the relationship between man and God, such as Shabbat, and one *mitzva* regarding which there is no presumption whatsoever that we understand the rationale, such as *kashrut* or family purity. An observant Jew must know from the outset that he will not be able to understand every *mitzva*.

We have spoken about the danger that a person will observe the *mitzvot* only because of their reasons. The Talmud also draws our intention to the reverse danger, namely, that a person who has learned the reasons for some commandments will come to treat lightly the other *mitzvot* whose reasons he does not understand. Thus, instead of the statutes influencing a person's attitude towards the judgments, the judgments will fashion his attitude towards the statutes. There is a danger that a person will scorn the *mitzvot* whose rationales he is unable to uncover. The Talmud therefore emphasizes: "'I am the Lord': I am the Lord who enacted them, you have no right to criticize them."

When a person succeeds in uncovering a satisfying reason for a particular *mitzva*, the danger exists that he will view the reason as the source of the obligation, and may even refrain from observing the *mitzva* in situations where he thinks that the reason does not apply. If fails to find a reason, the danger exists that he will scorn the *mitzva*. This argument, however, goes in two directions. It is possible to say that the danger arises when a person searches for a reason but fails to find one, and therefore it is preferable not to engage in the investigation. But it is also possible that it is precisely occupation with the reasons for the *mitzvot* that will save a person from this danger, for thus he will learn that most of the *mitzvot* have a comprehensible reason.

Maimonides was also aware of this danger. On the one hand, he encourages us to study the reasons for the *mitzvot* and try to understand them; on the other hand, he is aware of the danger of scorning *mitzvot* whose rationales have not been uncovered, and he struggles with this danger:

> It is fitting for man to meditate upon the laws of the holy Torah and to comprehend their full meaning to the extent of his ability. Nevertheless, a law for which he finds no reason and understands no cause should not be trivial in his eyes. Let him not break through to come up against the Lord, lest the Lord break forth upon him (Exodus 19:24). Nor should his thoughts concerning these things be like his thoughts concerning profane matters. Come and consider how strict the Torah was in the law of trespass! Now if sticks and stones and earth and ashes became hallowed by words alone, as soon as the name of the Master of the universe was invoked upon them, and anyone who comported with them as with a profane thing committed trespass and required atonement even if he had acted

> unwittingly, how much more should man be on guard not to rebel against a commandment decreed for us by the Holy One, blessed be He, only because he does not understand the reason; or to heap words that are not right against the Lord; or to regard the commandments the same way he regards ordinary affairs. Surely it is stated in the Torah: "Therefore shall you keep all My statutes, and all my judgments, and do them" (Leviticus 19:37). The Sages said: To give keeping and doing to the statutes as to the judgments. Doing is known, namely, that he should do the statutes. And keeping – that he be watchful regarding them, and not imagine that they are inferior to the judgments.
>
> (*Hilkhot Me'ila* 8:8)

Let us summarize the problems and dangers connected with searching out rationales for the *mitzvot*: (1) violation of religious innocence; (2) mistaken understanding of the true reason for the *mitzva*; (3) disregarding a *mitzva* when the supposed reason seems not to apply; (4) observance of the *mitzvot* because of their value and meaning, and not because of the divine command; and (5) making light of *mitzvot* that have no apparent rationale.

We have also seen ways to confront these problems. The bottom line is that many Torah giants have occupied themselves with the rationales for the *mitzvot*, and therefore it seems apparent that the potential benefits outweigh the possible dangers.

What Type of Reason?

Having concluded that the *mitzvot* do indeed have rationales and that it is fitting for us to discuss them, we face a new question: What type of reasons do the *mitzvot* have? Theoretically, the reasons could be social, ritual, mystical, psychological, or whatever. Of course, we cannot discuss here all the different ideas on the nature of the reasons for the *mitzvot*, but we shall try to address several pivotal questions. It is also reasonable to distinguish between different kinds of commandments, some having reasons of one type and others having reasons of another type.

Do the *Mitzvot* Benefit God or Man?

We shall quote here at great length from Nachmanides' classic discussion of the *mitzva* of setting the mother bird free before taking the eggs or chicks:

> "If a bird's nest chances to be before you" (Deuteronomy 22:6). This, too, is a commandment explained by the prohibition "You shall not kill it [the dam] and its young both in one day" (Leviticus 22:28). For the reason for both [commandments] is that we should not have a cruel heart and be without compassion. Or it may be that Scripture does not allow us to uproot a species altogether, though it permits slaughter [for food] within that species. And he who kills the dam and the young on the same day or takes them when they are free to fly [is regarded] as if he destroys that species.
>
> Now, the Rabbi [Maimonides] wrote in the *Guide of the Perplexed* (III, 48) that the reason for the commandment to release the mother bird when taking its nest and the prohibition against killing the dam with its young on the same day is to warn us not to kill the young in front of the mother, for animals feel great pain in such situations. There is no difference between the distress of man and the distress of animals for their young, because a mother's love and tenderness to her offspring are not the result of reason or speech, but are produced by the faculty of mental images which exists among animals just as in man.... [The foregoing is Maimonides' view.]
>
> It is more correct [to explain them as prohibitions] to prevent us from practicing cruelty.
>
> And the Rabbi [Maimonides] also said: "Do not raise an objection against me from what the Sages say: 'He who says in his prayer: Even to a bird's nest do Your mercies extend' [we silence him, for he treats the ordinances of God like acts of mercy,

whereas they are merely decrees]" (*Berakhot* 33b), for that is one of two views, namely the view of the Sage who maintains that the commandments have no other reason but the will of the Creator. We, however, follow the second opinion that all commandments have a reason." And the Rabbi raised an objection from what he found in Genesis Rabba [44:1], which states: "What difference does it make to the Holy One, blessed be He, whether an animal is slaughtered from the throat or from the back of the neck? Surely, the commandments were given only to refine man through them, as it is stated: 'Every word of God is refined' (Proverbs 30:5)."[8]

Now, this idea of the Rabbi's concerning the commandments, that they have a reason, is indeed very clear. There is a reason, benefit, and improvement for man in each of them, in addition to the reward from Him who commanded it, blessed be He....

But in my opinion, these aggadic statements presenting difficulty to the Rabbi[9] express the following idea: The benefit from the commandments is not derived by the Holy One Himself, blessed be He. Rather, the advantage is to man, to prevent him from suffering injury or some evil belief, or unfit character trait, or to recall the miracles and wonders of the Creator, blessed be He, in order to know God. This is what the Rabbis meant [when they said] that the commandments were given "to refine man," namely, so that he would become like refined silver. For he who refines silver does not act without purpose, but to remove all impurity therefrom. So, too, the commandments remove all evil beliefs from our hearts, and teach us the truth, so that we may remember it always....[10]

The Rabbis merely came to say that the benefit is not for

---

8. According to Maimonides, this midrash refers to the particulars of the *mitzvot*, and not to their general principles (*Guide of the Perplexed* II, 26).
9. Namely, the midrashim which seem to imply that the *mitzvot* are arbitrary and lack rationales.
10. Nachmanides ignores the possibility of a third explanation: that *mitzvot*

Him, exalted be He, that He needs the light of the *menora*, or that He needs the food of the offerings and the scent of the incense, as might appear from their simple meanings. Even regarding the memorial He made for His wonderful works, that He commanded us to perform in memory of the exodus from Egypt and the creation, the benefit is not for Him, but so that we should know the truth and merit to be worthy of His protection, for our mentioning and remembering of His wonders are regarded by Him as things of naught and vanity.

And the Midrash brought proof from [the law regarding] slaughter at the throat or the back of the neck, meaning to say that all the benefits are for us and not for the Holy One, blessed be He. For it is impossible to say concerning slaughter that there is more benefit and glory to the Creator, blessed be He, by cutting the throat than by cutting the back of the neck or by stabbing the animal. Rather, all these advantages are to us – to lead us in paths of compassion even at the time of slaughtering....

So, too, regarding what the Rabbis have stated: "Because he treats the ordinances of God like acts of mercy, whereas they are merely decrees" (*Berakhot* 33b). This means that it is not a matter of God's mercy extending to the bird's nest or the dam and its young, for His mercies do not extend so far into animal life as to prevent us from achieving our needs through them, for if so, He would have forbidden slaughter altogether.[11] But the reason for the prohibition is to teach us the trait of mercy and that we should not be cruel, for cruelty spreads in a man's soul, as it is known that butchers, those who slaughter large oxen and asses, are men of blood; and they that slaughter men are extremely cruel. It is on account of this [cruelty] that the

---

only have a general reason, namely acceptance of the yoke of Heaven, this being the "refinement."

11. It is not clear whether Nachmanides holds that animals do not suffer during slaughter or whether he maintains that God is not concerned about their suffering.

> Rabbis have said: "The most fit among butchers is a partner of Amalek" (*Kiddushin* 82a).
>
> We see then that these commandments with respect to cattle and fowl are not a matter of compassion upon them, but they are decrees given to us to guide us and to teach us good character traits. So, too, the Rabbis refer to all commandments of the Torah, positive and negative, as "decrees."
>
> (Commentary to Deuteronomy 22:6)

Maimonides had interpreted a midrashic statement as seemingly claiming that the *mitzvot* are arbitrary decrees, having no reasons whatsoever. Nachmanides explains that the midrash means to say that the purpose of the *mitzvot* is not to benefit God, but rather to improve us, men of flesh and blood, because God does not need the *mitzvot.*[12] Nachmanides argues this point forcefully, adducing many proofs. The idea that God needs the *mitzvot* is, however, very prominent in Kabbala, especially in the school of the Ari. (Rabbi Chayyim Volozhiner greatly developed this approach in his *Nefesh ha-Chayyim*, but he gave special emphasis to the educational significance, namely, the responsibility that such an idea places on man.) Anyone who before performing a *mitzva* recites the formula "*Le-shem Yichud*" ("for the sake of the unity of the Holy One, blessed be He, and His *Shekhina*") effectively believes that the *mitzva* is necessary for God. Even Nachmanides himself indicates that God's resting His *Shekhina* upon Israel was necessary not only for man but also for God Himself (Exodus 29:46). Here is what the kabbalist Rabbi Meir ben Gabbai said on this issue:

> For this is the ultimate goal of the toil of the perfect servant [of God], and toward it should he turn in all his efforts, and toward it should he direct himself in all his actions. He should

12. The central question is not whether the *mitzvot* are *beneficial* to us, but whether they are intended to have an *effect* upon us.

> strive to [fill] God's need, namely the unity mentioned above, and not his own need.
>
> (*Avodat ha-Kodesh*, introduction)

Obviously, the proponents of a more rationalistic religious outlook view this as a highly problematic position. It implies that God, as it were, is deficient and needs our help. Those who stress the element of fear in the service of God also have reservations about this position that are not connected to rationalism.

Do the *Mitzvot* Have a Psychological or a Real Effect?

In the course of his discussion, Nachmanides raises another significant question. According to Maimonides, the *mitzva* of setting the mother bird free has a concrete external goal – preventing the mother bird's suffering. Nachmanides suggests another possible concrete result – preventing the extermination of the species. He concludes, however, that the Torah is not concerned here with the birds; the objective of the *mitzva* is to enhance our sensitivity – to make us less cruel and more compassionate. We are dealing here with a fundamental question: are the *mitzvot* intended to improve the external world around us or the internal psychological world of the individual? Are the *mitzvot* directed outward or inward? Is the *mitzva* of charity intended to improve the condition of the poor or the morals and sensitivity of the rich? The difference between Maimonides and Nachmanides on this point is restricted to the *mitzva* of setting the mother bird free; there is no general dispute between them on the issue.

Spiritual Law or Halakhic Abstraction?

There is a fundamental disagreement about those *mitzvot* that fall into the category of *chukkim* ("statutes"), namely, *mitzvot* that are viewed as not based upon common sense. In this context, Rabbi Yehuda Halevi records a famous analogy:

> The conditions which render man fit to receive this divine

influence are not in the scope of human knowledge. It is impossible for him to gauge their quantity or quality, and even if he knew their essence, he would not know their time, place, composition, or manner of preparation. For all this, he needs divine knowledge, coming fully explained from God Himself.... But...such a person offers sacrifices and burns incense according to speculation and conjecture, not knowing the essence of what is needed for that purpose, or how much, in which way, in which place, at what time, by whom, in which manner, and many other details, the enumeration of which would take a very long time.

To what is this akin? To an ignoramus who enters the medicine chamber of a doctor who is known to all for his beneficial medications, at a time when the doctor is out. When he sees crowds of people congregating outside the chamber, seeking cures for their ailments, he begins to dispense medicines out of the vials, knowing nothing about the medications or the appropriate dosages for each person. Thus he kills people with the very medicines that could have cured them.

(*Kuzari* 1, 79)

Rabbi Yehuda Halevi sees the purpose of *chukkim* as directing divine influence in the world. The world is governed by spiritual laws that parallel the physical laws. The *mitzvot* are guidelines and principles that suit the spiritual laws that exist in the world.

In contrast, Rabban Yochanan ben Zakkai took a different approach to this question:

An idol worshipper once asked Rabban Yochanan ben Zakkai: "These rites that you perform seem like a kind of witchcraft. You bring a heifer, burn it, grind it, and take its ashes. If one of you contracts ritual impurity from a corpse you sprinkle upon him two or three drops and say to him: 'You are ritually pure.'" Rabban Yochanan asked him: "Have you ever been possessed by the demon of madness?" He said: "No." "Have you ever seen

> a man possessed by this demon of madness?" He answered: "Yes." "And what do you do for him?" He said: "We bring roots, and smoke them under him; then we sprinkle water upon the demon and it flees." Rabban Yochanan said to him: "Let your ears hear what your mouth speaks! Precisely so is this spirit a spirit of impurity; as it is written: 'And also I will cause the prophets and the impure spirit to pass out of the land' (Zechariah 13:2). Water of purification is sprinkled upon the unclean person and the spirit flees."
>
> When the idolater had gone, Rabban Yochanan's students said to him: "Master! This man you dismissed with a flimsy answer; what do you say to us?" He said to them: "By your life! It is not the dead that defiles nor the water that purifies! Rather, the Holy One, blessed be He, said: 'I have laid down a statute, I have issued a decree. You are not permitted to violate My decree.'" As it is written: "This is the statute (*chukkat*) of the law" (Numbers 19:2).
>
> (Numbers Rabba 19:8)

Rabban Yochanan ben Zakkai proposes an approach entirely different from Rabbi Yehuda Halevi's. The laws of ritual impurity constitute an area of Halakha that is perhaps best understood using the idea of spiritual laws. Yet even in this area, Rabban Yochanan ben Zakkai rejects such an understanding. Ritual purity and impurity have no spiritual significance as independent entities. To say that something is ritually impure is like saying that it is *muktze*: there is no ontological change in the article, no physical or spiritual change. The only thing that changes is its halakhic status.

Rabban Yochanan ben Zakkai does not explain the purpose or reason for the laws of ritual purity and impurity. In light of what we have seen above, there is no need, nor is it even reasonable, to assume that he is arguing that *mitzvot* have no rationales. Rabban Yochanan ben Zakkai is telling his disciples that we are dealing here with a halakhic abstraction which has no direct spiritual parallel ("it is not the dead that defiles, nor the water that purifies"), and whose reason is unknown to us. There is a reason – psychological, social, religious, or the like – but we do not know it.

There is one set of reasons that Rabban Yochanan ben Zakkai rejects, however – magical reasons, according to which the *mitzvot* have curative powers that blend in with the spiritual laws of the universe. It is very possible that he rejects such rationales on theological grounds, for they encroach upon God. Judaism shrinks from magic, and commands: "You shall be perfect with the Lord your God" (Deuteronomy 18:13). According to Rabban Yochanan ben Zakkai, it would be unreasonable for Judaism to deviate from this position precisely in the area of the *mitzvot*.

Two additional points are worthy of note. What stands out in the aforementioned story is the fact that Rabban Yochanan ben Zakkai's disciples immediately understood that their master had not given the heathen a serious answer. Many people in our own day would probably be persuaded by his argument, but this only demonstrates how the generations have declined. Similarly, many in our generation would probably see Rabban Yochanan ben Zakkai's response to his disciples as a "dismissal with a flimsy answer." His disciples, however, understood the depth of his answer – limited as it may be – and the shallowness of the detailed response to the heathen.

Mitzvot as Symbols

Rabbi Samson Raphael Hirsch argues that the *mitzvot* are symbols. The particulars of the various *mitzvot* convey a symbolic message, informing us of the spiritual and moral values that God wishes to bestow upon us. Our study of the *mitzvot* and their rationales clarifies the symbolic significance for us. Thus, for example, the obligation of wearing the ritual fringes (*tzitzit*) on four-cornered garments symbolizes, among other things, the blossoms (*tzitzim*) – the fruits and benefits – to be derived from doing God's will.

Prof. Shalom Rosenberg (*Be-Ikvot ha-Kuzari*, p. 181) notes the problematic nature of this position. According to Rabbi Hirsch, the *mitzvot* serve merely as a means of transferring speculative information. What is more, this is not even a particularly effective way of transferring such information, for most of the people who observe the *mitzvot* are oblivious to their rationales, and most of those who have in fact pondered their reasons have arrived at altogether different conclusions. Prof. Rosenberg argues that Rabbi Hirsch's proposal requires modification. He suggests that the symbolism of the *mitzvot* should be understood as directed not only at man's intellect, but at his emotions and subconscious. The *mitzvot* impart spiritual and moral values not only through intellectual study, but primarily through their subconscious effect on the personality.

According to this interpretation, the rationales for the *mitzvot* focus on their psychological effect on the individual observer, through symbols that give expression to spiritual values.

Historical Reason or Spiritual reason?

In *The Halakhic Mind*, Rabbi Joseph B. Soloveitchik states that the uniqueness of religion demands that we analyze it with its own tools, and not force upon religious research methodologies borrowed from other realms of knowledge. The title of his work faithfully reflects its primary objective: charting a path for the construction of a Jewish outlook based on Halakha. Rabbi Soloveitchik explains that Halakha is the objective norm that represents Judaism in the clearest and most faithful manner. Therefore, any attempt to construct a Jewish belief system must focus on an analysis of Halakha.

But how is it possible to extract from Halakha the value system upon which it is founded? Rabbi Soloveitchik deals with this question in the final chapters of his work. He distinguishes between two fundamental approaches: the causalistic or genetic approach, and the reconstructionist approach. Those who advocate the causalistic approach try to understand the development of religious institutions, beliefs, and laws, and the spiritual and conceptual background that shaped them. Rabbi Soloveitchik rejects this approach, and proposes in its place the method of reconstruction, whereby we take these "objective" religious facts as they are and try to understand what they tell us about the spiritual and conceptual principles of the religious person. As stated, Rabbi Soloveitchik claims that this methodology is particularly necessary in the realm of Halakha and understanding the reasons for the *mitzvot*.

Why does Rabbi Soloveitchik reject the causalistic approach? First of all, he says, because this method is highly speculative. It is very difficult, and perhaps even impossible, to uncover a causal connection in a realm that is so delicate, sensitive, and unstable. Who can guarantee that it was precisely this consciousness or that emotion that fashioned a particular *mitzva*? (*The Halakhic Mind*, p. 89). Human consciousness in general, and religious consciousness in particular, are so complex and complicated that any attempt to find systematic causality in them is extremely pretentious (pp. 95, 98).

In addition to the problem of the limitations of knowledge and cognition, Rabbi Soloveitchik raises another problem. The causalistic method tends to find causality within the realm of man's cognition – namely, causality that is sociological, historical, psychological, or the like (p. 98). Rabbi Soloveitchik does not deny that the origin of certain religious institutions and norms has a historical background; but he argues that this fact need not influence our assessment of their value in and of itself (p. 87).

Even when the causalistic method leads to an explanation of the value of a *mitzva*, the explanation remains in the realm of human values, be they moral, aesthetic, hygienic, or the like. Thus the autonomy of religion is denied, and it is subjugated to explanations from a different realm (p. 95). Against this approach, the religious realm is autonomous, and we should not seek moral or aesthetic rationales for religious norms (p. 90).

Rabbi Soloveitchik argues that it was precisely for this reason that the chapters dealing with the reasons for the commandments in Maimonides' *Guide of the Perplexed* never enjoyed widespread influence in the Jewish world. Maimonides' discussion adopted the causalistic method and attempted to explain *why* the *mitzvot* were legislated as they are. By choosing this method, the Maimonides was perforce drawn to historical-developmental explanations, and these, according to Rabbi Soloveitchik, "neither edify nor inspire the religious consciousness" (p. 92).

In contrast to this developmental-causalistic approach, Rabbi Soloveitchik proposes the method of reconstruction. This approach respects the autonomy of the religious realm, and makes no attempt to construct religious edifices on foundations borrowed from other realms. The proponents of this approach take the objective religious phenomenon – in our case, the *mitzva* – and try to understand the spiritual and conceptual principles that are implied by and contained within it. No attempt is made to uncover why a particular *mitzva* was legislated, or how a particular custom developed; all that is asked is what these tell us in their present configuration.

Let us summarize, then, the uniqueness of the method of reconstruction: Owing to the shift of emphasis from the reason to the meaning, it does not pretend to uncover clear and unequivocal causal relationships, but merely to expose fundamental conceptual motifs stemming from the *mitzva*. So, too, it does not slide into historical and sociological explanations or to moral and aesthetic rationales; the method of reconstruction attempts to reveal the meaning of the *mitzva* to the believer who clings to it, and to examine how it fits into his religious consciousness. It respects the autonomy of religion, and does not hang religious phenomena on explanations external to them.

In order to illustrate the difference between the two methods, we shall recount two examples that Rabbi Soloveitchik himself mentions. The first is taken from Maimonides' *Mishne Torah*, which in clear contrast to the *Guide*, according to Rabbi Soloveitchik, reflects the method of reconstruction:

> Although the blowing of the *shofar* on Rosh Hashana is a decree

> of the Holy Writ, nevertheless there is a hint to it, as if saying, "Ye that sleep, bestir yourselves from your sleep, and ye that slumber, emerge from your slumber. Examine your conduct, return in repentance and remember your Creator."
>
> (*Hilkhot Teshuva* 3:4)

Rabbi Soloveitchik notes that there is no attempt here to uncover the "real" reason for the obligation to blow the *shofar*. Maimonides opens with the assertion that the blowing of the *shofar* on Rosh Hashana is a "decree of the Holy Writ." Nevertheless, he adds that "there is a hint to it," that is to say, it is possible to extract spiritual meaning from the law of *shofar* blowing. The emphasis here is not on the question of why the law of *shofar* blowing was instituted, but on the spiritual message that rises from it, and on the *shofar*'s meaning to the believer. In contrast to this approach, Rabbi Soloveitchik (p. 95) cites the words of Rabbenu Sa'adya Gaon, who relates to the historical functions of the *shofar* as an alarm or as a summons to joyous celebration. This is the causalistic method, which Maimonides took pains to avoid in his *Mishne Torah.*[13]

As his second example, Rabbi Soloveitchik mentions the dispute between Maimonides and Nachmanides on the issue of sacrifices. According to Maimonides in his *Guide*, the sacrifices were meant to further an educational-social objective that was dependent upon the historical circumstances – to wean the children of Israel away from the worship of idols, whose primary mode of worship at the time was through the offering of sacrifices. In contrast, Nachmanides points to the eternal and universal meaning of the sacrifices – a sacrifice helps a person internalize the recognition that essentially he should have offered himself as a sacrifice to God.

These two explanations differ from each other in their very

---

13. Regarding the differences between Maimonides' approaches to the reasons for the *mitzvot* in the *Guide* and in the *Mishne Torah*, see Isidore Twersky, *Introduction to the Code of Maimonides*, pp. 430 ff.

essence. Maimonides offers a causalistic explanation (why God established the laws of sacrifices), which by its very nature tends to the historical-relativistic realm. Nachmanides gives an explanation based on the method of reconstruction, and extracts from the laws of sacrifices eternal meaning for all believers in every generation (p. 131, n. 108).

It is not always possible to differentiate the two methods. Sometimes a causalistic explanation remains within the realm of religion, and sometimes the reconstructionist explanation looks like a cause. Fundamentally, however, Rabbi Soloveitchik succeeded in clarifying that we are dealing here with two separate approaches that are different in both their objectives and their results.

Rabbi Soloveitchik establishes the nature of the rationale that he seeks: he is looking not for a historical or sociological explanation, but for a totally spiritual explanation that relates to man's eternal nature, and not to passing social circumstances. In addition, he proposes a method: one should not attempt to uncover what God meant when He legislated the *mitzva*, but only to understand what the *mitzva* means to the believer.

The Reasons for the *Mitzva* of Circumcision

Sanctification Above Nature. The conceptual significance of the *mitzva* of circumcision will become more apparent from an examination of the following famous midrash:

> The wicked Turnus Rufus [once] asked Rabbi Akiva: "Whose deeds are more seemly – those of the Holy One, blessed be He, or those of man?" He said to him: "Those of man are more seemly." The wicked Turnus Rufus said to him: "Surely the heavens and the earth – can you do what they do?" Rabbi Akiva said to him: "Don't answer me with something that is above people, over which they have no control, but rather with something that is found among men." He said to him: "Why do you circumcise yourselves?" He said to him: "I knew that

> eventually you would ask me this, and so I went first and said to you: The deeds of man are more seemly than those of the Holy One, blessed be He. Bring me sheaves and baked goods." He said to him: "These are the handiwork of the Holy One, blessed be He, and these are the handiwork of man. Are these not seemly?"
>
> (*Midrash Tanchuma*, ed. Buber, *Tazri'a* 7)

The provocative heathen claims that the natural world, the handiwork of God, is complete and perfect, and needs no correction or improvement. With his sharp intuition, Turnus Rufus understands the special meaning of circumcision in this context: circumcision symbolizes nature's imperfection and the need to refine and improve it. In the ancient world, circumcision was indeed regarded as a mutilation of man, as an offense committed against his innate natural perfection. It was for this reason that circumcision so disgusted the civilized peoples of the Hellenistic world. We also know that the Sages vigorously fought against the Hellenizers who would "stretch their foreskin" in order to disguise the fact that they had been circumcised. Modern scholars have concluded that the mass conversion to Judaism during the first century before the common era came to end because, among other reasons, the heathens recoiled from circumcision. As was stated above, Turnus Rufus saw in circumcision an exemplification, as well as a symbol, of his general complaint against Judaism: Why doesn't Judaism accept nature, the handiwork of God, as it is, and instead ruins it?

How does Rabbi Akiva respond to Turnus Rufus' defiant argument? He answers without hesitation: Man's handiwork is more seemly! Just as a loaf of bread, the handiwork of man, is more becoming than the grain growing in the field, so, too, circumcised man is more becoming than one who is uncircumcised. God created nature with imperfections, and it falls upon man to improve and develop it. Why? The midrash provides us with an answer: "Why is [man] not born circumcised? Because the Holy One, blessed be He, gave Israel the *mitzvot* only in order to refine them thereby" (ibid.). That is to say, God deliberately designed nature with imperfections, so that we would be able to perfect it.

It must be emphasized that we are not required to fight against nature, but to improve it. The difference between the two is the difference between human sacrifice, despised by God and an abomination in His eyes, and circumcision. The removal of the foreskin emancipates man from his subjugation to the indifferent natural world around him; his body is no longer chained to the mold cast for him by nature. He gives up a small part of his body for the sake of God, thus refashioning his body and demonstrating that he is not subject to nature, but to his Creator. The difference between one who is circumcised and one who is not is found not in the foreskin that has been removed, but in the body that remains. Following circumcision, the body is no longer a mere lump of clay; it is now the body of a servant of God, which has been given new form and is no longer bound by the form in which it came into the world.

In this sense, circumcision gives expression to a powerful spiritual message: Nature is blemished and imperfect. We are not to accept the events and phenomena of the natural world that surrounds us on the outside, and certainly not the natural inclinations and desires that are found within us. We are not commanded to fight against nature – but we are to perfect it, not accepting it as we find it. Not everything that is natural is also good, and not everything that is good is also natural. Much of nature is chaff.

> "I found Israel like grapes in the wilderness; I saw your fathers as the first ripe fruit in the fig tree at her first season" (Hosea 9:10).... Rabbi Yudin said: Just as a fig has no waste other than its stalk, remove it and the blemish is gone, so, too, the Holy One, blessed be He, said to Abraham: There is no waste in you other than your foreskin; remove it and the blemish is gone; "Walk before me, and be perfect" (Genesis 17:1).
>
> (Genesis Rabba 46, 1)

Circumcision as a Sacrifice. The idea of circumcision as an improvement upon nature and as the removal of chaff is accompanied by an additional meaning: circumcision as a sacrifice to God. The conceptual significance that we have found in circumcision led the Sages to relate to circumcision as a miniature sacrifice:

> Whoever presents his son for circumcision is regarded as if he were a High Priest offering his meal-offering and libation on the altar. (*Yalkut Shimoni*, 81)[14]

One who undergoes circumcision, giving his foreskin to God, is essentially offering God a sacrifice of sorts. It is interesting that the midrash sees circumcision as a sacrifice offered by the parents of the newborn, rather than by the one undergoing circumcision. Maharil likens circumcision to a sacrifice brought by the *sandak* who holds the infant during the circumcision ceremony:

> Mahari Segal, when he was appointed *ba'al berit* – or as referred to by the Sages, the *sandak* – would bathe and undergo ritual immersion in order to bring the infant into the covenant in a state of ritual purity. And he would say that the *mitzva* of the *ba'al berit* is greater than the *mitzva* of the *mohel*, because the legs of the former are likened to the altar, as if he were burning incense to heaven. (*Sefer Maharil, Hilkhot Mila*)[15]

The idea of comparing circumcision to a sacrifice may be

---

14. See also: "Rabbi Isaac said: If for someone who builds an altar for My sake, I reveal Myself to him and bless him, for Abraham who circumcised himself for My sake, all the more so. Rabbi Levi opened: 'Also a bullock and a ram for peace offerings, to sacrifice before the Lord...[for today the Lord will appear to you]' (*Leviticus* 9:4). He said: If for someone who offered a bullock and a ram for My sake, I reveal Myself to him and bless him, for Abraham who circumcised himself for My sake, all the more so" (Genesis Rabba 48, 4–5).
15. See also *Noda be-Yehuda, mahadura kama, Yore De'a* 86; Chatam Sofer, *Orach Chayyim* 158–159.

connected to one of the laws governing circumcision. A newborn child is circumcised when he is eight days old. Some have suggested that this parallels a similar law in the realm of sacrifices:

> Rabbi Yitzchak said: The law governing man and the law governing an animal are the same. The law governing man – "And on the eighth day the flesh of his foreskin shall be circumcised" (Leviticus 12:3), and the law governing an animal – "[Then it shall be seven days under its dam;] and from the eighth day and thenceforth it shall be accepted [for an offering made by fire to the Lord]" (Leviticus 22:27).
>
> (Leviticus Rabba 27, 10)

Rabbenu Bachya writes in a similar vein:

> Homiletically speaking, the *mitzva* of circumcision is like a sacrifice. Just as the blood of a sacrifice achieves atonement on the altar, so, too, the blood of circumcision achieves atonement. For this reason it is a *mitzva* on the eighth day, for a sacrifice is not fit until the eighth day, as it says: "And from the eighth day and thenceforth it shall be accepted." And just as it says about a sacrifice, "And they shall eat those things with which atonement was made" (Exodus 29:33), for the eating of a sacrifice is for atonement, so Israel celebrates a festive meal on the day of circumcision. It is even greater than a sacrifice, for a sacrifice involves a person's property, and circumcision, his body.... Therefore it is regarded for him as a binding and a sacrifice, as if he had bound himself [as an offering]. As it says: "Those that have made a covenant with me by sacrifice" (Psalms 50:5).
>
> (Commentary to Genesis 17:13)

One might add to the words of Rabbenu Bachya that it may be possible to connect the idea of circumcision as sacrifice to another law regarding circumcision:

> Circumcision may only be performed during the day following sunrise, whether on its designated time on the eighth day or not on its designated time from the ninth day on. As it is stated: "On the eighth day" – during the day, and not at night.
>
> (Maimonides, *Hilkhot Mila* 1:8)

There is reason to think that circumcision may only be performed during the day, because it is perceived as a sacrifice, and sacrifices may only be offered during the day:

> All sacrifices must be offered only during the day. As it is stated: "On the day that He commanded the children of Israel to offer their sacrifices" – during the day and not at night.
>
> (Maimonides, *Hilkhot Ma'ase ha-Korbanot* 4:1)

Maimonides formulates these two laws in a very similar fashion. Circumcision is a human sacrifice, and therefore its laws parallel the laws of sacrifices. We have already noted the instructive fact that man is not asked to offer his entire body as a sacrifice to God, but only his foreskin. In any event, however, this is a sacrifice.

Rabbi Soloveitchik views circumcision as an allusion to the halakhic way of life, which demands many sacrifices of man but does not encourage renunciation of all pleasures or asceticism. The Jewish sacrifice expresses our readiness to give up what is most dear to us for the sake of God. Restrictions on sexual life, for example, do not imply that this realm is evil in the eyes of God, but rather that it is sufficiently important that we should express through it our acceptance of the yoke of heaven, by way of retreat and withdrawal:

> Jewish thought always understood the act of sacrifice as a renunciation of something that man's variegated vital or imaginative impulse craves for.... Sacrifice is not identical with destruction. The Torah is interested in life and loathes death. An altar is built not alongside a man's grave, but next to his cradle.

> On the eighth day he is sacrificed to God; this ceremony symbolizes the continuous burnt-offering in Jewish life. His table, his bed, his store, his palace – all turn into altars on which man offers himself daily and sanctifies his personality through the conquest of his routine passions.
>
> (*Ra'ayonot al ha-Tefila, Ish ha-Halakha: Galui ve-Nistar*, p. 261)

National Covenant. Thus far we have related to circumcision as an act pertaining to the individual. As we all know, however, circumcision does not pertain only to the isolated individual; it is a national covenant pertaining to the entire Jewish people. This element is evident even in the earliest command regarding circumcision:

> And God said to Abraham, You shall keep My covenant, you, and your seed after you in their generations. This is My covenant, which you shall keep, between Me and you and your seed after you; every man-child among you shall be circumcised. And you shall circumcise the flesh of your foreskin, and it shall be a token of the covenant between Me and you.
>
> (Genesis 17:9–11)

There are only two positive precepts whose violation is punishable by *karet* ("excision"): the paschal offering and circumcision. These two *mitzvot* give expression to the national covenant between God and the Jewish people. Therefore, anyone who shirks one of these obligations is liable to *karet*, which is understood as being cut off from the Jewish people: "That soul shall be cut off from his people" (regarding circumcision, Genesis 17:14; regarding the paschal offering, Numbers 9:13). When the Israelites entered the Promised Land, they immediately observed the *mitzvot* of circumcision and the paschal offering, through which they entered into a covenant with God (Joshua, chap. 5). We also find a special connection between these two *mitzvot* in that an uncircumcised person is specifically forbidden to eat of the paschal offering: "No uncircumcised person shall eat of it" (Exodus 12:48).

In Man's Sexual Organ. Circumcision involves the removal of the foreskin from man's sexual organ. According to the Sages over the generations, this is no mere coincidence, but a message for all times. Maimonides saw in this point the primary focus of circumcision:

> Similarly with regard to circumcision, one of the reasons for it is, in my opinion, the wish to bring about a decrease in sexual intercourse and a weakening of the organ in question, so that this activity be diminished and the organ be in as quiet a state as possible.... The bodily pain caused to that member is the real purpose of circumcision. None of the activities necessary for the preservation of the individual is harmed thereby, nor is procreation rendered impossible, but violent desire and lust that goes beyond what is needed are diminished.
>
> (*Guide of the Perplexed* II, 49)

It is possible to develop Maimonides' direction of thought without reaching his conclusion that circumcision weakens the sexual organ. As is well known, there is no medical basis for Maimonides' assertion: circumcision does not harm man's member in any way. On the contrary, removing the foreskin is beneficial in that it reduces the likelihood of infection. It may still be argued, however, that there is special significance to the fact that circumcision is performed on man's sexual organ. We have already explained that one of the central messages of circumcision is man's capacity to perfect nature by sacrificing a part of himself to God. This sacrifice relates, among other things, to sexual desire, which man is sometimes asked to conquer by divine demand. Circumcision serves as a constant reminder of this obligation.

We mentioned Maimonides' rationale for the *mitzva* of circumcision. Maimonides brings an additional reason – circumcision serves as a physical sign common to all members of the nation. In his *Sefer ha-Mitzvot*, Maimonides counts the *mitzva* of circumcision (positive precept 215) among the *mitzvot* relating to sexual intercourse – procreation, marriage, rejoicing with one's wife during the first year of marriage, levirate marriage, and *chalitza*. This fits in with what he writes in the *Guide*, where he connects circumcision to the control of sexual desire. In his *Mishne Torah*, however, Maimonides treats the *mitzva* of circumcision in *Sefer Ahava*, alongside *keri'at shema*, *tefillin*, blessings, and the like. In his introduction to *Mishne Torah*, Maimonides explains why he included circumcision in *Sefer Ahava*:

> Included in this group is circumcision, because it is a sign in our flesh, serving as a constant reminder, even when there are no *tefillin*, *tzitzit*, or the like.
>
> (Maimonides' [third] introduction to the *Mishne Torah*)

Here Maimonides emphasizes the sign of circumcision, and not the sanctification of sexual intercourse. Circumcision involves not only sacrifice and the control of one's natural inclinations, but also is a constant reminder of the covenant we made with God by way of that sacrifice. In his introduction to the *Mishne Torah*, Maimonides emphasizes the sign of circumcision on the personal level. As we have explained, however, circumcision serves not only as a personal sign, but also as a national sign of the Jewish people as a whole. Seforno connects this point to the question of why circumcision is performed on man's sexual organ:

> Since this covenant is performed on the organ that brings about the eternity of the species, it points to the eternity of the covenant; and since it is performed on the reproductive organ, its sign indicates the continuity of the covenant to the sons.
>
> (Seforno, Genesis 17:13)

We explained earlier how the fact that circumcision is

performed on man's sexual organ fits in with the rationale for circumcision on the individual level. Seforno explains that even in relation to the rationale for circumcision on the national level, there is special significance to the fact that circumcision is performed on that organ.

The Problem of Evil

What Is the Problem?

The problem of evil or the apparent lack of justice in the world is a very ancient issue. Philosophers refer to it as "theodicy," the attempt to vindicate divine justice even though it allows evil to exist. Traditional Jewish sources talk about the problem of "a righteous man who is in adversity, a wicked man who prospers." The earliest known expression of the problem long antedates such formulations. Abraham our father, the first believer, rose up against what he perceived as injustice in the world:

> And the Lord said, Because the cry of Sodom and Gomorrah is great, and because their sin is very grievous.... And Abraham drew near, and said, Will You also destroy the righteous with the wicked? Perhaps there are fifty righteous within the city; will You also destroy and not spare the place for the fifty righteous that are therein? Far be it from You to do after this manner, to slay the righteous with the wicked; and that the righteous should be as the wicked, far be it from You; Shall not the Judge of all the earth do right? And the Lord said, If I find in Sodom fifty just men within the city, then I will spare all the place for their sakes.
>
> (Genesis 18:20–26)

It is important to note that Abraham did not question the fate awaiting the righteous in and of itself, but only in comparison to that which awaited the wicked. This is a fundamental characteristic of the problem of evil in the world: If everyone faced adversity, we might understand that this is God's system of justice. What is particularly upsetting is the apparent lack of justice and absence of equality.

The prophets also struggled with this issue:

> Right would You be, O Lord, if I were to contend with You, yet I will reason these points of justice with You: Why does the way of the wicked prosper? Why are all they happy that deal very treacherously?
>
> (*Jeremiah* 12:1)

We have not yet even mentioned the book of Job, the whole of which addresses this very issue. In fact, the problem of evil is the only conceptual issue to have merited an entire book of Scripture. It may be surmised that this is because we are dealing here not with an abstract philosophical issue, but with a disturbing existential matter.

The question of evil in this world is grounded upon some of the most fundamental assumptions of Judaism: The two main things that we know about God are (1) that He is the ultimate in goodness and truth, and (2) that He enjoys ultimate power and strength. Taken together these two assumptions give rise to the problem of evil in the world: If God is both good and all-powerful, why hasn't He fashioned a world that is good and just?

The British historian Arnold Toynbee once said that the fact that the Jews are so proud of having been the first to adopt a monotheistic creed teaches that even in the religious arena, numbers are the only thing that matters to Jews. Truth be said, what is the fundamental difference between believing in three or even in twenty gods, and believing in one God? One answer is that belief in one God combines morality and power in a single Being. When there are several gods, power may be divided between them. Morality, however, is indivisible. One half-justice and another half-justice add up to one great injustice. It is for this reason that the pagan gods were utterly immoral, as is evident from the stories of Greek mythology, the moral value of which was already held in contempt by the Greek philosophers.

The Gnostics, an ancient idolatrous quasi-Christian philosophical sect, believed in two gods: a good but weak god, and a powerful but evil god who rules the world (known as the "demiurge"). This takes to the extreme the idolatrous tendency to separate power and goodness. Judaism believes in the unity of power and goodness, and therefore expects that the world should operate according to the dictates of morality.

There is another thing that we may learn from this. Einstein's general theory of relativity revolutionized modern science. In 1919, there was a solar eclipse. It was carefully measured because the figures would be able to confirm or refute the theory. In November of that year, the final results were announced. They corresponded to Einstein's predictions. When one of Einstein's students asked him how it felt to receive the telegram with the news that his theory had been confirmed, he looked at her in astonishment and said: "I already knew that my theory was correct." Einstein was confident that the theory of relativity did not need empirical proof: its validity was evident from the equations themselves. As this demonstrates, there are certain beliefs that stem not from an analysis of empirical reality, but from pure logic. And for that very reason, reality can neither confirm nor refute them.

Some people claim that the Holocaust has made it impossible to believe any longer in God's justice. Emotionally, hewing to this belief is indeed difficult, especially for the survivors. Essentially, however, no historical event, even a cruel and monstrous catastrophe like the Holocaust, can undermine our faith in God's justice. The reason is simple: Our belief in divine justice does *not* follow from an analysis of God's actions in history, and therefore it cannot be undermined by history. As we saw in the words of Einstein, a definitive conclusion arrived at through theoretical intellection cannot be refuted by reality. What does not follow from reality, cannot be refuted by it.

We believe that God is just and righteous, abundant in love and truth, not because these traits have been impressed upon us by His actions in history, but because our most primal notion about God is that He is just and righteous. "He is the Rock, His work is perfect, for all His ways are justice; a God of truth and without iniquity, just and right is He" (Deuteronomy 32:4). Our religious experience embraces the conviction that morality constitutes one of God's basic traits. Since this conviction follows from our basic experience as servants of God, it precedes our analysis of reality, and so reality cannot undermine it.

As was stated above, the problem of evil in the world arises precisely because of this axiom. Even if it cannot undermine our belief in God's goodness and power, we are still left with a serious question that awaits a fitting answer.

The World-to-Come

One common answer to the problem of evil claims that all apparent injustices in this world will be resolved by God in the world-to-come. We see only a small part of the picture, and therefore our reckoning is partial and imprecise.

This is what follows from a story related in the Jerusalem Talmud about the life of Elisha ben Avuya, one of the greatest *Tannaim*, who became an apostate. The Talmud raises the question: What brought Elisha ben Avuya to become an apostate?

> Once he was sitting and studying in the Ginosar Valley when he saw someone climb to the top of a date-palm, remove the dam from its chicks, and then climb down in peace. The next day he saw another person climb to the top of the palm, take the chicks and send off the dam, and then climb back down, only to be bitten by a snake and die. He said: "It is written: 'You shall surely let the mother go, and take the young to you; that it may be good with you, and that you may prolong your

> days' (Deuteronomy 22:7). Where is this one's good, where is this one's prolonged days?" And he was unaware that Rabbi Jacob had already interpreted the verse "That it may be good with you" as meaning in the world-to-come, which is entirely good; "and that you may prolong your days" as in the future, which is entirely prolonged.
>
> (Jerusalem Talmud, *Chagiga* 2:1)

The Babylonian Talmud also cites Rabbi Jacob:

> Rabbi Jacob says: There is no command in the Torah accompanied by a promise of reward to which resurrection is not appended. Regarding honoring one's father and mother it is written: "That your days may be prolonged, and that it may go well you" (Deuteronomy 5:15). Regarding sending away the mother-bird it is written: "That it may be good with you, and that you may prolong your days" (Deuteronomy 22:7). If his father said to him: "Climb up to the castle, and bring me pigeons," and he climbed up to the castle, and sent away the mother-bird, and took the chicks, and on his way down, he fell and died – where is the good of his days, and where is the prolongation of his days? Rather, "That it may go well with you" – in a world that is entirely good; "and that your days may be prolonged" – in a world that is entirely prolonged.
>
> (*Kiddushin* 39b)[1]

The point of departure in the Babylonian Talmud is not the gap between the righteous and the wicked, but the gap between the reward described in the relevant biblical verses and the reward actually dispensed; the principle, however, is one and the same.

1. The Talmud explains that Rabbi Jacob witnessed such a case, which led him to conclude that there is no reward in this world for the performance of a *mitzva*. It is stated there that Rabbi Jacob was the grandson of Elisha ben Avuya. Thus we see how two members of the same family confronted the very same situation in two entirely different ways.

The Best Possible World

Maimonides provides a different answer, one with a more philosophical inclination:

> Often it occurs to the imagination of the multitude that there are more evils in the world than there are good things. As a consequence, this thought is contained in many sermons and poems of all the religious communities, which say that it is surprising if good exists in the temporal, whereas the evils of the temporal are numerous and constant. This error is not found only among the multitude, but also among those who deem that they know something….
>
> The explanation of this lies in the fact that all the evils that befall man fall under one of three species. The first species of evil is that which befalls man because of the nature of coming-to-be and passing-away, I mean to say because of his being endowed with matter. Because of this, infirmities and paralytic afflictions befall some individuals either in consequence of their original natural disposition, or they supervene because of changes occurring in the elements, such as corruption of the air or a fire from heaven and a landslide. We have already explained that divine wisdom has made it obligatory that there should be no coming-to-be except through passing-away. Were it not for the passing-away of the individuals, the coming-to-be relating to the species would not continue….
>
> The evils of the second kind are those that men inflict upon one another, such as tyrannical domination of some of them over others. These evils are more numerous than those belonging to the first kind….
>
> The evils of the third kind are those that are inflicted upon any individual among us by his own action; this is what happens in the majority of cases, and these evils are much more numerous than those of the second kind. All men lament over the evils of this kind…. This kind is consequent upon all vices, I mean concupiscence for eating, drinking, and copulation, and

> doing these things with excess in regard to quantity or irregularly or when the quality of the foodstuffs is bad. For this is the case of all corporeal and psychical diseases and ailments.... Thus every ignoramus who thinks worthless thoughts is always sad and despondent because he is not able to achieve the luxury attained by someone else. In most cases such a man exposes himself to great dangers, such as arise in sea voyages and the service of kings; his aim therein being to obtain these unnecessary luxuries. When, however, he is stricken by misfortunes in these courses he has pursued, he complains about God's decree and predestinations.
>
> (*Guide of the Perplexed* III, 12)

Maimonides, effectively proffers several answers. First of all, it is incorrect to say that the world is evil. Overall, the world is good and just, and the exceptional instances of evil can be accounted for. Maimonides divides the evil occurrences in the world into several categories.

1. *Evils stemming from the fact that we are material beings*. In effect, Maimonides argues that there is a certain randomness in the world, about which there is nothing to be done. From the moment that God decided to create a material world, all created beings have, of necessity, been subject to the laws of nature. We saw in one of the earlier chapters that according to Maimonides, God does not intervene in the laws of nature, but only watches over man through the human intellect. Hence, God is not guilty for the fact that nature has its problems; this is inevitable. Leibniz referred to this position as "the best of possible worlds": our world may not be perfect, but it is the best world that God could have created.[2]

In essence, Maimonides is saying that God could not have created a perfect world in which there is no evil whatsoever. Such a

2. Leibniz , who had learned the writings of Maimonides, sang his praises with great enthusiasm.

statement is typical of Maimonides' approach, which argues time and again that even God is subject to reason. Thus, according to Maimonides, God could not have created a triangle with four sides, legislated a Torah that would fit the needs of each and every individual, or created a material world that contains no evil. We have noted that the problem of evil arises from a combination of the assumptions that God is both good and all-powerful. Maimonides' first answer diminishes the force of the second assumption.

2. *Evils that men inflict upon each one another.* God's intervention with regard to such evils is also limited. I once heard someone say that just as we ask God how the Holocaust could have occurred, He asks us the very same question. In the final analysis it was men of flesh and blood who murdered human beings.

3. *Evils that men inflict upon themselves.* According to Maimonides, these constitute the majority of evils and injustices. A person smokes cigarettes for thirty years and then complains to God because he has developed lung disease. A person drives recklessly, and then complains because he was injured in a traffic accident. Maimonides believed that if a wise man conducts his affairs in accordance with reason, he will for the most part be spared injury and harm.

This answer is also conditioned on Maimonides' position that, generally speaking, God does not intervene in the laws of nature. For even if we say that a person who fails to wear a seat belt is responsible for his injury, traffic laws do not recognize negligence as a capital offense. Thus, we are not dealing here with moral reward and punishment, but with laws of nature.

There are a number of weaknesses in Maimonides' position: (1) It is based on the assumption that God does not intervene in the laws and affairs of nature. (2) The moral question still remains: Why doesn't God intervene in what happens in the world if He sees that the world, in and of itself, is unjust? (3) It assumes that our world is the best of possible worlds. This is both a statement about the world, that overall it is good and just, and a statement about God, that He could not have fashioned a better world. Are these two statements true? At least from an experiential perspective, we are not always persuaded.

There Is No Answer

A third school of thought maintains that the problem of evil in the world has no answer. The Sages long ago expressed themselves in this direction:

> Three things did Moses ask of the Holy One, blessed be He, and they were granted to him. He asked that the Divine Presence should rest upon Israel, and it was granted to him.... He asked that the Divine Presence should not rest upon the idolaters, and it was granted to him.... He asked that He should show him the ways of the Holy One, blessed be He, and it was granted to him. For it is said: "Show me now Your ways" (Exodus 33:13). Moses said before Him: "Lord of the Universe, why is it that some righteous men prosper and others are in adversity, some wicked men prosper and others are in adversity?"...The righteous man who prospers is a perfectly righteous man; the righteous man who is in adversity is not a perfectly righteous man. The wicked man who prospers is not a perfectly wicked man; the wicked man who is in adversity is a perfectly wicked man. Now this is in opposition to the saying of Rabbi Meir. For Rabbi Meir said: Only two [requests] were granted to him, and one was not granted to him. For it is said: "And I will be gracious to whom I will be gracious" (Exodus 33:19) – although he may not deserve it; "And I will show mercy on whom I will show mercy" – although he may not deserve it.
>
> (*Berakhot* 7a)

According to Rabbi Meir, even Moshe Rabbenu was denied an answer to this troubling question, the question of the adversity of the righteous and the prosperity of the wicked. Moreover, Abraham our father was also denied an answer to this question. When Abraham expressed his astonishment at God's decree to destroy Sodom, God did not answer: "Be silent, they will receive their reward in the world-to-come." The questions posed by Abraham and Jeremiah testify to the fact that they did not accept the answers suggested above, for were this not the case, there would have been no room for their questions. Our forefathers apparently were not convinced that this is "the best of possible worlds," and as for the world-to-come, they seem to have expected, as inhabitants of this world, an answer within the bounds of this world. Their questions remained unanswered.

And furthermore, a philosophical answer does not resolve existential distress, as Rabbi Soloveitchik noted:

> On the one hand, we know that this metaphysic has worked miracles with our people, whose history is a continuous tale of martyrdom and suffering. The Jewish community found, in this metaphysic of evil, relief, hope and courage. Yet what seemed apodictic and simple to our ancestors, inspired by indomitable faith and passionate transcendental experiences, might prove to be an extremely complicated matter for contemporary egotistic man, who is spiritually uprooted, homeless, and perplexed. I can state with full candor that I personally have not been too successful in my attempts to spell out this metaphysic in terms meaningful to the distraught individual who floats aimlessly in all-encompassing blackness.... I tried but failed, I think, miserably, like the friends of Job.
>
> (*Out of the Whirlwind*, pp. 99–100)

Rabbi Soloveitchik notes that modern man is not satisfied with answers that push him off with a denial of the reality of evil and suffering. Modern man seeks more existential answers. He feels the reality of suffering and is unable to deny his immediate experiences.

The French-Jewish philosopher Emmanuel Levinas argues that there is a theological problem with the demand always to understand God's ways:

> What can this suffering of the innocents mean? Is it not proof of a world without God.... This is also the sanest reaction for all those for whom previously a fairy primary sort of God had dished out prizes, inflicted punishment or pardoned sins.... But with what lesser demon or strange magician have you therefore filled your heaven, you who claim that this is empty? And why, under an empty sky, do you continue to hope for a good and sensible world?
>
> (Levinas, *Difficult Freedom*, Baltimore, 1997, p. 143)

In other words, when we are conscious of the suffering that abounds in the world and the absence of justice, the emphasis moves to man himself. Man no longer seeks help and support from above, and instead assumes responsibility for the world.

Rabbi Soloveitchik follows in the same direction and develops this idea further in his classic article, "Kol Dodi Dofek." He does not condemn reliance upon God, but he, too, emphasizes the obligation that suffering imposes upon man. In his eyes, this is the key to our confrontation with evil, for Judaism adopts a realistic attitude toward the world, and therefore understands that it is impossible to blur the fact that there is evil in the world. Every philosophical attempt to solve the problem of evil leads to disillusionment.[3] "Evil is an incontrovertible fact; there is evil, there is suffering, there are infernal afflictions in the world."

Without a doubt, God has an explanation for the evil found in this world. God is abundant in love and truth, and we wholeheartedly believe that He governs the world in the path of truth and justice. This explanation, however, is beyond our reach. Rabbi Soloveitchik likens the world to an intricately designed carpet that

3. There is a great difference between what Rabbi Soloveitchik says here and what he says in the passage cited earlier from *Out of the Whirlwind*. There, Rabbi Soloveitchik described modern man's inability to be satisfied with a metaphysical answer as a weakness; here he argues that a philosophical-metaphysical answer to the question of evil in the world is beyond man's reach.

we perceive from the wrong side, so that all we see is a whirlpool of meaningless colors.

Accordingly, there is no theoretical answer to the question of evil in the world. The matter is beyond our comprehension. We must therefore reformulate the question. Instead of asking why a certain thing occurs, we must ask how are we to deal with it. "The most important question is: What obligations do afflictions impose upon man?...We do not seek the cause of evil nor its objective, but only its repair and elevation; how should man conduct himself in times of trouble?" At this point the philosophical question of injustice turns into an existential question of suffering. It is not the injustice that is troubling, but the suffering. How then is man to respond to suffering and affliction?

> The halakhic response to this question is very simple. Afflictions come to elevate man, to purify his spirit and sanctify him, to clean his thought and refine it of all dregs of superficiality and crudeness; to ennoble his soul and broaden the horizons of his life. To summarize: The role of afflictions is to perfect what is blemished in man's personality.[4]...Woe to man if afflictions do not bring him to a spiritual crisis, and his soul remains frozen and without pardon! Woe to the sufferer if his soul is not heated by the flame of affliction!
>
> (*Kol Dodi Dofek*, in *Divrei Hagut ve-Ha'arakha*, pp. 13–15)

Rabbi Soloveitchik calls upon us to shift the problem of evil from the intellectual to the existential plane, and to use it as a driving force for self-improvement. Times of suffering and distress are opportunities for spiritual growth. Note that he does not ask us to set the question aside or ignore it. When he says that there is

---

4. Rabbi Soloveitchik's formulation notwithstanding, it is clear from the context that he does not mean to say that God imposes afflictions in order to purify us, for he himself said earlier that we do not understand the reason for human suffering. We are dealing here with an existential outlook that focuses upon man's obligations rather than upon God's intentions.

no intellectual answer to the question of evil, this does not mean that we are to repress the distress that the question causes. On the contrary, one should channel the energies that are aroused in the right direction and use them to power spiritual progress. This is the key to the processes of personal growth that can take place precisely in situations of suffering and affliction.

Halakha and Morality

Does Religion Recognize the Existence of Morality?

The relationship between Halakha and ethics is by no means simple. The classic starting point for discussing this question is the famous passage from Plato's *Euthyphro*, already cited in our consideration of the reasons for the *mitzvot* in Chapter 19. Plato raises there a fundamental question: Can a religious worldview encompass morality and good as independent and objective standards? On one side of the dilemma, good has independent, objective value, and God chooses the good because it is good. On the other side, there is no inherent difference between good and evil. God chooses arbitrarily; that which He desires is good, and that which He rejects is evil.

Many generations later, Rabbi Jacob Charlap formulated the same dilemma:

> Regarding the verse which states: "Its ways are ways of pleasantness" (Proverbs 3:17) – are the ways themselves by their very nature pleasantness and truth, peace and tranquility, and it is only that we do not know what they are, and God, blessed be He, revealed them to us; or does their pleasantness and sweetness exist [only] after we were commanded [to follow them] and because of the command.
>
> (*Responsa Malki ba-Kodesh* IV, p. 80).

We have already noted that this is a very difficult question from a religious perspective. On the one hand, it is difficult to say that good exists independently of God's will, for that would diminish God's power. On the other hand, it seems unreasonable to say that there is no inherent difference between charity and murder, and that God arbitrarily chose the one and loathed the other.

Neither position is simple; but we have already observed that Judaism strongly inclines toward the first position, which recognizes the existence of objective good. This tendency seems to have been greatly influenced by the dialogue between Abraham and God regarding God's desire to destroy Sodom:

> And the Lord said, Because the cry of Sodom and Gomorrah is great, and because their sin is grievous; I will go down now, and see whether they have done altogether according to the cry of it, which is come to me; and if not, I will know. And the men turned their faces from there, and went toward Sodom; but Abraham stood yet before the Lord. And Abraham drew near, and said, Will You also destroy the righteous with the wicked? Perhaps there are fifty righteous within the city; will You also destroy and not spare the place for the fifty righteous that are therein? Far be it from You; shall not the Judge of all the earth do right? And the Lord said, If I find in Sodom fifty just men within the city, then I will spare all the place for their sakes.
>
> (Genesis 18:20–26)

One cardinal point stands out in Abraham's exchange with God: Abraham assumes that God acts according to moral criteria. And furthermore, God's moral criteria are understandable to man. The argument might have been made that absolute standards of good and evil do in fact exist, but are incomprehensible to man. Abraham, however, does not accept such a position. Abraham approaches God with a moral claim: "Shall not the Judge of all the earth do right?" God does not reject Abraham's contention; He accepts it. This is apparently the primary source for the Jewish position that assumes the existence of an absolute moral good that is not determined arbitrarily by God.[1]

A classic example of the Jewish view may be found in the writings of Maimonides. He maintains that God's will is moral and rational. He then takes a further step, applying this position to the world of *mitzvot*. Maimonides argues that God's commandments are not arbitrary, but stem from moral and reasoned rationales (*Guide of the Perplexed* II, 31).

Thus far we have maintained that Judaism, as a rule, recognizes the position of morality. We have seen that for Maimonides this also holds with regard to the *mitzvot*. Now let us examine the degree to which Halakha accords with human morality in actual practice.

Mitzvot That Seem Morally Wanting

Many of the *mitzvot* can be easily reconciled with our standards of morality. These include most of the social *mitzvot*, such as "You shall not steal" and "You shall love your neighbor as yourself." The problem begins with those moral imperatives that are not expressed in the *mitzvot*. How are we to relate to moral values that find no expression in the halakhic system? Nachmanides, in his commentary to the verses "You shall be holy" (Leviticus 19:2) and "And you shall do that which is right and good" (Deuteronomy 6:18), says that the Torah prohibits being a "scoundrel by permission of

1. It is interesting to note in this context the famous dictum, "Had the Torah not been given, we would have had to learn modesty from the cat, theft from the ant, illicit sexual relations from the dove, and *derekh eretz* from the rooster" (*Eruvin* 100b). My revered teacher, HaRav Aharon Lichtenstein, *shelita*, proves from this that Judaism recognizes, at the very least, natural morality, if not natural law. Prof. E.E. Urbach questioned the relevance of this source to the issue of natural law in Judaism. He believed that the statement speaks of what would have happened had the Torah not been given, but since the Torah was in fact given, all this is irrelevant. Prof. Y. Englard raised a question from a different direction: the statement assumes the preexistence of a system of norms that would teach us that we should imitate the rooster in the realm of *derekh eretz*, and not in the area of modesty.

the Torah." This clearly implies that any indecent behavior, even if not explicitly mentioned by the Torah, is forbidden.

The author of *Dor Revi'i*, a great-grandson of the Chatam Sofer, raises an important argument regarding the prohibition on eating human flesh. Technically, it is merely an *issur aseh* – a prohibition that is not stated in the Torah in the form of a negative commandment, but is inferred from a positive commandment. The moral taboo that accompanies it, however, gives it great weight:

> And furthermore, you should know that as to all the loathsome things that man finds despicable, even if the Torah had not forbidden them, anyone eating such things would be regarded as being far more abhorrent than one who violates an explicit Torah prohibition.... According to Maimonides, [the eating of] human flesh is only forbidden by way of an inference from a positive commandment, and according to Rashba it is outright permitted by Torah law. But tell me now, a mortally ill patient having to choose between meat from an improperly slaughtered or congenitally defective animal...and human flesh – which should he eat? Do we say that he should eat the human flesh, which is not forbidden by a Torah prohibition – even though it is forbidden by the moral code accepted by civilized man, so that anyone eating or feeding another person human flesh is cast out from the community of men – rather than eat meat which the Torah forbids with a negative commandment? Would it enter your mind that we, the chosen people, a wise and understanding people, should violate this moral code in order to save ourselves from violating a Torah prohibition?... For whatever is abhorrent in the eyes of the enlightened nations is forbidden to us...by virtue of the commandment "You shall be holy." Whatever is forbidden to the entire species of enlightened man by virtue of a moral code cannot possibly be permitted to us, a holy people.
>
> (Introduction to *Dor Revi'i* on *Chullin*)

The *Dor Revi'i* argues that in a case where one's life is in danger, it is preferable to eat non-kosher meat and not human flesh, despite the fact that the prohibition of eating human flesh, halakhically speaking, is less severe. This case is highly problematic, for it involves a moral claim that directly collides with a solid halakhic prohibition. We may, however, derive from *Dor Revi'i* the following principle: even that which is not explicitly prohibited by the Torah may be forbidden to us by virtue of a universal moral code. To illustrate this point he cites the prohibition of going out naked into the street. Is it possible that a man is forbidden to dress in a woman's clothing but is permitted to go about in public stark naked? The *Dor Revi'i* bases these prohibitions on the general *mitzva* "You shall be holy," as explained by Nachmanides.

It might be argued that reliance on the general commandment of "You shall be holy" leaves us still in the realm of the halakhic imperative, and does not take us beyond it. The next source relates to non-Jews, the descendants of Noah, regarding whom this argument cannot be raised, because they are not subject to the command of "You shall be holy." Rav Nissim Gaon argues that all human beings are bound by moral imperatives, even when there is no explicit divine command. In the absence of such a command, man's conscience can bring him to recognize God's will.

> All the mitzvot that depend upon reason and the heart's understanding were already binding upon all men from the day that God created man on earth.... Even though these mitzvot [i.e., the seven commandments binding upon all the descendants of Noah] are derived from Scripture...they are not merely received commandments, for the obligation to know God and to obey and serve Him is fitting by way of the law of the intellect; and the shedding of innocent blood and stealing are forbidden by virtue of the path of reason.
>
> (Introduction to *Sefer Mafte'ach*)

That is to say, all human beings must obey the norms of morality even when they are not explicitly spelled out by scriptural commandment.

Thus far, we have discussed moral values that are not explicitly mentioned in the Torah. Another issue, very similar to this, involves those *mitzvot* which appear to be directed toward the perfection of morality but nonetheless do not seem to satisfy our moral standards. The classic example is slavery. The Torah restrained the worst injustices of slavery, but it did not sweepingly do away with it. In this case the Torah does not seem to stand up to our moral standards.

The Sages confronted this issue with respect to the law regarding non-Jewish female prisoner-of-wars, which allows the capture of non-Jewish women in wartime. The Sages assert that the *mitzva* has a moral objective, but since God understood that the Jewish people of that generation would be unable to observe an absolute prohibition, He was satisfied with restrictions that would minimize the moral offense.

> Our Sages have taught: "[Woman] of beautiful appearance." [Here] the Torah only speaks in consideration of the evil inclination. It is better that Israel eat the flesh of animals on the point of death but ritually slaughtered, rather than eat of carcasses unslaughtered.
>
> (*Kiddushin* 21b–22a)

Nachmanides defined the problem with a female prisoner-of-war as lying in the injury it causes to the sanctity of Israel. Maimonides, however, understood that we are dealing here with a moral issue:

> Even though his evil inclination overcomes him and patience is impossible for him, he must obligatorily bring her to a hidden place.... And as [the Sages] have explained, he is not permitted to do her violence during the war. And he is not allowed

> sexual intercourse with her for the second time before her grief has calmed down and her sorrow has been quieted. And she should not be forbidden to grieve, to be disheveled, and to weep;...Therefore the Torah has had pity on her and gave her the possibility to do so until she is weary of weeping and of grieving.
>
> (*Guide of the Perplexed* III, 41)

Maimonides explains that the Torah took pity upon this unfortunate woman, but was unable to totally prohibit the injustice done to her. Therefore it tried to minimize the damage to the extent possible. The Sages provide us with a key to understanding those *mitzvot* that do not appear to satisfy our moral standards. In many such instances, the Torah aims to counteract the evil inclination. It knows, however, that it cannot totally dislodge deeply rooted negative practices, but can only limit them as much as possible. In such cases, the Torah would certainly look favorably upon further developing the goal of the *mitzva*, to the point of absolute negation of the moral injustice.

Immoral *Mitzvot*

The problem arises in its most acute form with regard to *mitzvot* that unquestionably seem to contradict our moral standards. The starting point must be that we are required to follow the *mitzva* even when it contradicts our moral principles. Proof of this may be adduced from the story of the *Akeidah*. The very same Abraham who expected God to act morally seems to have been prepared to execute an absolutely immoral divine command without protest or hesitation. Our duty to God supersedes our duty to moral principles.

In general, however, we try to avoid situations of this kind. But from where do we derive the authority to fashion the *mitzvot* in such a manner that they do not clash with morality? We can learn from the example presented by Moshe Rabbenu:

> And the Lord spoke to me, saying…Behold, I have given into your hand Sihon the Amorite, king of Heshbon, and his land; begin to possess it, and contend with him in battle…. And I sent messengers out of the wilderness of Kedemot to Sihon king of Heshbon with words of peace, saying…
>
> (Deuteronomy 2:2–26)

God commanded Moses to fight Sihon, and yet Moses sent peace emissaries to him. How did Moses dare to deviate from instructions received directly from God? Rashi explains as follows:

> Although the Omnipresent had not commanded me to proclaim peace upon Sihon, I learned to do so from what happened in the wilderness of Sinai, that is, from an incident that relates to the Torah which preexisted the world. For when the Holy One, blessed be He, was about to give the Torah to Israel, he took it round to Esau and Ishmael. It was manifest before Him that they would not accept it, but yet He opened unto them with peace. Similarly, I first approached Sihon with words of peace. Another explanation:…. Moses said to God, I learned this from You…. You could have sent one flash of lightning to burn up the Egyptians, but You sent me from the wilderness to Pharaoh, to say, Let my people go.
>
> (Rashi ad loc.)

The Sages tell us why Moses dared to veer from the simple meaning of God's instructions. When Moses interpreted God's words, he took into consideration what he knew of God's moral nature. The plain meaning seemed to indicate that God wanted an immediate engagement in battle. If, however, we consider the moral values to which God had already demonstrated that He was devoted, we must interpret His words differently: God apparently meant that we must first approach Sihon with words of peace, and only afterward, if there is no other alternative, must we go out in battle against him.[2] In this case, the moral consideration does not contradict God's word, God forbid, but rather it serves as an exegetical tool that may help us to understand the true will of God.

This principle is reiterated many times in the words of the Sages. Once again, it should be emphasized that we are not dealing here with a "show" or a perversion of God's word. We are using moral values as an exegetical tool, based on the sincere belief that they can truly help us to decipher God's will. Obviously, there are other exegetical considerations that must be taken into account.

---

2. As for Moses and Sihon, one might argue that we are dealing here merely with a tactical maneuver for the purpose of public relations, for it was clear that Sihon would not agree to peace. The Sages, however, seem to imply otherwise: "Whatever Moses decreed, the Holy One, blessed be He, approved. How so? The Holy One, blessed be He, did not tell [Moses] to break the tablets. Yet Moses went and broke them on his own. From where do we know that the Holy One, blessed be He, approved? For it says: 'Which (*asher*) you broke' – be thanked (*yishar*) for having broken them. The Holy One, blessed be He, told him to wage war against Sihon, as it says: 'And contend with him in battle.' But he did not do so. Rather, 'And I sent messengers, etc.' The Holy One, blessed be He, said to him: I told you to wage war against him, but you opened with peace. On your life, I shall fulfill your decree: Any war that [Israel] wages, they must open with peace, as it says: 'When you come near to a city, etc.'" (Deuteronomy Rabba 5:13). By implication, this means that Moses understood God's deeper intention regarding the conduct of war in general. Similarly, we find in another source: "'Her ways are ways of pleasantness, and all her paths are peace.' Whatever is written in the Torah was written for the sake of peace. Even though the Torah speaks of wars, even wars were written about for the sake of peace. You find that the Holy One, blessed be He, annulled His decree for the sake of peace. When? When the Holy One, blessed be He, said to Moses: 'When you shall besiege a city a long time,' and the entire passage, the Holy One, blessed be He, said to destroy them, as it says: 'You shall utterly destroy them.' But Moses did not do that, but rather he said: Shall I go now and smite him who sinned together with him who did not sin? Rather, I shall approach them with peace, as it says: 'And I sent messengers out of the wilderness of Kedemot to Sihon king of Heshbon with words of peace, saying, Let me pass through your land.' When he saw that [Sihon] was not coming in peace, he smote him.... The Holy One, blessed be He, said: I said: 'You shall utterly destroy them,' but you did not do so. On your life, as you said, I shall do, as it says: 'When you come near to a city to fight against it, proclaim peace to it'" (*Midrash Tanchuma Tzav*, 3).

These may sometimes overwhelm the moral considerations, in which case we will find ourselves facing a *mitzva* that, in our eyes, contradicts morality. In such a situation, we must prefer the *mitzva* to our moral principles, on the assumption that God understands better than we what is good and what is fitting. In general, however, we try to the best of our ability to interpret the *mitzvot* in such a manner that they correspond to the moral values reflected in the Torah and, in our opinion, reflect the will of God.

Let us now consider some examples where moral values are treated as legitimate exegetical tools. First, the famous halakha that "an eye for an eye" means financial compensation:

> "An eye for (*tahat*) an eye" (Exodus 21:24). Even though it is possible to explain the word *tahat* in its literal sense, the Sages decided to support the tradition that the verse refers here to money. For the Sages understood the Torah's thinking, for its ways are pleasant, and the Torah cannot possibly have commanded something that will bring no benefit to the community and only damage to the individual. This is not the case if we interpret the word *tahat* as referring to money, for the injured party will at least receive monetary compensation for the loss of his eye.
>
> (*Torah Temima*, no. 171)

Rabbi Barukh Epstein argues in *Torah Temima* that the Sages interpreted "an eye for an eye" as referring to financial compensation, because if the words were understood in their literal sense, we would be left with a cruel law that in no way benefits the injured party. This is a moral consideration.

A second example is found in the commentary of Ibn Ezra to Exodus 20:1:

> And the second kind are the *mitzvot* with hidden rationales, regarding which it was not stated explicitly why they were commanded. And heaven forbid that one of those *mitzvot* should

> contradict sound reasoning. It is just that we are obligated to keep everything that God has commanded us, whether or not its secret has been revealed to us. And if we should find that one of them contradicts sound reasoning, it is not right to believe that it must be understood literally. Rather, we must seek its rationale in the works of our Sages of blessed memory, when it is to be understood metaphorically. And if we do not find this in writing, we should seek it ourselves and search for it to the best of our ability, perhaps we can fix it. And if we are unable to do so, we should let it rest as is, and admit that we do not understand it. As in the case of "And you shall circumcise the foreskin of your heart" – did He cruelly command us to kill ourselves?

Ibn Ezra makes clear that we explain the verse "And you shall circumcise the foreskin of your heart" as a metaphor because we know God's moral ways and understand that He would never command us to cut our hearts. Our world of values serves here as an exegetical consideration in the understanding of God's word.

A final example of moral values serving as an exegetical tool to help us understand God's will is found in the words of Rav Chayyim Volozhiner, father of the Lithuanian yeshiva world, regarding dispensations enabling *agunot* to remarry:

> I see that regarding most things we are headed in the same direction. It is just that he inclines toward stringency, since the matter is not cast upon him. Just like him, I too did not turn to the allowances that emerge from study before the burden of decision-making was placed upon my shoulders. Now, however, as a result of our many sins, our environs have been orphaned of its sages, and the yoke of ruling for the entire area was placed on my shoulders.... And I calculated with my Maker, and I saw it a personal obligation to gather all my strength in order to persevere in finding a remedy for the *agunot*.
>
> (*Responsa Chut ha-Meshulash* I, no. 8)

Rav Chayyim Volozhiner admits that according to formal legal considerations, the unfortunate *aguna* should be forbidden to remarry. Moral considerations, however, incline him toward leniency. Rav Chayyim genuinely believes that this is truly God's will. Compassion for the widow leads him to search for a valid halakhic dispensation, and serves as an element in understanding God's will.

It is not always possible, however, to find a halakhic exegesis that accords with the world of moral values that we attribute to God. The moral factor is not the only factor, and sometimes it must be set aside by other considerations.

Here is an example of a divine command that gives rise to a moral problem that cannot be circumvented.

> When the Holy One, blessed be He, told Saul to "Go and smite Amalek," he said: Now, if for a single soul the Torah said to perform the rite of *egla arufa*, surely this is so for all these souls. And if man sinned, how did the cattle sin? And if the adults sinned, how did the children sin? A heavenly voice issued forth and said to him: "Be not overly righteous" (Ecclesiastes 7:16).
>
> (*Yoma* 22b)[3]

---

3. Another example of this tension is found in the Talmud's discussion of capital punishment by burning. According to the Sages, this does not refer to actual burning, but rather to destruction of the internal organs: "*Mishna:* The obligation regarding those who are liable to [death by] burning. They would sink him in manure up to his knees, and place a stiff kerchief inside a soft one, and wrap [it] around his neck. This one would pull to him, and that one would pull to him, until he opens his mouth. Someone would heat up the strip, and cast it into his mouth, and it would go down to his entrails, and scald his bowels.... Gemara: From where do we derive [this]? 'Burning' is learned from 'burning' from the company of Korah. Just as there, burning of the soul, and the body remaining intact, so, too, here, a burning of the soul, and the body remaining intact.... Rav Nachman said in the name of Rabba bar Avuha: The verse states: 'Love your neighbor as yourself' (Leviticus 19:18) – select for him a humane death. And since there is that of Rav Nachman, why do I need a *gezera shava* [analogy]? If there were no *gezera shava*, I might have said [that] burning the soul with the body remaining intact is not burning at all. And if because of

We shall not always – or perhaps almost never – succeed entirely in resolving the moral difficulties that arise in Halakha. But we are duty bound to walk in the paths of the Sages of Israel, and, at the very least, to strive to minimize as much as possible the clash between Halakha and morality.

'Love your neighbor as yourself,' let him add bundles of branches so that he burns quickly. Therefore, it teaches us" (*Sanhedrin* 52a). This source clearly indicates the tension between the moral consideration and other, more formal, exegetical considerations. If there were no formal source to teach us that even burning that does not involve external kindling may still be called burning, we would have to invoke the moral consideration in a more diminutive manner (i.e., by adding bundles of branches).

The Binding of Isaac

Akeidat Yitzchak, the binding of Isaac, is one of the most impressive events in Scripture and all of Jewish history. In this chapter we shall attempt a conceptual analysis of some of the fundamental ideas arising from the *Akeida*. The ideas connected to it are many and richly varied; we shall, therefore, limit ourselves to some of the more basic concepts.

Man's Standing Before God

We begin with the human aspect of the story. What were Abraham's feelings? What did God want Abraham to feel? What is the *Akeida*'s message regarding our own service of God?

Rabbi Joseph B. Soloveitchik, among others, stressed the idea that the *Akeida* evoked the ultimate feeling of sacrifice and suffering that at times accompanies the religious experience. He writes that "his soul loathes" expositions that revolve around one point: that the observance of *mitzvot* is beneficial, say, for family life, good digestion, sweet dreams, or social position. In contrast to this superficial understanding of the religious world, Rabbi Soloveitchik states that the authentic religious position is based primarily on spiritual tension and inner affliction. God demands of man that we obey His orders and offer Him sacrifices expressed through the conquest of our natural impulses. In this context, Rabbi Soloveitchik sees the trial of the *Akeida* as a foundational experience:

> God says to Abraham: "Take now your son, your only one, whom you love, Isaac," and so on. That is to say, I demand of you the greatest sacrifice. I want your son who is your only son, and also the one whom you love. Do not fool yourself into thinking that after you obey Me and bring your son up for a burnt-offering, I will give you another son in place of Isaac. When Isaac is slaughtered on the altar, you will remain alone and childless. You will not have another child. You will live your life in incomparable solitude. I want your only son, who is irreplaceable. Neither should you think that you will succeed in forgetting Isaac and remove him from your mind. All your life you will think about him. I am interested in your son whom you love and whom you will love forever. You will spend your nights awake, picking at your emotional wounds. Out of your sleep you will call for Isaac, and when you wake up you will find your tent desolate and forsaken. Your life will turn into a long chain of emotional suffering. And nevertheless, I demand this sacrifice.
>
> (*Divrei Hashkafa*, pp. 254–255)

Rabbi Soloveitchik underscores the fact that joy awaits us at the end of our road of sorrows; in the end, Abraham was able to remove Isaac from the altar. But we must not blur the beginning of the trek, which conveys the primary message that sacrifice is demanded of those who serve God. According to Rabbi Soloveitchik, Abraham offered his sacrifice by binding his son and standing ready to slaughter him. This may be why we, too, refer to this incident as the *Akeida* – the "binding." The very act of binding Isaac was already a sacrifice. Elsewhere, Rabbi Soloveitchik writes as follows:

> We would be mistaken if we were to say that the *Akeida* was not actually carried out. God forbid! Abraham did indeed sacrifice his son and offer him to God. From the very moment that God said to him: "Take now your son...and offer him there for a burnt-offering," Isaac was no longer under Abraham's authority, but in the domain of God. Abraham himself saw Isaac as having already been offered as a burnt-offering, and he withdrew from him immediately.
>
> (*Yemei Zikaron*, p. 196)

A number of midrashim and *piyyutim* develop this point that a sacrifice actually transpired during the *Akeida*:

> When Isaac our father was bound upon the altar and turned into ashes, and his ashes were cast upon Mount Moriah, the Holy One, blessed be He, immediately brought dew upon him and restored him to life.
>
> (*Shibbolei ha-Leket ha-Shalem*, p. 9)

So, too, in a *piyyut* by Rabbi Ephraim of Bonn:

> He quickly put his knees upon him, and like a warrior he strengthened his arms. With steady hands he slaughtered him in their midst, slaughtering him and making him ready. Resuscitating dew fell upon him and he was restored to life. He grabbed him for slaughter a second time. Scripture attests [to this], and the matter has a basis: "And the angel of the Lord called to Abraham out of heaven the second time" (Genesis 22:11).
>
> (*Jubilee Volume in Honor of Alexander Marx*, p. 543)

According to the tradition embodied in the *Shibbolei ha-Leket* and in this *piyyut*, Isaac our father was indeed slaughtered and killed, and afterwards he was restored to life. From Abraham's perspective, his sacrifice was complete. The tradition apparently wishes to emphasize Abraham's sacrificial act rather than to change the plain meaning of the verses. The description of Isaac as dying and then brought back to life is intended to emphasize, in picturesque fashion, that from his own perspective, Abraham was indeed ready to slaughter Isaac, and this was his sacrifice.

The same understanding is also found in a more famous midrash:

> "And Abraham came to bewail Sarah, and to weep for her" (Genesis 23:2). From Mount Moriah, for Sarah died from that distress. This is why the [narrative beginning] "And the life of Sarah was" follows immediately upon that of the *Akeida*.
>
> (Genesis Rabba 58, 5)

And in a comment by Rashi:

> The narrative of the death of Sarah follows immediately on that of the Binding of Isaac, because through the announcing of the *Akeida* – that her son had been made ready for sacrifice and had almost been sacrificed – her soul flew from her and she died.
>
> (Rashi, Genesis 23:2)

What is the message of this midrash? It seemingly wishes to emphasize the element of sacrifice in the *Akeida* story. There is a fundamental difficulty in understanding the emotional strengths of the heroes of the *Akeida*. We know that the tale has a happy ending, but Abraham did not know this. From his perspective, he was called upon to perform a real sacrifice. Abraham was truly prepared to sacrifice his son. In order for us to share in this experience, the Sages emphasize that the story did not have an entirely happy ending: Sarah died. The *Akeida* did indeed involve a sacrifice. A religious person is expected to sacrifice.

Across the generations, many have asked what is unique about the *Akeida* story: surely, many pagans sacrificed their children to their gods; and the Torah, in fact, condemns those who sacrifice their children to their deities![1]

One of the first thinkers to make this point was Philo of Alexandria. He saw himself as struggling with "quarrelsome critics who misconstrue everything" by insisting that many other people besides Abraham had offered their children for the sake of their country or out of religiosity. Philo answered that other people who sacrificed their children did so because it was the custom, or because they thought that they would save their countries by doing so, or under compulsion of higher powers, or perhaps out of a desire for glory and honor. In Abraham's case, all of these factors were irrelevant:

> We must therefore examine whether Abraham, when he intended to sacrifice his son, was mastered by any of these motives, custom or love of honor or fear. Now in Babylonia and Mesopotamia and with the nations of the Chaldeans…the custom of child slaughter does not obtain…. Surely, too, he had nothing to fear from man, since no one knew of the oracular message which he alone had received; nor was he under the pressure of any public misfortune which could be remedied only by the immolation of a child of special worth….
>
> Thus, everyone who is not malignant or a lover of evil must be overwhelmed with admiration for his extraordinary piety.
>
> (Philo, *On Abraham*)

Philo makes several important points. The most important is that Abraham did not expect to derive any benefit from killing Isaac. When Mesha, King of Moab, sacrifices his son,[2] he wishes

1. See *Tanya*, *Iggeret ha-Kodesh*, letter 21.
2. II Kings 3:27; following the understanding of the Sages in *Sifrei*, Deuteronomy, *piska* 148.

thereby to achieve victory in war. Abraham, on the other hand, seeks no benefit; he wishes only to obey the will of his Creator.

Kierkegaard held the same view:

> With Abraham it is different. In his actions he overstepped the ethical altogether, and had a higher telos outside it, in relation to which he suspended it.... It is not to save a nation, not to uphold the idea of the state, that Abraham did it, not to appease angry gods.
>
> (*Fear and Trembling*, p. 88)[3]

But in Jewish and general history, we know of many similar incidents. Abraham may have been the first, but after him many others sacrificed themselves and their children, giving up their lives for the sake of their religious belief, and not for some personal or national interest. Already during the Second Temple period, the Sages raised this question: Was Abraham unique only in being first? Or is he in some way different from all those who suffered a martyr's death throughout the generations?

Here are the words that the Sages put into the mouth of a woman who sacrificed her seven sons so that they would not bow down before an idol during the persecution by Antiochus:

> His mother said to him: "My son, Let not your heart faint, and be not afraid. You are going to your brothers, and you shall be placed in the bosom of Abraham our father. And say to him in my name: 'You built a single altar, and did not sacrifice your

3. We shall not discuss Kierkegaard's position at length. Kierkegaard argues that Abraham's greatness expressed itself in his faith in the absurd, in the paradox: Abraham believed at one and the same time that he would sacrifice his son, and that God's promise regarding a son would be fulfilled through Isaac. This, according to Kierkegaard, was Abraham's greatness and the greatness of the *Akeida*. Clearly operative here is the Christian motif of faith in the absurd. But it is interesting to note that parallel motifs may be found in Chasidic literature. See *No'am Elimelekh* 9c; *Mei ha-Shiloach*, vol. 1, p. 29.

> son. But I have built seven altars, and I have sacrificed my sons upon them. Moreover, in your case it was a test, while in my case it was real.'"
>
> (Lamentations Rabba [Buber], 1)

What then is the true difference between Abraham and everyone else who sacrificed a child for the sake of the sanctification of God's name? Yeshayahu Leibowitz gave a profound answer to this question:

> The trial that Abraham was made to withstand involved the forgoing not only of natural human emotions, but also of collective human values; not only of his paternal relationship with the son of his old age, his only son, but also of the covenantal promises connected to Isaac. All aspects of human consciousness, whether they relate to man as an individual or to the problems of all of humanity, are set aside by the worship of God.
>
> (Leibowitz, *Emuna, Historiya ve-Arakhim*, p. 58)

Abraham offers up not only his love for his son, but his entire faith system, his values, and his understanding of the world. Until now, he was an honorable man, both in his own eyes and in the eyes of others; from now on, he will be a murderer. Until now he believed that God was abundant in love; this belief is now shattered into pieces. Until now he believed in God's promise "For in Isaac shall your seed be called" (Genesis 21:12); this, too, he is ready to forgo. Those who died a martyr's death in later generations understood what they were dying for. Their death had meaning. Abraham gave up even on meaning.

Rabbi Shlomo Aviner wrote in a similar vein:

> Abraham had to give up on everything that he felt and understood as a human being – as a most superior human being; he had to erase all his thoughts and ideas, all the feeling of goodness in him, in order to fulfill God's command. This

> teaches us in a most drastic way that we do not fulfill God's commandments because it is good for us to do so, or because we understand them, or because we experience pleasantness in their performance, but rather because they are God's commandments.
>
> (Aviner, *Tal Chermon*, pp. 49–50)

It is important, however, to mention the end of the *Akeida* story – something which Leibowitz does not do. In the end, as Rabbi Soloveitchik emphasizes, Isaac is not sacrificed, and Abraham enjoys everlasting joy. God does not demand that we give up on our whole world. What we learn from the *Akeida* story is that God demands of us that we be *ready* to give up on our whole world. The *Akeida* story establishes man's priorities for once and forever: serving God is above all else – above all values, above all feelings. And the service of God means doing what God says, even in the absence of identification and understanding.

According to the thinkers thus far mentioned, the message of the *Akeida* emphasizes the worship of God through fear and acceptance of His yoke. This is also what follows from the plain sense of Scripture, which, following the *Akeida*, designates Abraham as "one who fears God." Those who advocate other approaches can argue, of course, that the *Akeida* gives expression to only one element of religious experience. Rabbi Abraham Isaac Kook, who emphasizes loving God and identifying with Him, refused to accept this interpretation even partially, and even with respect to the *Akeida* itself:

> "And Abraham rose up early in the morning" (Genesis 22:3). The peace of mind of the holy soul, of the holy father, the mighty native, did not cease.... He passed the night in the restful and gaily holy sleep of the upright, and the time of rising arrived as usual....
>
> This holy old man went off to this amazing task, the opposite of all the natural ways of the human soul, neither stooped

> nor with failed strength, but fully erect and girded in might. His entire journey was powered by the fullness of supremely elevated love.
>
> (*Olat Ra'aya* 1, pp. 86–87)

How different Rabbi Kook's words are from those of Rabbi Soloveitchik! In contrast to the sleeplessness described by Rabbi Soloveitchik, Rabbi Kook speaks of "the restful and gaily holy sleep of the upright." As opposed to the sacrifice emphasized by Rabbi Soloveitchik, Rabbi Kook speaks of "supremely elevated love."

As we stated earlier, one may adopt Rabbi Kook's theological approach without forcing this idea onto the *Akeida*. It would suffice to argue that whereas Abraham's initial feeling may have been one of sacrifice, what may perhaps be most important from our perspective is what happened at the end: Isaac's ultimate rescue, which, it might be argued, is the dominant element that has been impressed in the hearts of believers. Rabbi Kook went a step further, emphasizing the love that was in Abraham's heart throughout the entire *Akeida* saga.

Religion and Morality

Over and above the subjective emotional issue that has thus far occupied us, the *Akeida* story raises another question: What is the relationship between religion and morality, between the religious command and morality? As the Sages emphasized, the *Akeida* story ended on a happy note, leaving no contradiction or tension between religion and morality:

> "Which I did not command them" (Jeremiah 19:5), regarding Jephthah; "and I did not speak" (ibid.), regarding Mesha king of Moab; "Nor did it come into my heart" (ibid), that Abraham should sacrifice his son on the altar.
>
> (*Sifrei*, Deuteronomy, *piska* 148)

The piercing practical question remains, however: What

should one do when religion and morality seem to conflict? Which should one choose? Abraham, when faced with this conflict, chose God's command and rejected the demands of morality.[4]

There are those who claim that no such conflict ever existed:

> [God] spoke to [Abraham] in language bearing two meanings: one that would be understood by the masses, and another that would be understood by [select] individuals. When [God] said to him: "And offer him there for a burnt offering" (Genesis 22:2), its meaning to the masses is what would appear to be the plain sense of Scripture, namely, "And offer him as a sacrifice."... But its meaning to [select] individuals is: "And raise him up on one of the mountains in place of a burnt offering."...Abraham, may he rest in peace, did not understand this esoteric meaning, but rather he understood [God's command] according to its manifest meaning.
>
> (Ibn Janach, *Sefer ha-Rikma*, pp. 58–59)[5]

Rabbi Yona ibn Janach argues that God never told Abraham to slaughter Isaac, but only to bring him to the mountain. It is not clear from this whether Rabbi Yona means that God intended for Abraham to misunderstand him or that He would have preferred that Abraham understand him, but Abraham erred in understanding the commandment as it would have been understood by the masses. In any event, Rabbi Yona is clearly trying to reduce the tension between God's command and morality.[6]

---

4. In my opinion, this is the answer to the famous question of why Abraham argued with God about His plan for Sodom, but was silent regarding the *Akeida*. In the latter case, Abraham received a command, and his first duty was to fulfill it. In the former case, God shared certain facts with Abraham, facts that did not require immediate action on his part. Thus, the door was open for questions and objections.

5. Support for this position may be found in Genesis Rabba 56, 12.

6. The words of Ibn Janach, the eleventh-century Spanish grammarian, may be

Some understand just the opposite, holding that there was no conflict because there is nothing with which to conflict: morality has no meaning other than "what God desires":

> Now the nations of the world, even the best of them, think that truth exists independently, and that God commanded the truth because in and of itself it is true.[7].... This is in contrast with Israel, who say: You are the God of truth; He, may He be blessed, is truth, and there is no truth outside Him. All the truth in the world is [true] only because so God commanded and willed. Since He, may He be blessed, is truth, therefore this, too, is truth. One is forbidden to steal because the God of truth so commanded. Because of the command of the true God, this is true as well. But when God commands the opposite – that property declared ownerless by a court is ownerless – then that becomes the truth, that this person's property is ownerless. And when God commanded our father, Abraham, to bind up his son Isaac [as an offering], then it was the truth to bind him. Had He not said to him afterwards, "Do nothing to him," it would have been the truth to slaughter him.
>
> (Admor of Piasetzno, *Eish Kodesh*, p. 68)[8]

Note that the proof from the *Akeida* is inconclusive. The *Akeida* story only shows that in a case where there seems to be a conflict between the two, God's command takes priority over mo-

---

understood against the backdrop of the religious polemics between Jews and Muslims. The Muslims claimed that if God was able to retract His command that Isaac was to be brought as a sacrifice, he could also have taken back the Torah given to Moses and replaced it with the Law given to Muhammad. Ibn Janach argues that God never retracted His command regarding the *Akeida*, because He never actually commanded that Isaac be killed (see Aviezer Ravitzky, "*Ha-Akeida ve-ha-Berit*," in *Abraham Avi ha-Ma'aminim*, p. 30).

7. This is reminiscent of Plato's famous words in *Euthyphro*.

8. The statement of the Admor of Piasetzno must be understood against the backdrop of the atrocities of the Holocaust, which in his eyes made any attempt to explain God's ways seem ludicrous.

rality. Abraham's initial understanding seems to have been that there is no such thing as morality. But is this also the conclusion? The simple meaning seems to be that after Abraham was commanded not to slaughter Isaac, he understood that God's commands and morality are basically in harmony. That is to say: Abraham thought at first that he would have to give up morality, but in the end he understood that God's commands are in consonance with it.[9] Even according to the conclusion, God's command prevails when there is a conflict; but the normal situation is one of correspondence rather than conflict.

Rabbi Ezra Bick proposed a slightly different understanding.[10] Even at the outset Abraham did not think that he was about to perform an immoral act for the sake of heaven. He certainly saw the act as moral even though he was unable to understand why. This approach is the total opposite of that of the author of *Eish Kodesh*: Whereas the Admor of Piasetzno argues that even at the end God is immoral, Rabbi Bick claims that from the very beginning it was clear to Abraham that God is moral even if he did not understand how this could be so.

Whatever Abraham's initial assumptions may have been, it is clear that in a conflict, real or imagined, between a divine command and morality, priority must be given to the divine command; whether because God's command is necessarily moral, or because God can command us to give up our moral standards. It also seems that God's command and morality are in harmony at the end of the *Akeida* story, this being the normal situation.

---

9. In the first half of this chapter, which dealt with the emotional component of Abraham's experiences, we emphasized his initial understanding, because on the emotional plane Abraham experienced the sacrifice of Isaac as a real event. On the objective moral plane, however, of greatest import is what actually occurred.

10. Rav Ezra Bick, "Bein ha-Maimonides le-Kierkegaard," *Sefer Daf Kesher* 6 (Yeshivat Har Etzion), p. 85.

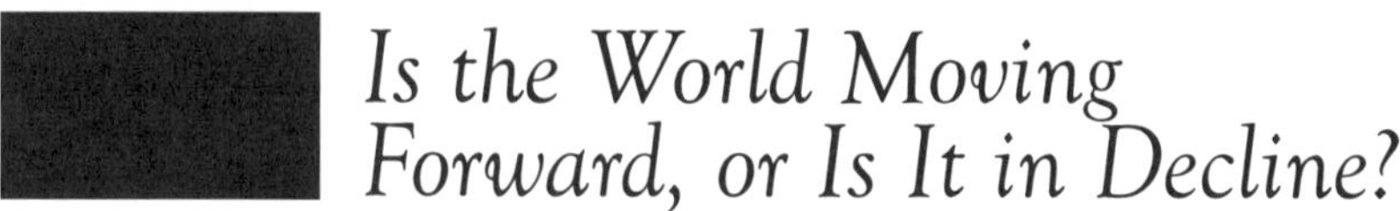

Is the World Moving Forward, or Is It in Decline?

Retreat or Progress?

The midrash on *Parashat Chayyei Sarah* cited by Rashi contains one of the sharpest expressions of the idea that man has declined over the course of the generations:

> Rabbi Acha said: The ordinary conversation of the patriarch's servants is more pleasing than even the Torah of their children. For the chapter of Eliezer, two or three pages [long], is stated and repeated, whereas [the laws of] creeping creatures are a fundamental aspect of the Torah, and [we] only [know] that its blood imparts ritual impurity like its flesh from a superfluity in Scripture.
>
> (Genesis Rabba 60, 8)

The starting point of this midrash is the astonishing fact that the Torah describes in detail what happened to Abraham's servant, and then reports what the servant said to Rebecca's family, which merely repeats what had been related earlier. The Sages explain that there is special value to the words of those who were connected to the patriarchs. The plain sense of the text permits other explanations of the repetition. Nechama Leibowitz has taught us to pay attention to the differences between the account of Abraham's servant and the original events, and to learn important lessons from the discrepancies. Nevertheless, the words of the Sages may be understood even on the level of the plain sense: the lessons that may be derived from the conversation of the servants of the patriarchs are more important than the Torah of their children.

In any event, these words of the Sages teach us about the superiority of the generation of the patriarchs in comparison to their descendants. There are many other sources in which the Sages refer to the decline of the generations:

> Rabbi Zera said in the name of Rava bar Zimuna: If the earlier [scholars] were sons of angels, we are sons of men; and if the earlier [scholars] were sons of men, we are like asses, and not [even] like asses of Rabbi Chanina ben Dosa and Rabbi Pinchas ben Ya'ir, but like other asses.
>
> (*Shabbat* 112b)

> Rabbi Yochanan said: The hearts of the earlier Sages were as broad as the entranceway to the porch of the Temple, and those of the later Sages were as broad as the entranceway to the Sanctuary, but our hearts are as narrow as the eye of a very fine sewing-needle.
>
> (*Eruvin* 53a)

Rabbi Ezekiel Landau, author of the *Tzelach*, based certain halakhic decisions on these considerations. As is well known, an acute problem arose, and the authorities noticed that calculations based on talmudic measurements of length came out much larger – actually, twice as large – than calculations based on measurements of volume. Rabbi Landau suggested two solutions, and decided between them:

> And you must conclude that something has changed in our time: either the thumbs have increased in size, so that they are larger than the thumbs in the days of the *Tannaim*, or eggs

> have diminished in size, so that they are now smaller than what they were in the days of the *Tannaim*. And it is known that the generations continually decline, and so it cannot be that our thumbs are larger than the thumbs in the days of the talmudic Sages. You must therefore conclude that the eggs of our day have diminished in size.
>
> (*Tzelach, Pesachim* 116b)

Rabbi Landau utilized the argument that "the generations continually decline" to make a practical decision regarding halakhic measurements. He expanded the scope of this consideration to include the physical plane.

On the other hand, there exists an important principle in Judaism that seems to contradict this idea. Let us briefly examine the following midrash:

> It was taught in the school of Eliyahu: Six thousand are the years of the world: two thousand years of chaos, two thousand years of Torah, and two thousand years of the days of the Messiah.
>
> (*Avoda Zara* 9a)

This midrash clearly points in the direction of historical progress: from "chaos" to "Torah" to "the Messiah."[1] We are not talking here about some haphazard midrash. The very mention of the Messiah and redemption forces us to understand that the generations are progressing, not retreating, for surely the pinnacle and culmination of human existence lies yet ahead of us! This argument, however, is not necessarily true, as has been emphasized by Prof. Gershom Scholem:

---

1. The *Chazon Ish* understood, however, that we are dealing here with a retreat of sorts. He argues that even if medical advances render certain defects once considered fatal as no longer life-threatening, the Halakha does not change, for it was established according to the reality of the "two thousand years of Torah" (*Chazon Ish, Yore De'a, Hilkhot Terefot* 5, 3)

> Scripture and the apocalyptic revelations do not recognize historical progress that leads to redemption. Redemption is not the result of self-development, as the term has come to be understood according to the modern Western explanation given to it ever since the Enlightenment.... Redemption is essentially a transcendental experience that breaks into history, a breach that conveys the nonexistence of history, which turns over in its ruins because it had been struck by a ray of light from some source outside of it.
>
> (Scholem, *Devarim Bego*, p. 164)

Scholem argues that the coming of the Messiah may be seen as a one-time event that breaks into history, unconnected to any historical development that preceded it. According to this understanding, belief in the redemption is not necessarily connected to an outlook that recognizes historical progress. Clearly, however, there were schools of Jewish thought that saw in history development and progress toward the coming of the Messiah. The coming of the Messiah was not seen as a break in history, but as its climax, the end of historical progress:

> And as I have heard from my master in explanation of the verse, "In His hand are the deep places of the earth," and so on (Psalms 95:4). He asked: Why did the philosophers in ancient times believe in the eternity of the world, which is not the case now, when they believe that the Blessed One is the One and only? And he answered: This was because of the turbidity of the material comprising the earth, which at that time was much greater, but that is not the case now.
>
> (*Toledot Jacob Yosef, Parashat Vayeshev*)

Interestingly, the Ba'al Shem Tov connects the progress of the world with the progress of science and philosophy, and their correlation with the religion of Israel. The Admor of Radzin voiced similar ideas regarding the progress and perfection of the world.[2]

In the twentieth century, Rabbi Abraham Isaac Kook saw the ideas of progress and evolution as extremely important:

> The theory of evolution, which is now conquering the world, is in greater accord with the secrets of the world of Kabbala than any other philosophical theory.... And when we penetrate into the innermost aspects of the foundation of evolution, we find that the divine idea is illuminated in it in absolute clarity, that an infinite *in realia* actualizes that which is infinite *in potentia*.... All of existence evolves and becomes elevated, as is clearly evident in parts thereof.
>
> (*Orot ha-Kodesh* II, p. 537)

Rabbi Kook's outlook was intimately connected to his spiritual world, which was primarily inspired by the Kabbala. The Nazir explained that the kabbalistic creed is a sound philosophical basis for the idea of progress: the world returns to its source in a manner similar to the law of connected vessels, which asserts that a liquid will rise to the level from which it descended:

> The elevation of the world is based on sublime emanation. As for the modern theory of evolution, its philosophical foundation, if not its biological foundation, is shaky. From where [comes the belief] in progress in an ascending line, without ups and downs, or in a circle? This is not the case with the elevation of the world based on sublime emanation, the fall of the world and its repair, which rises, like the mechanical law of connected vessels, to the same level from which it had descended, to its previous lofty position.
>
> (*Mavo le-Orot ha-Kodesh*, pp. 20–21)

2. The Admor of Rozin, *Sod Yesharim, Pesach*, p. 121.

The world progresses and develops only because it originated in the celestial worlds. The development of the world is essentially a return to its source. The Nazir went so far as to argue that the rise in the status of women and the yearning for spiritual equality between men and women were expressions of the world's progress.[3]

Reconciling the Approaches

As we have seen, some Jewish sources speak of the decline of the later generations, and others speak of continuous progress. Can these diverse approaches be reconciled? Is it possible to accept the idea of progress and at the same time hold fast to the notion that the generations have declined over time? Or is it impossible, because only one of the two approaches can be adopted? Moreover, perhaps both types of sources, those that refer to progress and those that refer to a decline, are merely midrashim, and do not express an overall and obligatory idea. Many Jewish thinkers have given serious consideration to these questions and have suggested various models for reconciliation between them.

1. *Accumulation over Time*. The most famous of the models we will discuss here is found in the writings of Rabbi Yeshaya of Trani (the Rid), and it was borrowed, we should note, from the Christian thinkers of his day. The Rid asserts that it is in our power to disagree with the Sages of the early generations, even if individually they were wiser than us, because we are "dwarfs riding on the backs of giants" (*Responsa Rid*, 62). In other words, the total body of knowledge increases over time. As individuals, the *Rishonim* were greater and wiser than the *Acharonim*, but knowledge accumulates. We start out today at the point reached by the *Rishonim*, and therefore, despite our lesser ability, have a head start in dealing with the big questions.

3. Cited by D. Schwartz, *Ha-Tziyonut ha-Datit bein Higayon li-Meshichiyut*, pp. 323–324.

Rabbi Tzadok Ha-Kohen of Lublin develops this point along kabbalistic lines, speaking not only about the accumulation of knowledge, but also about the accumulation of holiness:

> Every soul in Israel has its own special force in holiness, and as is the number of generations that have already passed, so is the number of holy forces and words of Torah that have been revealed in the world. Therefore, in each and every generation, holiness becomes ever more revealed, even though the generations are in decline, as is well known. The reason is that that which was revealed in the early generations has already been revealed, as is known by way of the parable of the dwarf sitting on top of the giant.
>
> (*Tzidkat ha-Tzadik*, p. 116)

Rabbi Kook also mentions the accumulation of holiness in the people of Israel. Although as individuals we steadily diminish in stature, the accumulated holiness continually grows.[4]

2. *Distinguishing Between Different Periods.* It is sometimes argued that in the past the idea of the decline of the generations was correct, but in our day, owing to the impending redemption, the generations are growing in stature. According to this approach, there are two focal points: past revelation and future redemption. These two points create sort of an inverted bell curve, at both ends of which there are generations of great stature. Rabbi Pinchas of Koritz writes in this vein:[5]

> As for Ibn Ezra who complained about Kalir,[6] the Rav said: I like to defend the Ibn Ezra.... The *Tannaim* and the *Amoraim*

4. *Iggerot ha-Ra'aya*, I, p. 369. Compare to *Orot ha-Kodesh* II, pp. 217–219.
5. Rabbi Pinchas, however, emphasizes the period of the Temple, and not necessarily that of the revelation at Sinai, as the focus of holiness in the past.
6. See *Ecclesiastes* 5:1, where Ibn Ezra attacks the *piyyutim* of Kalir.

> were close in time to the destruction of the Temple, which still gave illumination, having only recently been removed. And the recent *Tzadikim* in these generations are close to the light of the Messiah; there is no novelty, then, in their attaining the truth.... But Ibn Ezra was far removed from the destruction [of the Temple] and also far removed from the Messiah, and, therefore, he did not attain the level of Kalir.
>
> (*Midrash Pinchas*, p. 82)[7]

3. *Distinguishing Between Different Realms.* A third approach holds that in some realms there has been a rise, whereas in others there has been a decline. This approach seems quite reasonable, for we see that alongside the sharp drop over the last two hundred years in the proportion of the Jewish people that has remained Torah-observant, there has been a steep rise in other realms. Thus writes Rabbi Tzadok of Lublin in the name of the Admor of Peshiskha:

> While the souls diminish from one generation to the next, nevertheless the point in the heart becomes more purified in each successive generation.
>
> (*Peri Tzaddik*, p. 217).

While it is not clear what the Admor of Peshiskha means here by "the point in the heart," he is certainly describing a complex twofold process. Rabbi Tzadok's point of departure, as we mentioned earlier, is the issue of redemption: If the generations are steadily diminishing in stature, how can we be getting closer to the redemption?

Rabbi Kook proposes another distinction between the realms:

> The collective has been elevated at the expense of individuals, which is the general process of human development. In most

7. Cited by S. Sperber, *Hemshekh ha-Dorot*, in *Ha-Ra'aya*, pp. 45–46.

> periods of history we find distinguished sages, masters of spirit, in the early generations. We are astounded by their greatness and the might of their spirit. But the collective is in a degraded situation, both in intellect and in morality.... In the later generations there are fewer ignoramuses, but there are also correspondingly fewer geniuses and righteous men, and they are of lower caliber.
>
> (*Eider ha-Yakar*, p. 111)

Rabbi Kook describes an interesting phenomenon: the nation's leaders become progressively smaller, but the masses continue to improve.

Attitudes in the Non-Jewish World

Generally stated, the idea of progress and development is widely accepted in the modern world. This perception feeds primarily on a single fact: the tremendous technological advances that nobody can deny. The idea of progress accorded well with the image of the world projected by the thinkers of the Enlightenment. It was primarily the philosopher Georg Wilhelm Friedrich Hegel who provided the idea of progress with philosophical backing. Hegel saw the history of the world as the development of the world-spirit, which finds expression in every realm of life. Regarding the subject at hand, Hegel was convinced that the world was headed in one direction: progress. Some have suggested that Rabbi Kook was influenced either by Hegel's writing or by the Hegelian spirit of the time.[8]

Later in the twentieth century, however, given the realities of Auschwitz and Hiroshima, doubts about the idea of progress began to surface. Is mankind really moving ahead? These doubts were the first seeds of what would later be called post-modernism. The scholar and philosopher Isaiah Berlin wrote in his *The Sense*

---

8. See the Nazir's description of the spirit of the modern period in his introduction to *Orot ha-Kodesh*, p. 31.

of Reality that the century's brutal leaders – Lenin, Stalin, Hitler – had returned the world to barbarism, something that should have been impossible according to the nineteenth century's theory of progress. Ideas once considered as inseparable from the advanced stage of human development were shattered or distorted beyond recognition. The entire concept of progress collapsed.

In this context and with his customary pungency, Professor Yeshayahu Leibowitz notes that for several generations the Western world has been undergoing a process of barbarization. Many, he said, fail to recognize this, due to naiveté or to an affection of naiveté, and continue to speak glibly of "the darkness of the Middle Ages" as opposed to our "enlightened and cultured world." Leibowitz reminds us that nothing in the Middle Ages even came close to the horror of the two world wars. As an example of the moral deterioration of our era, Leibowitz points to the lowering of moral sensitivity to suffering and atrocities:

> As an example of the change that has taken place in the psychological background of the social reality, let us mention an event that occurred three generations ago, one that at the time shocked not only the entire Jewish world, but also a large portion of the non-Jewish world – the Kishinev pogrom.... Now, in Kishinev 41 Jews were killed and several tens of Jewish houses and stores were looted. This was the reality less than a hundred years ago. In the last seventy or eighty years, human society has undergone a process of barbarization, and human life no longer has any value.
>
> (*Emuna, Historiya, va-Arakhim*, pp. 171–172)[9]

An interesting comment in this connection was voiced by someone who was neither a philosopher nor a historian. When the

9. See also the similar position voiced by Leo Strauss, "Progress or Return?", in *The Rebirth of Classical Political Rationalism: Essays and Lectures by Leo Straus*, pp. 227–270.

"who is a Jew" question first arose in Israel at the end of the 1950s, David Ben-Gurion initiated a typically grandiose project: he sent letters to fifty "Jewish sages," asking them for their positions on the matter. The responses to Ben-Gurion's question were published only a few years ago (A. Ben-Rafael, *Zehuyot Yehudiyot*, Sde Boker, 2001).

As it happened, the letter sent to the philosopher Dr. Yosef Schechter was accidentally delivered to an Israeli physician also named Dr. Yosef Schechter. The latter expressed surprise that the Prime Minister had bothered to ask for his opinion, inasmuch as his field of expertise was very far from questions of this sort, but nonetheless did not refrain from offering his opinion. If the truth be told, Dr. Schechter's response put forward one of the wisest reasons against deviating from the halakhic track; and it touches upon the question that has been the subject of our discussion:

> The argument that the position of the ancient authorities no longer fits the spirit of our time will undoubtedly be voiced. There is no need for deep analysis to convince ourselves that our time is one of the darkest, and almost certainly the darkest in history – a period whose crimes have brought mankind to the verge of destruction, similar to the generation of the flood and the people of Sodom. Can anyone seriously argue that we should bring the law of Moses, which bears the seal of God, into harmony with the spirit of our time?
>
> (*Zehuyot Yehudiyot*, p. 296)

In summary, the issue is not unequivocal. There are realms of life which demonstrate progress and advance, but there are others which show decline or no movement at all. There is no way to say that mankind is moving altogether in one direction or the other; we must therefore be careful in our formulation of the question. It is most reasonable to say that the world is not unequivocally moving in any one direction.

Prayer

The Efficacy of Prayer

It is in *Parashat Toledot* that we first encounter man praying to God:

> And Isaac entreated the Lord for his wife, because she was barren; and the Lord was entreated of him, and Rebecca his wife conceived.
>
> (Genesis 25:21)

At this point, as with every mention of prayer, a serious difficulty arises: How can prayer alter a divine decree? Isaac's prayer seems to have changed God's will. There are many other examples of this in Scripture. The most striking example is the prayer of Hezekiah:

> In those days Hezekiah fell mortally sick. And the prophet Isaiah the son of Amoz came to him, and said to him, Thus says the Lord, Set your house in order; for you shall die, and not live. Then he turned his face to the wall, and prayed to the Lord, saying, I beseech You, O Lord, remember now how I have walked before You in truth and with a perfect heart, and have done that which is good in Your sight. And Hezekiah wept bitterly. And it came to pass, before Isaiah was gone out into the middle court, that the word of the Lord came to him, saying, Turn

> back and tell Hezekiah the prince of My people. Thus says the Lord, the God of David your father, I have heard your prayer, I have seen your tears; behold, I will heal you; on the third day you shall go up to the house of the Lord. And I will add to your days fifteen years; and I will deliver you and this city out of the hand of the king of Asshur; and I will defend this city for My sake, and for My servant David's sake.
>
> (II Kings 20:1–6)

How could Hezekiah's prayer have changed God's balanced and righteous decree? How in general can prayer affect God's decisions? Rabbi Yosef Albo, author of the *Book of Principles*, formulates the question as follows:

> The reason which leads men to doubt the efficacy of prayer is the same as that which leads them to deny God's knowledge. Their argument is as follows: Either God has determined that a given person shall receive a given benefit, or He has not so determined. If He has determined, there is no need of prayer; and if He has not determined, how can prayer avail to change God's will that He should now determine to benefit the person, when He had not so determined before?
>
> (*Book of Principles* IV, chap. 18)

And in the words of Immanuel Kant:

> It is, further, not only a preposterous but also a presumptuous illusion to try to divine whether, through the persistent importunity of one's request, God cannot be diverted (to our present advantage) from the plan of His wisdom.
>
> (*Religion Within the Limits of Reason Alone*)[1]

1. Kant, indeed, rejects traditional prayer.

The Sages suggested the following answer in regard to the specific case involving the patriarch Isaac:

> Rabbi Yitzchak stated: Why were our ancestors barren? Because the Holy One, blessed be He, longs to hear the prayer of the righteous. Rabbi Yitzchak further stated: Why is the prayer of the righteous compared to a pitchfork? As a pitchfork turns the sheaves of grain from one position to another, so does the prayer of the righteous turn the dispensations of the Holy One, blessed be He, from the attribute of anger to the attribute of mercy.
>
> (*Yevamot* 64a)

If we accept the notion that God denied the patriarchs children because He longed for their prayers, we can understand why their prayers were able to change the situation: From the very outset they had never deserved to be barren. This resolution, however, raises other, no less serious problems about the way God runs the world. And in any event, the very same Rabbi Yitzchak who suggested this answer resolutely asserts in the continuation of the passage that the prayers of the righteous can indeed affect God, and so we are back where we started.

Rabbi Yosef Albo's answer to the question reflects the classic position of Jewish thought:

> The influences from above come down upon the recipient when he is in a certain degree and state of preparation to receive them. And if a person does not prepare himself, he withholds the good from himself.... Our idea, therefore, is that when a benefit is determined in favor of anyone, it is conditional upon a certain degree of right conduct. This must be taken to be a general principle as regards the promises of the Torah. In the same way, when a certain evil is determined upon someone, it is also conditional upon his being wicked in a certain degree or of being predisposed to it. And if the degree of wickedness

> or predisposition thereto changes, the predetermined event or fate changes also, necessarily for the better or the worse.... In this way it is clear that prayer and right conduct help to prepare the person to receive the good influence or to nullify the evil that has been decreed concerning him, because he changes from the evil state in which he was.... As for the objection that the divine will cannot be changed by prayer, the answer is that the divine will, in the first place, is that the decree will be realized if the person in question continues in the same state, and the decree will be changed if the person's state changes.
>
> (*Book of Principles* IV, chap. 18)

Rabbi Yosef Albo explains that we are dealing here with a precise calculation of merit: When a person prays, God does not answer his prayers because of love for him or because of a personal connection between them. The person's prayers add to the sum of his merits, and thus he now deserves additional reward, which can alter the decree that was issued against him. One could just as well give charity or redeem a first-born ass, and the results would be the same.

It must be admitted that a person who is engaged in prayer does not feel this way, nor is this the impression we are left with from a reading of Scripture. When Moses entreats God to show mercy to the children of Israel, Scripture implies that God answered his prayer because of the prayer, and not because Moses' merit tilted the balance and overcame the sin of the people of Israel regarding the Golden Calf. This is explicitly stated by one of the *Rishonim,* Rabbi Chasdai Crescas, in his *Or ha-Shem*:

> The tenet that hangs upon this *mitzva* is that we must believe that the Blessed One listens to the entreaty of him who prays and truly places his trust in Him.... For while he is not worthy, nor does he deserve to receive what he wants, without prayer, with prayer – *in addition to the reward for the mitzva* – it is

> possible for him to attain it, since he truly places his trust in Him.
>
> (*Or ha-Shem* II, pt. II, chap. 1)[2]

Rabbi Chasdai Crescas states explicitly that there are times when God answers prayer, not because the person by praying added to his tally of merits, but because God responds directly to the supplications of one who turns to Him in prayer and puts his trust in Him ("in addition to the reward for the *mitzva*"). This is difficult to understand from a theological perspective, but it seems to be the plain sense of Scripture, as well as the plain understanding of the heart. When we pray to God, we feel that He listens to our prayers, and we hope that He will answer them in the same way, as it were, that we fulfill a request made by a friend, and not because of a reckoning of our merits and failings.

In any event, according to all opinions, we are not dealing here with magic, that is to say, an attempt to force God in some way to bestow His goodness upon us. Ultimately, what happens is unquestionably in God's hands and depends upon His will and love. Another point that differentiates Jewish prayer from magic is the emphasis Jewish prayer places on intention, as opposed to the power of a text and the manner in which it is uttered (as emphasized in *Rosh ha-Shana* 3:8).

Prayer Uttered in Vain

The Sages endow us with two fundamental approaches to the issue of God's providence and its relationship to the laws of nature. The difference between the two is embodied in their respective attitudes to "prayer uttered in vain." This issue is closely connected to an incident alluded to in the book of Genesis.

The Mishna in *Berakhot* states:

> But to cry over the past is to utter a vain prayer. If a man's wife

2. Ed. Rabbi S. Fisher (Jerusalem, 5750), pp. 372–373.

> is pregnant and he says, "[God] grant that my wife bear a male child," this is a vain prayer. If he is coming home from a journey and he hears cries of distress in the town and says, "[God] grant that this is not in my house," this is a vain prayer.
>
> (*Berakhot* 9:3)

The Mishna's guiding principle here is found in the first line of the aforementioned passage: "To cry over the past is to utter a vain prayer." The Mishna implies that it is forbidden to pray for a change in the laws of nature. If this is true, how does God intervene in what takes place in this world?

The gemara in *Berakhot* 60a raises an objection against this mishna from an incident alluded to in the book of Genesis. According to the midrash, Leah was supposed to have given birth to another boy after Zebulun, but in order not to shame Rachel, the male child in her womb was turned into a female, and she give birth to Dinah. This implies that one is permitted to pray for his wife to give birth to a male child, against what is stated in the Mishna.

The gemara gives two answers: (1) "We make no mention of miraculous acts." (2) The incident involving Leah took place during the first forty days following conception, at which time the sex of the fetus is not yet determined.

The first answer recognizes the existence of miracles that transcend nature, even though one is forbidden to pray for them. We are dealing here with an important conceptual principle that sees routine nature as the normal and even desired situation, and an open miracle as an undesired breach of nature.

The second answer is important for a different reason. According to this idea, which better matches the idea of "prayer uttered in vain," the framework of the laws of nature is not hermetic. There are places where natural determinism is not valid, so that the "hand of fate" – or for us, the hand of God – influences what happens.[3]

---

3. See, however, *Responsa Maharil Chadashot*, no. 15. His explanation seems difficult to me. Our understanding of the mishna and the gemara is supported

If so, the mishna in *Berakhot* is trying to limit God's breaches of the laws of nature, and for that purpose it must reduce the scope of these laws from the beginning. During the first forty days following conception, the laws of nature do not absolutely determine the sex of the embryo. Thus, God's intervention does not fall into the category of miracles, and it is possible to offer prayers and make supplications about it.

A very different note is sounded in another tannaitic source:

> If one prays over that which had been measured, weighed, or counted, so that he should receive a blessing, this is a prayer uttered in vain.
>
> (*Midrash Tanna'im*, Deuteronomy 15:10)

And similarly we find in a *baraita* recorded in *Bava Metzia* 42a:

> Our Rabbis taught: Someone who goes to measure [produce in] his granary says: "May it be Your will, O Lord our God, that You send blessing upon the work of our hands."...[If] he measured [the produce] and afterwards said a blessing, this is a prayer uttered in vain, because blessing is not found, neither in something that is weighed, nor in something that is measured, nor in something that is counted, but [only] in something that is hidden from the eye.
>
> (*Bava Metzia* 42a)

What is the underlying idea? These *baraitot* are dealing with the issue of God's providence versus the laws of nature, but the principles they propose are entirely different. The validity of the laws of nature is not breached on the subjective plane: God does not

---

by a comparison to the conflicting opinion: "Even when she is sitting on the birthing chair, he may pray that she give birth to a male child, for the Holy One, blessed be He, has no difficulty changing females to males and males to females" (*Midrash Tanchuma, Vayetze* 8).

change the laws of nature in way that is evident to the human eye. However, as opposed to what is implied in tractate *Berakhot*, He certainly changes them in ways that we cannot perceive. It is entirely possible that whenever we turn our heads, the birds swim in the sea, the hills fly into the air, and purple clouds cover the skies. But the moment we look back over our shoulders, we once again see the world of nature that we are accustomed to.

The two different positions on vain prayer presented here focus on the dispensation to pray, but we can use them to present two approaches regarding God's providence. The two approaches to prayer do not deal with open miracles; they may both recognize that in rare situations God openly breaches the laws of nature that He has planted in the world. But they present new ways to deal with covert miracles and God's constant providence. The one argues that there are breaches in nature itself that leave room for divine intervention; the second maintains that God breaches His absolute laws – but only when human beings are not aware of what is happening. From man's perspective, the laws of nature remain valid and in force.

Since the time of Newton, the idea of the determinism of the laws of nature has prevailed. Modern science sees the world as a giant machine that operates in accordance with fixed and measured laws. The French scientist Laplace argued that if we knew all of the facts about the state of the world at a given moment in time, and all of the rules according to which the world operates, we would know precisely how the world will look in another hundred, thousand, or even a hundred thousand years.[4]

How does God's constant providence fit into such an understanding of the world? Here we go back to the two possibilities found in the words of the Sages. We can, of course, adopt the second possibility, and say that God breaches the laws of nature

4. We shall note below that this is no longer the accepted view of modern science. Without a doubt, however, it is the intuitive approach that rules our consciousness today.

whenever He is out of our view. In doing this we would be imposing upon God a mission that is not so simple – whenever He wanted to cause a storm, for example, He would have to hide behind all the weather satellites up in space. Those who advocate this approach can do so if they wish. But it is also possible to adopt the first possibility presented above, which assumes the existence of breaches in nature that allow God to act without changing the laws of nature that He has willed into being.

Where are the breaches? It seems to me that in the modern scientific world of the beginning of the twentieth-first century, we can locate two such breaches: the smallest and the largest. Quantum mechanics makes the revolutionary claim that the laws of nature are not absolute but statistical: generally speaking, and *almost* always, atomic particles obey the laws of nature.

It was against this "almost" that Einstein's wrath raged; it cannot be, he argued, that God plays dice with the universe. Einstein inclined to pantheism, as is well known and as was elaborated in an earlier chapter, and he saw profound religious meaning in the existence of regular laws of nature. But we can say just the opposite. Since the laws of nature are only statistical, God's actions on the subatomic level, which obviously have direct ramifications for the visible world, do not contradict the laws of nature.

Statistical laws of nature always allow for the possibility that instead of being pulled down to the ground, the dropped dish will rise upwards. The chances of this happening are indeed very small (and therefore it is not advisable to conduct such an experiment at home), but they exist. What is unique about divine providence is its timing and the meaning that is found in the revelation of God's will – and not the events themselves, which in and of themselves correspond to the laws of nature.[5]

The second breach is the largest: man. While most scientists today incline to a deterministic understanding of man's actions,

5. A. Barth offers a similar explanation in his *Dorenu Mul She'elot ha-Netzach* (Jerusalem, 5715), p. 100.

they hold this view merely on faith, for it has never been proven. Against their faith, we set our faith: Man is not subject to the laws of nature. Therefore, just as God interfered with the judgment of men in the past and changed it to suit His needs – we mention Pharaoh, Sihon, and Cyrus as examples – so, too, it is possible that He does the same today.[6] Thus God governs nature and also history, and our belief in His providence does not in the least contradict our clinging to the regular laws that direct nature.

Rabbi Soloveitchik on Prayer

We shall now mention some of the ideas of Rabbi Joseph B. Soloveitchik on the topic of prayer.

1. *The atmosphere of prayer.* As is well known, Maimonides and Nachmanides disagree about whether there is an obligation to pray in Torah law. Maimonides claims that there is a positive precept to pray every day, and Nachmanides counters that the Torah obligation to pray applies only in times of acute distress.

Rabbi Soloveitchik makes a daring suggestion regarding the *mitzva* of prayer:

> The views of Maimonides and Nachmanides can be reconciled. Both regarded prayer as meaningful only if it is derived from a sense of *tzara* [distress]. They differ in their understanding of the word. Maimonides regarded daily life itself as being existentially in straits, inducing in the sensitive person feelings of despair, a brooding sense of life's meaninglessness, absurdity, lack of fulfillment. It is persistent *tzara*, which exists *bekhol yom* [every day].
>
> (*Reflections of the Rav*, pp. 80–81)

Rabbi Soloveitchik proposes that Maimonides actually agrees

6. I am aware of the problems that this understanding creates in the realm of free will, as was long ago discussed by Maimonides in the sixth chapter of *Hilkhot Teshuva*. There is more to say, but this is not the appropriate forum.

with Nachmanides that what obligates man to pray is the sense of distress. According to Maimonides, however, every day is a time of distress: internal trouble, discomfiture of the soul. For Rabbi Soloveitchik, the defining feature of prayer is crying out from distress. He lays down three key principles: (1) Prayer must stem from identification and agitation. (2) Prayer must flow from a feeling of distress rather than comfort. Rabbi Soloveitchik here makes a veiled criticism of "progressive" synagogues where families sit together in order to feel more comfortable during the service. He insists that it is not by chance that the traditional synagogue bars comfortable, pleasant, happy family prayer. Prayer is not a social pastime, but the penetrating outcry of the individual in isolation. (3) Prayer must be our response to the exigencies of life, we are to bring all of our difficulties, tensions, and uncertainties to God.

Rabbi Soloveitchik rejects not only the seating arrangement in Reform synagogues, but also the style of the prayer and even the architecture of the buildings. He finds profound meaning in the traditional approach to all of these:

> One must never sever service of the heart from life.... As opposed to the church, Jewish synagogues never developed architectural and decorative elements to charm a person and cause him to fall into a sleepy state of supernaturalness.... In our synagogues, partial darkness never ruled: the bright light of the sun was never kept out by narrow stained-glass windows. Rich sounds of organ playing and choir singing, hidden from the eyes of the congregation, never echoed in the synagogue in order to create an atmosphere of mystery. There was never an attempt to remove the Jew from the real world and bring him together with spirits. Just the opposite is true: We always demanded that prayer be an extension of a man's life, and that through it he admit the truth. Therefore, all the Catholic-Christian dramatization is so alien to our religious consciousness, and for this reason Halakha is so greatly opposed to what is

> called modernization of the prayer service, which wipes out all that is unique and original in the service of the heart.
>
> ("Tefilatam shel Yehudim," *Ma'ayanot* VIII, p. 11)

2. *The content of prayer.* Prayer has a specific content. Maimonides rules that the Torah does not fix the text of our payers but nevertheless prescribes that they must include certain themes:

> The obligation in this precept is that everyone should daily, according to his ability, offer up supplication and prayer; first uttering praises of God, then, with humble supplication and petition, ask for all that he needs, and finally offer praise and thanksgiving to God for the benefits already bestowed upon him in rich measure.
>
> (*Hilkhot Tefila* 1:2)

According to Maimonides, the order of the *Amida* prayer is the order of prayer required by Torah law: praise, followed by petition, followed by praise and thanksgiving. The focus of prayer, as established by the Sages, is the middle section: the supplication. The great majority of the blessings are petitions for the fulfillment of our needs, spiritual needs as well as simple material needs.

The emphasis upon needs and requests raises two problems: egoism and materialism. In *Chassidus* as well as in other streams of Jewish thought, there are many who reject the focus upon man's needs. A Chasidic tract, *The Ethical Will of Rivash*, attributed to the Ba'al Shem Tov, states: "Pray not for that which you lack, for your prayer will not be answered" (ed. 5708, p. 17). So, too, writes the Besht's disciple, the Maggid of Mezhirech:

> A person should not pray for his needs; he should always pray only for the *Shekhina*, for its redemption from exile. And thus the Zohar refers to those who pray for themselves, and not for the *Shekhina*, as greedy dogs who bark, "Give, give."
>
> (*Maggid Devarav le-Jacob*, ed. Shatz, p. 81)

A similar idea is expressed by one of the great *mitnaged* leaders, Rabbi Chayyim Volozhiner:

> The essence of prayer is that one's entire intention should be to strengthen holiness. Just as a soldier casts away all his affairs and needs, and willingly dedicates his life exclusively to the needs of the king, that he achieve the royal crown of that country and that his kingdom be exalted, so, too, it is extremely fitting that the upright man should set all of his intention and the purity of his thought in his prayer exclusively upon adding strength to the holy worlds...and not at all upon his own affairs and needs.
>
> (*Nefesh ha-Chayyim*, gate 2, chap. 11)[7]

Rabbi Soloveitchik, however, sees the focus of Jewish prayer upon petitioning for our human needs as a fundamental principle in our general outlook:

> As we have explained, prayer also requires praise and thanksgiving: nevertheless, the power and vitality of prayer lies in petition. Halakha is interested in psychosomatic man, in his actual body. It is not pleased by an ecstatic separation of the soul from the body during prayer.... He cannot escape his material chains and petty needs.... Ordinary man is commanded to pray for the sick in his household, for his wine that turned sour, for his grain that was stricken.
>
> ("Ra'ayonot al ha-Tefila," *Ish ha-Halakha: Galui ve-Nistar*, p. 265)[8]

---

7. Thus writes one of the leading *musar* masters, the Saba of Kelem: "The purpose of prayer is to allow a person to see that everything comes from God, blessed be He.... Asking for one's needs is only a way of reminding a person that every minute he is in the hand of God, may He be blessed" (*Chokhma u-Musar* II, 1). His words, however, lack the theurgical dimension that is so striking in the words of the Maggid and Rabbi Chayyim Volozhiner.
8. See also what Rabbi Soloveitchik writes there, pp. 80 ff.

Rabbi Soloveitchik repeatedly explains that anyone who attempts to sever the true servant of God from the real world is making two mistakes: (1) If admonished to withdraw from the real world, man will usually not reach the desired level and give up his material pursuits, but instead will remove his day-to-day activities from the supervision of religion. This is Rabbi Soloveitchik's major critique of Christianity. (2) A more substantial critique: God does not want man to be unconnected to this world. He wants man to lead a normal human life in the context of which he serves his Creator.

It is for these two reasons that Rabbi Soloveitchik views the centrality of petition in our prayer as an absolutely desirable feature: When man engages in prayer, he approaches God with his true worries, his troubles, his requests, and his needs. Only in that way can he truly serve God with his entire personality.

Acknowledgements

Judaica Press for permission to reprint selections from Charles Chavel, translator, *Ramban: Commentary on the Torah*, © 1971.

Judaica Press for permission to reprint selections from Rabbi Dr. H. Freedman and Maurice Simon, translators, *Midrash Rabbah*, © 1939, Soncino Press.

Judaica Press for permission to reprint selections from S.R. Hirsch, *Pentateuch*, Translated by Isaac Levy, © 1956, 1962.

Feldheim Publishers for permission to reprint selections from A.M. Silbermann and M. Rosenbaum, translators, *Pentateuch and Rashi's Commentary*, © 1973.

Index

C

D

E

I

L